Advance Praise for *Embrace Your Freedom*

"I loved reading this book. It's filled with so much wisdom. It does a wonderful job of synthesizing all the advice college students need."

—Adam S. Weinberg, PhD,
President, Denison University

"This book is truly fabulous—it made me want to start college all over again. I love it! I want to buy copies for all the students and parents I work with."

—Judy Campbell, Founder,
Emeritus College Counseling

"This is indeed a book I wish I'd read when I was eighteen!"

—Dennis Johnson, Co-founder and
Publisher, Melville House

"Philip Glotzbach may be the last of a breed of educators who believe students can learn to think critically for themselves, by far the greatest freedom a college education can impart. He also provides invaluable guidance for parents to help them support their student in this journey."

—John R. MacArthur, Publisher of *Harper's Magazine* and Skidmore Parent

"This book does a fine thing for generations of students (and their parents) who will profit from its wisdom. Above all, it offers them two things that are sadly in short supply today: empowerment and hope."

—Moisés Kaufman, Founder and Artistic Director, TECTONIC Theater Project

"This book speaks to the many issues that affect the day-to-day lives of today's college and university students—including questions relating to mental health, drug and alcohol use, cyberbullying, and much more. Practical as well as inspirational, it represents an invaluable guide book for contemporary undergrads and their parents, and it offers them a good measure of hope and encouragement."

—W. Rochelle Calhoun, Vice President for Campus Life, Princeton University

EMBRACE YOUR FREEDOM

EMBRACE YOUR FREEDOM

Winning Strategies to Succeed in College and in Life

PHILIP A. GLOTZBACH

Post Hill
PRESS

A POST HILL PRESS BOOK
ISBN: 979-8-88845-436-7
ISBN (eBook): 979-8-88845-437-4

Post Hill Press
New York • Nashville
posthillpress.com

Published in the United States of America
1 2 3 4 5 6 7 8 9 10

For future college students
Barrett, Reid, and Trevor,
their parents, Jason and Kristi, and
in memory of Elizabeth Marie (Liz)

CONTENTS

PART THREE: FOR PARENTS, AN IMPORTANT SUPPORTING ROLE

INTRODUCTION—LET'S GET STARTED

You're going to college—terrific!!! First of all, hearty congratulations! I trust you're looking forward to starting your college journey. It's a time of beginnings and endings, excitement and anticipation, and maybe some anxiety and even a few tears. Author Gail Blanke has written that these transitional moments can make us feel like we're "between trapezes."[1] You've let go of one bar but not yet caught hold of the next one. You're flying free. The experience can be exhilarating—like riding a mountain bike down a steep hill or skiing a run that's just a little too intense for comfort. Or it can be scary. Most often, it's both at once. Especially if you don't know exactly what to expect when you grab on to the new bar ahead of you.

Heading off to college is a signature event in anyone's life. You're moving from the minor leagues to the majors—up to "the show," where fastballs will be faster, curve balls will break harder, and everyone will still expect you to hit them. It's where you'll do so much to shape the adult you want to become, and you'll

---

[1]   Gail Blanke, *Between Trapezes: Flying into a New Life with the Greatest of Ease* (Emmaus: Rodale, 2005); please see Additional Resources at the end of this book.

experience an enormous sense of satisfaction as you do. This book will give you ideas about how to begin this exciting phase of your life and then carry it through to a terrific conclusion—to win your personal College World Series!

Congratulations, as well, to parents, stepparents, guardians, and other relatives and friends invested in this student's success! This moment marks a symbolic passage from your child's final stage at home to their initial steps into independent adult life. You've nurtured this young person from their early years through high school, and you've helped them navigate and survive the sometimes daunting and too often anxiety-provoking college admissions process. Now that the transition is finally here, it can serve up a new set of uncertainties and anxieties for *you* as well. This book will help you think through these issues and understand the positive role you still can play in your student's new college life and beyond. In a very real sense, your family is heading off to college too.

But now what? What's next for you as a student? What do *you* need to do to make everything work out? You probably have other questions too: *Will I fit in and feel that I belong? How can I make new friends? Will I be able to handle my classes? How do I pick a major?* And the big ones: *What is college for? What's its real goal—what should I be trying to get out of it? And what do I need to do to succeed?*

Parents, of course, have their own questions: *How do I connect with my child's new college life? How can I figure out the school's complex (and sometimes confusing) array of offices and departments? What's my role as my child makes choices about what to study and do after college? What are my options if they seem to be having serious difficulties? After graduating, will my child be equipped to find a job and begin a successful professional life?* And the big ones: *Will my student be able to succeed? And how will all of this change my child's relationship with me?*

This book aims to remove much of the mystery, uncertainty, and anxiety surrounding the transition to college and the years that follow. Its goal is to help you, as a new student, take full advantage of everything your school offers, from the moment you first step on campus to your final walk across the stage at commencement. To make it all less overwhelming and, in the end, as satisfying and successful as it can be—for both students *and* parents.

What you'll find in the following pages may be rather different from what you're expecting. In fact, some things I say will run counter to much of what you've been told about college, seen in the media, or encountered in popular culture. But frankly, there's a lot of confusion today about just what a college education is *for* and how best to pursue it. So, it's useful for us to start out with some clarity on these topics. I just ask you to approach what you'll read with an open mind.

Overall, I suggest that you see this book as *an integrated picture of a good undergraduate life*—one that brings together some more abstract discussions of key ideas with a lot of focused, down-to-earth, and sensible advice. The first nine chapters speak directly to students, and the final two to parents. But the best plan is for students and parents alike to read all of it. The student chapters provide important information for parents, and it will be useful for students to read the parents' section. The first chapter, especially, frames the entire book—for everyone—by talking about the enduring values of a college education in today's complex world.

Your college years quite literally represent a once-in-a-lifetime, life-changing opportunity that will remain with you forever. The word "transformative" is often overused. But in this context, it's completely appropriate. If you approach it in the right frame of mind, your college experience can truly *transform* you in countless ways that won't be clear at the start and may only begin to become evident by the time you graduate.

Yes, college can be challenging at times for everyone involved. But it can and *will* be incredibly rewarding—even more than it's possible to anticipate in advance—provided you do your part. For traditional students, it's a full-time job that demands commitment and hard work. For parents, it requires—how best to say it?—an adjustment. But you still have a very important role to play in partnership with your student: to be supportive but not intrusive in their life.

A STRANGER IN A STRANGE NEW LAND

On your first day on campus, a college or university can seem like an eccentric, exotic place to anyone. A new student can easily feel like a traveler who's landed on the shore of a strange new land. But once you settle in, you'll soon begin making sense of it all. This book will help. We'll talk about ways to connect with people and make great new friends. You'll find strategies for handling your new—and sometimes unfamiliar—academic challenges.

Though it includes plenty of insider information, this book is not a collection of deep, dark secrets about your new college or university. It's more like a guidebook for a traveler crossing into an unfamiliar country. You may have to learn a new language and realize that not everyone will be fluent in the dialect you were comfortable with in high school. In fact, you'll probably find it useful to practice switching back and forth between different ways of speaking—some people refer to this as "code switching"—depending on whom you are conversing with (new friends, professors, and so on). You'll also have to get used to some exotic customs. But the people you'll meet will turn out to be more like you than different from you, and there will be many professionals eager to assist. Equipped with this guidebook, you'll soon feel at home, begin enjoying your new college or university surroundings, and get focused on what you're there to do.

To illustrate some main points, I've included stories of students I've known over the years—people who've already made the journey you are about to take—mostly from my experience as Skidmore's president. I'm grateful to these grads for giving me permission to share their experiences and for checking to make sure that what I say about them is accurate. I've used just their first names, but let me emphasize that each of these brief narratives is genuine, not fictional. You'll also read about several other individuals who've made their mark in the world and whose stories are more public. You may already be familiar with many of them.

These examples, of course, illustrate successes—often some pretty amazing ones. But they also touch on the obstacles many of these people had to overcome. Contrary to what you may see in your friends' social media feeds, *everyone* (!) runs into problems now and again; sometimes we hit a brick wall. In that case, what you do *next* is the most important thing. For the student, I hope these stories spark your imagination and encourage you to think of *your* college journey in richer and more ambitious terms than you might have before.

Some of these examples may strike you as pretty far removed from your experience—they may even be a bit intimidating. ("No way I could ever do that!") If so, it may help to remember that *none* of the outcomes you'll read about was guaranteed in advance. Every one of these individuals started off as a young person just like you, with their own doubts, fears, and uncertainties.

Some came from modest or even extremely challenged beginnings, from which no one could have predicted where they eventually would end up. And they all were new college students at some point in their lives. So, let these stories encourage you to begin thinking of your own life in audacious ways—to help you envision a spectacular future far beyond your current horizons and expectations! (More on this in Chapter 3.)

WAYS TO BE A COLLEGE STUDENT (AND PARENT)

There are practically as many ways to be an undergraduate as there are types of colleges and universities to choose from. You may be a traditional eighteen- or nineteen-year-old setting off to a four-year college or university straight out of high school. You could be traveling some distance away or staying closer to home. You may be going to a community college. You might be a transfer student, starting over at a new school after having tried out another one the year before. Or you may be an older, "non-traditional" student returning to complete your degree or even starting out for the first time. Rather than belabor these differences, as you've already seen, I've written as though my most likely reader is a traditional-aged student entering a four-year college or university for the first time. But whatever your personal circumstances, the ideas you'll find here should be useful to you. So, please try to see yourself in the following pages.

Likewise, there are many ways to be a college parent. You may already have sent one or more children off to college. (In which case, you may feel that *you* should be writing this book!) You may have undergrad or even post-grad experience yourself. Or you may be saying goodbye to the first one in your family to attend a college or university. Whatever your situation, I trust the advice you'll find here will be helpful to you as well.

For the student, even before you arrive on campus, you can discover quite a bit more about your new college or university than you learned in the admissions process. You can further explore its web pages to review the graduation requirements, look more deeply into the variety of programs and classes you'll choose from, see what clubs or other student organizations you might join, and so on. You can learn more, too, about the town or city in which your school is located to see what it has to offer. You should be able to get in touch with your new roommate(s) and classmates through social media or other ways of connecting your school will provide. (Many schools also support online parent communities.) Lastly, please read through the orientation materials your school will send out, including any relating to a required summer reading. (And, of course, if there is a summer reading, you need to complete it *before* you arrive on campus.) These sources of information can help get you off to a great start![2]

OPTIONS IN HIGHER EDUCATION

Before we go any further, let's talk more generally about higher education in the United States. As with any organization, our colleges and universities are not perfect; there are lots of issues

---

[2] For more helpful tips about what you can do during the summer before you begin, see Adam Weinberg, "So, you've gotten into a college. Now what?" CNN, May 15, 2022, https://www.cnn.com/2022/05/15/perspectives/graduation-college-freshmen-tips/index.html. For a quick introduction to some of the ideas you'll read in this book, you might also check out his article, "Essential advice for first-year college students," The *Chicago Tribune*, August 25, 2023, https://denison.edu/campus/president/speeches/151453. Adam Weinberg is President of Denison University.

any president could name. Even so, our system of colleges and universities remains the envy of the world, in part because it features such a wide variety of schools. This fact represents both a major strength for our country and a significant advantage for students and families because it provides such a broad range of choices: from small private (and in some cases, public) liberal arts colleges to Ivy League schools and large private and public research universities, from medium-sized liberal arts universities to Historically Black Colleges and Universities (HBCUs), and from public community colleges to for-profit institutions.

Historically, most private colleges and universities in the United States were founded by religious communities. Though many ended those affiliations over time, others still maintain a religious identity in some form or another. So, the religious/secular distinction is one more overlay to use in considering your options within US higher education. In sum, there are so many possibilities that at least one should be right for just about anyone who wants to go to college, at any point in their life's journey. And so, for you!

In the admissions process, unfortunately, many students and parents focus far too much on commercially published ratings of colleges and universities—and the perceived prestige of the best known and most highly ranked ones. However, schools at the upper end of these classifications receive so many applications, and therefore are so highly selective, that many are able to admit fewer than 10 percent of their applicants—in some cases, it's closer to 2–3 percent! This means that *more than 90 percent* of students who apply to these schools will *not* be admitted, including many (very many!) who certainly could do well there. This is just a fact of the admissions picture as it is today.

Yes, the various college guidebooks can be informative—especially in their descriptions of academic programs and campus life. But looking at them just (or primarily) as ranking scorecards can obscure the unique factors at a given school that might well end up being most meaningful to *you*: the great teaching you'll experience from learned and caring professors, the way the campus community welcomes you and helps you feel at home and the friends you'll meet, and the unique experiences and opportunities you'll discover in and out of the classroom. *None* of which can be found anywhere else.

I do hope you're truly excited about the college or university you're about to attend. But if you didn't gain admission to your first-choice school, you might be tempted to start your college career already feeling somewhat disappointed. If you're in this situation, let me encourage you to pause and take a step back. Try to approach your new school with a positive attitude and an open mind about what you'll find there. As I've just suggested, give yourself the chance to discover the unique programs, people, and opportunities at your college or university that speak to your particular interests and plans. In short, give yourself the emotional space to fall in love with your new school and then make the most of it.

In my experience, many students who weren't admitted where they initially wanted to go landed in colleges and universities that actually suited them *much better* than those "first-choice" schools would have. The main point is that *the choices you make and the effort you give when you get there—to take best advantage of the special opportunities your school offers to you—will end up meaning far more than the name of the school on your diploma.* And if you're not convinced by what I've been saying, check out Frank

Bruni's excellent book, *Where You Go Is Not Who You'll Be*.[3] But if your school really doesn't offer what you want, you always have the option to transfer to somewhere else, and that's okay too.

FINANCING YOUR EDUCATION AND WHY ACCREDIDATION MATTERS

Let's acknowledge up front that your family's financial resources, the quality of the primary and secondary schools you've attended, and other opportunities you've already had (or not had) may make it easier or harder for you to attain your goals for college and beyond. The world is not always *fair*, and it's important that we all commit to doing what we can to improve it. (We'll return to this topic in Chapter 8.) But we all have to start off playing the cards we've been dealt.

Even so, each of us has the ability to choose how we respond to our unique circumstances. Going to college opens up an enormous range of possibilities and opportunities that can enable you to overcome even the most difficult life situations or personal issues you may have faced in the past—provided you're willing to apply yourself and persist in working hard to achieve your goals. The ideas you'll encounter in this book will help you figure out how to do this.

Nearly every private college or university offers financial aid, and public institutions are increasingly providing it as well. If you haven't yet finalized your choice of school, try not to be put off by a college or university's advertised "sticker price"; schools have lots of creative ways to "discount" it through various forms of financial aid. So, take a serious look at the colleges or

---

3   Please see Additional Resources.

universities that seem most promising or appealing, and find out whether their aid packages can make them affordable for you and your family.

Of course, most people reading this book are well past that point—you've already settled on your school of choice. Even so, I encourage you to stay in touch with your high school or pre-college guidance counselor(s), along with the financial aid office at your college or university. It's especially important to talk with them about how to minimize any debt you might need to take on. Moreover, if you or your family encounters a new or unexpected financial challenge along the way, let a counselor in the financial aid office know that your situation has changed. There are no guarantees, but there's a good chance they'll be able to adjust your aid package to enable you to stay enrolled.

Regardless of your situation, *please be cautious about taking on excessive debt.* Look closely at any "gap" between the total aid package your school offers to you and your family's "demonstrated need for financial aid"—as determined by the FAFSA (the Free Application for Federal Student Aid), which you and your family most likely have already filled out. The larger the gap, the more you or your family may need to borrow. Responsible colleges and universities work hard to narrow this difference as much as possible, and the best-resourced ones meet "full demonstrated need," which eliminates the gap altogether.

But whatever borrowing choices you may be facing, please make sure you know what they will mean—not just for your first year but for your entire time at college and beyond. Let me emphasize this point: *Before you start your first term*, it's important to do everything you can to *understand what the total cost of your college education will be.* Make your financial choices with your eyes fully open to their long-term implications. And if at all possible, *try to borrow no more than you reasonably can expect to earn in your first year out of college.* Although this is just a rule of thumb, it's a good target to keep in mind.

Please be especially careful about borrowing if you have chosen a for-profit institution. There are reputable for-profit schools that have positioned their graduates to improve their lives and advance themselves professionally. But unfortunately, this segment of higher education also includes far too many disreputable schools, which encourage their students to borrow the maximum amount available in federal and other loans and then fail to deliver on their educational promises. Some students end up not graduating at all yet still remain burdened with serious debt. Others complete their course of studies and only then discover that, because the school is not fully accredited, the degree they've earned is *not* recognized by graduate or professional schools or potential employers. Such "degrees" are essentially worthless in the larger world.

Accreditation is the federal government's official seal of approval for a college or university. It's your guarantee that a given school is financially sound and meets its educational obligations for its students. Most of all, a degree from an accredited institution will be recognized by other colleges and universities, professional schools, or graduate schools—as well as by employers. Almost every non-profit college or university is accredited, so you usually don't have to worry about it at one of these schools. But *if you're considering a for-profit institution, make sure to do your due diligence to assure it's fully accredited.* Here's the bottom line: *If a school is not fully accredited—regardless of how attractive it might seem or whatever promises people there might have made to you—do not attend it!* Instead, seek good advice to find an *accredited* alternative that works for you.

There's plenty of information available regarding any college or university—public, private, or for-profit. For example, the average amount of debt its graduates carry, the percentage of first-year students who return for their second year (this number is usually called "retention"), and the percentage of entering students who graduate within six years (the standard completion benchmark in higher education). Your high school or pre-college guidance counselor, or even a reference librarian at your local public library, should be happy to assist you in finding out what you need to know.

In the end, one of the most important ways to keep your student debt to a manageable level is to complete your degree in four years if possible. Obviously, every year in school contributes to your overall loan obligation. But going beyond four years can exhaust certain lower-cost state and federal resources and force you to borrow at higher interest rates with less favorable repayment terms. And of course, you'll be paying for extra years of housing and food—all the while *not* being full-time in the workforce and earning a paycheck.

Not all pathways to commencement are straight lines. Sometimes, circumstances beyond a student's control (for example, a car accident, serious illness, or a family issue) can extend the time to graduation. Some schools, unfortunately, do not have sufficient places in required courses to enable their students to complete certain majors in four years. (That's one more reason to check on a school's average time to graduation *before* you choose to attend it!) Some students switch their majors, transfer to another college or university, take a year off, or do something else that extends the time needed to earn their degree. Often, the decision to change direction turns out, in the long run, to be a great move, and you'll decide that the additional semester(s) or quarter(s) required to finish have been well worth it. Maybe not immediately, but soon and for the rest of your life.

In short, it's best to *begin* with the goal of finishing in four years. But if the route to your degree takes some unexpected turns, make the most of them! *The most important thing is to persevere in completing your undergraduate degree*—either at the school where you started or at another to which you've transferred, no matter how long it takes.

A PERSONAL NOTE

This book reflects a long career in higher education—in fact, more than five decades. During those years, I met thousands of students as they progressed from being brand-new, sometimes hesitant, first-year undergrads to confident seniors walking proudly across the commencement stage. Along with their parents, I celebrated their victories and, on occasion, shared the pain of their setbacks.

My own academic journey began at the University of Notre Dame (BA in philosophy); then on to graduate school at Yale University (MA, MPhil, and PhD in Philosophy). From there, I taught for fifteen years in the Department of Philosophy at Denison University (a national liberal arts college in Granville, Ohio). After that, I spent eleven years as the Dean of the College of Arts and Sciences and then Vice President for Academic Affairs at the University of Redlands (a private, liberal arts university in Redlands, California). And lastly, I served seventeen years as President of Skidmore College (a national liberal arts college in Saratoga Springs, New York). In short, the ideas in this book reflect my experience as an undergrad, grad student, professor, academic administrator, and president at both small colleges and major universities all over the US.

In addition, my wife Marie Glotzbach and I raised two children and saw them through their college years and beyond. So, we can add *parent* to the list of credentials. Marie, too, has always been an educator—sometimes in vocal music but primarily as a teacher and director in theater—at both secondary and college levels. So, it's fair to say that we've both dedicated our professional lives to helping young people achieve their dreams through education.

This book's more specific roots trace back to talks I gave to new students and their parents: in earlier versions at Denison and Redlands and more recently to each entering class at Skidmore in the college's fall opening convocation. Frankly, I would have loved to sit down with each new student and parent over a cup of coffee and talk about their dreams, anxieties, and concerns. I would have enjoyed hearing what was on their minds, and then I would have done my best to answer their questions and suggest some things to think about.

But of course, that wasn't possible. So, I summarized what I thought would be most useful for new students and parents to hear in those annual presentations. Speaking to each entering class was always a highpoint of the academic year for me. I loved sharing my passion for what college students experience, along with my sense of how important it is to get your college years off to the right kind of start. I also enjoyed encouraging parents to embrace their continuing role as partners in this enterprise.

After hearing those talks, parents frequently asked for a copy of my remarks; sometimes, students did as well. I resisted these requests because my talking points were never formatted as a text that could stand on its own, and they continued to evolve from year to year. Moreover, there were things I wanted to say, even then, that didn't fit into the time constraints for those events. Now, having retired from the Skidmore presidency, I've turned those notes and the additional ideas and stories into this book.

It would be terrific if we could get together in person and talk face-to-face. But I hope this book can be the next best thing. Whether you're a first-time college student, returning student, transfer student, or a parent or guardian, my most sincere wish is to share with you some pointers about making the most of this remarkable, once-in-a-lifetime opportunity. Even so, please try to imagine that we're having a conversation.

As you would expect, the chapters build on one another. So, students, if you run into one that doesn't particularly speak to you, I would encourage you to work through it anyway, and then move on to the next. And if you come upon some places where things seem a little complicated, just keep in mind that this is a *college-level conversation*. So, hang in there! Give yourself the chance to connect with what we're talking about. You *will* be able to work through it—just like you'll do in your new college courses.

TWO QUESTIONS, BEFORE WE MOVE ON

In this book, we'll have a lot to say about *freedom* and *choice*. In fact, I strongly believe that *understanding and embracing the new level of freedom you'll experience in college will be the foundation of everything else you'll accomplish*. The beginning of your college career is the perfect moment to take charge of your life in new and more satisfying ways than ever before—to fully engage the project of shaping the autonomous, self-directing adult you want to become. So, let me conclude this section with two questions that also relate to choices—one for students and a second for both students and parents.

First, to the student: *Why are you going to college at all?* Everyone is pretty much required to complete high school, but no one is forced to go to college—and you certainly don't have to go right away. So, please have a better reason than just taking the expected next step after high school. Here's just a small sample of alternatives you might pursue instead. You could:

- take a year off to work or travel—to make sure you're really ready for college;
- volunteer your service for some worthy cause or organization;
- enter the military and go to college later using the financial aid benefits you'll earn;
- attend a trade or culinary school or consider a different apprenticeship.

There are many other possibilities as well.

In the current labor market, increasing numbers of companies are considering applicants who haven't yet completed college but are willing and able to learn on the job. This is called skill-based hiring, and it reopens some important avenues for upward social mobility for people who don't hold a college degree. As economist Ben Wildavsky reports, "Fourteen states, including ten in [2022] alone, have dropped degree requirements for many state jobs."[4] But Wildavsky also notes that these advertised opportunities may not always amount to what they seem. For example,

---

[4]   Ben Wildavsky, "Let's Stop Pretending College Degrees Don't Matter," *New York Times*, August 21, 2023, https://www.nytimes.com/2023/08/21/opinion/skills-based-hiring-college-degree-job-market-wage-premium.html.

hiring decisions may still reflect employers' preferences for a college degree, despite what is stated in a job advertisement.

So, let me be very clear: *I'm not at all trying to discourage you from going to college.* Both the short- and long-term earnings prospects for college graduates still far exceed those of non-college grads. As Wildavsky writes,

> The economic advantage of getting a college degree remains at just about an all-time high when compared with the average earnings of Americans with only a high school diploma. In recent years, a typical college graduate earned a median wage premium of more than $30,000, or almost 75 percent more than those who had completed just high school, a 2019 New York Fed analysis found.

In the long run, over the course of an entire professional life, college graduates can expect to earn, on average, at least $1 million more than those lacking a college degree. And throughout this book, we'll discuss many other important reasons to seek a college education *beyond* preparing to enter the workforce. In fact, as I hope you'll agree, the most meaningful reasons to pursue a college career extend well beyond the work you'll do and the money you'll earn.

But I am urging you *not to go to college by default*—just because you've always seen it as the next step after high school, or because it's what other people assume you will do. Instead, *think about what you want to accomplish, where you want to be when you finish, and how college fits into those plans.* You don't need to have all the answers worked out right now, and we'll spend a good deal of time on these topics later on. But please approach this exciting next stage in your life—and the enormous opportunities for intellectual and personal development that are at its core—with a sense of personal agency. Embark on your undergraduate career as *an intentional project*—as something you're setting out to do on purpose.

Second, to both students and parents: *What are you prepared to do* together *to gain the absolute most from these precious college years?* Succeeding in college takes determination, perseverance, and sometimes sacrifice, on *everyone's* part—students and parents alike. Reflecting on your role in the process and reaffirming your commitment to it will help you keep your eyes on the prize. And let me add that you, as a student, need to define what will count as success in college—and after college—for *you*. This is one of the most important ways of embracing and owning your new freedom. As you go through this book, you'll find lots of ideas, specific strategies, and I hope, encouragement that will help you do so.

Now let's move ahead to a chapter that sets the stage for everything else that follows.

PART ONE

THE BIG PICTURE

CHAPTER 1

WHAT'S A COLLEGE EDUCATION
FOR—WHAT WILL THE WORLD ASK
OF *YOU* WHEN YOU GRADUATE?

The mind once enlightened cannot again become dark.
—*Thomas Paine*

I n May 2023, venture capitalist Katherine Boyle tweeted, "The decline in liberal arts degrees bodes well for society on almost every dimension. College students now know that majoring in Book Club won't get you a great job. This is progress."[5] She was responding to a study by the National Student Clearinghouse Research Center that reported the following: while the number of US students seeking four-year degrees in computer and information sciences rose 34 percent from 2017 to 2022, the number

---

5   Katherine Boyle (@KTmBoyle), "The decline in liberal arts degrees bodes well for society on almost every dimension," Tweet, May 20, 2023, https://twitter.com/KTmBoyle/status/1659943789337640960.

of English majors fell by 23 percent, and the number of history majors fell 12 percent.[6]

These statistics are real. But Boyle's conclusions are dead wrong. In fact, she herself is a liberal arts graduate with a BA in government. And so, she should be better informed about the value of this kind of education—both for graduates' future employment prospects and for the personal and intellectual growth they should expect to gain from college.

Boyle's comment threw fuel on an already burning debate about the "usefulness" of studying certain subjects—especially the humanities—rather than technology, business, or other fields often regarded as more "practical." As a faculty member and administrator, I encountered similar concerns from students and parents throughout my career. But this discussion has gained intensity year over year, as each new student cohort faces ever-greater pressures to realize the maximum economic value from the steep undergraduate tuition their families are paying or the significant loans they've taken on.

For the rest of this chapter, we'll talk about the core of what you'll be up to in college, how to think about your choice of major, and what the world will need—and, indeed, *expect*—from you after you graduate. There are two parts to this discussion: The first addresses *personal* questions about positioning yourself for both professional success and personal fulfillment in your post-college life; the second, which we'll get to in a few pages, looks at the significant but all-too-often-overlooked *social value* of your college education.

---

[6] Nick Anderson, "College is remade as tech majors surge and humanities dwindle," *Washington Post*, May 20, 2023, https://www.washingtonpost.com/education/2023/05/19/college-majors-computer-science-humanities/.

LEARNING TO ADAPT TO CHANGE

Let's begin with a story.

Preparing for a job that doesn't yet exist: Chris

In the fall of 2001, a student named Chris arrived at Skidmore College, where I would soon begin serving as President. He took courses in a variety of areas, cultivated his love for literature and writing, and joined the staff of the student newspaper. He also maintained a commitment to music, performing with a campus a cappella group for four years.

After graduating in 2005, Chris set out to become a professional writer, pursuing jobs in publishing and media. But none of them led to a positive career trajectory. He recalls, "While I was able to land pieces in some major newspapers and national magazines, I never felt like I was building anything—the flywheel never seemed to gain enough momentum."

Then in 2008, a friend suggested Chris learn to design iPhone apps, which had become a red-hot field following Apple's release of its first iPhone in 2007. It took several years, but he eventually landed a job at the *New York Times*—not as a journalist but as a *senior software engineer*. To his surprise, Chris discovered he thoroughly enjoyed developing the code that powered the paper's smartphone and tablet apps and kept them from crashing. Today, he runs his own successful software company creating new apps focused on music.

As an undergrad, Chris never took a single computer science or business course, and he certainly never considered becoming a mobile app developer. How could he? At that point, *mobile apps didn't even exist!*[7] Although he had learned HTML (the markup language for web pages) on his own while starting an online magazine, he never thought of college as preparation for a tech career.

But Chris was able to evolve into a successful young tech entrepreneur because he graduated with a set of incredibly effective cognitive skills. Among these were the ability to access knowledge from different fields, the flexibility to change his mind and pivot when necessary, and inner confidence in his own judgment. Most importantly, *he learned how to continue learning.*

***

You could have two quite different takeaways from this vignette: Boyle would likely say that Chris wasted his college years by not studying computer science or business. He could have gotten to his tech career more quickly and easily, without those early

---

[7]   To be technically accurate, a few features on some cell phones were essentially proto-apps, but they were primitive and not very interesting—hardly foreshadowing the industry we know today.

missteps and dead-end jobs. Alternatively, I would maintain that Chris was wise to pursue a course of studies that equipped him with the incredibly useful cognitive skills mentioned above—which positioned him to succeed in a rapidly changing and unpredictable professional environment, as both it and his career goals evolved.

In arguing for the second take-away, I would ask people tempted to think like Boyle to remember this projection: on average, you and other college grads will change careers—not just jobs, *careers*—*nine* times over your working lifetime. Like Chris, ten years out from graduation, you might find yourself exploring a field that wasn't even imagined when you were in school. His is just one story. But it exemplifies countless others I could tell about broadly educated college graduates who went on to accomplish extraordinary things, often in areas apparently unrelated to what they studied in college.

To not just survive but to *thrive* in the rapidly changing professional world of the twenty-first century, you'll need a *powerful and adaptive intellectual toolkit*—you might picture it as a cognitive Swiss Army knife.[8] Specifically, like Chris, you'll need to be broadly educated, flexible in your thinking, and able to draw upon multiple areas of knowledge. Above all, you'll need to be adept at *continuing to learn*. Equipping yourself with this toolkit will give you what you most need to pursue your personal dreams and achieve success. Let's explore in more detail what this is all about.

---

[8]   David Epstein uses this term in his excellent book *Range: Why Generalists Triumph in a Specialized World*. Please see Additional Resources.

WHAT DOES "LIBERAL ARTS EDUCATION" REALLY MEAN?

*We are drowning in information, while starving for wisdom.
The world henceforth will be run by synthesizers, people able
to put together the right information at the right time, think
critically about it, and make important choices wisely.*
—E. O. Wilson

Most teachers at the college and university level would place the key intellectual abilities we've been talking about under the headings of "*liberal arts education,*" "*the liberal arts,*" or "*liberal learning.*" The notion of *liberal education* traces its origin to the Roman orator Cicero's[9] use of the Latin word "*liber*" meaning *free*. First and foremost, he said, a *liberal education* provides the appropriate intellectual training for a *free citizen*. "Free" and "freedom" are words people toss around a lot these days, but we don't always stop to consider what they mean.

A *truly* free person is someone who is not only able to *choose what to do* but who also accepts responsibility for *deciding what to think*—for determining which beliefs to hold, which to reject, and which to set aside for further consideration. They also accept responsibility for not being "willfully blind" (a legal term) regarding facts that add up to an obvious conclusion that reasonable people would accept.

A liberal education challenges you to acknowledge and embrace these profound personal responsibilities, which are the foundation for all other kinds of freedom. (We'll have more to say about freedom in Chapter 2.) Most importantly, it empowers you to live up to these responsibilities. At its core, *liberal learning* aims to free you from the grip of received opinion, unexamined

---

9   Cicero lived from 106 to 43 BCE.

assumptions, and inherited prejudices by developing your own critical and self-critical intellectual faculties. It encourages you to explore a broad range of viewpoints on important issues. As you do this, you earn the right to come to your own conclusions about them.

The specific goals of liberal education encompass a number of key proficiencies:

- reading carefully and insightfully
- thinking critically and distinguishing between more justified and less justified statements in what you read, see, and hear
- formulating cogent and persuasive arguments
- communicating effectively in writing, speech, or electronic media
- drawing upon knowledge from different academic areas, realizing that each field represented in the undergraduate curriculum has its unique way of exploring the world, generating knowledge, and creating meaning
- as E. O. Wilson suggests in the above quotation, the crucial ability to sort through the deluge of information inundating us today
- understanding how the sciences work—the physical and life sciences (including psychology), mathematics and computer science, and the social sciences—and appreciating how they develop and test hypotheses and theories, how they collect relevant data, how they evolve and correct earlier mistakes, and how they reflect the social world in which they exist
- seeing how appeals to data, evidence, and facts of any kind—*empirical claims*—need to be grounded in legitimate inquiry

- understanding how well-grounded empirical claims should inform political discussions and decision-making
- being aware of the limits of what we can know at any given time, but also understanding why a great many beliefs can reasonably be regarded as true
- knowing how public information is produced (in news reports, on social media platforms, etc.) and learning how to distinguish more and less reliable sources
- learning about cultures beyond your own, appreciating what they may have to teach you, and affirming the humanity of their people
- learning a new foreign language or extending your previous knowledge, at least to a first level of proficiency, which opens a window into a foreign culture and gives you fresh insights about the structure of your first language
- strengthening your creative imagination—both to help you be a better problem solver and to enhance your ability to relate to people whose situations and life experiences may be unlike your own
- and perhaps most importantly, as I've been urging, developing both *the capacity and the inclination* to be a curious, lifelong learner—someone who can change their mind in response to new facts, ideas, or arguments

You've actually been working on these abilities since elementary school. Now it will serve you well to develop them on purpose—to keep them front and center in your undergraduate studies.

As these bullets indicate, the liberal arts are much broader than just the humanities (English literature, philosophy, history, etc.). In fact, liberal learning comprehends the full breadth of the traditional undergraduate curriculum: the humanities, the social sciences, the visual and performing arts, the physical and biological sciences, and more recently data science. It's prudent to enhance your intellectual toolkit by doing at least some academic work in each of these areas.

The good news is that you can cultivate these essential cognitive skills no matter which course of study you pursue—whether it's one of the traditional liberal arts disciplines or a pre-professional program like business, engineering, or pre-med. In fact, you'll need these abilities just as much in one of those careers as in any other line of work. Especially in today's rapidly evolving work world, these intellectual capacities are incredibly valuable.

And by the way, research shows that heads of large and small companies alike look for these skills in people they want to employ. Quite a few Fortune 500 CEOs themselves have degrees in the humanities. Their earlier experience in theater, for example, was cited as important "by the Governor of New Jersey, ... the Canadian Ambassador to the United Nations, Canadian Prime Minister Justin Trudeau (who taught theater in high school), US Senator Ted Cruz, and Supreme Court Justice Ketanji Brown."[10] In other words, pursuing a liberal arts education is about the most "practical" thing you can do.

"LIBERAL EDUCATION" DOESN'T MEAN "POLITICALLY LIBERAL"

Before we go any further, let's put aside another common misunderstanding about liberal learning. You may have noticed that I've been talking about this educational framework *without* bringing in politics. Specifically, I've *not* been contrasting liberal vs. conservative political views.

---

[10] Madison Malone Kircher, "Grown-Up Theater Kids Run the World," *New York Times,* August 20, 2023, https://www.nytimes.com/2023/08/20/style/grown-up-theater-kids.html.

Among other things, a liberal education helps you develop the capacity to *make up your own mind* about political matters. To say this another way, it equips you with the intellectual tools to evaluate different perspectives across the political spectrum: conservative vs. liberal vs. progressive vs. whatever. It positions you to *thoughtfully* determine which one(s) you personally choose to embrace and, if appropriate, to change your mind later on in response to new things you've learned.

So, whatever might be said about the political climate at a particular college or university, a liberal education is not at all designed to indoctrinate you into becoming a political liberal. Instead, as I've been emphasizing, it's intended to teach you *to think for yourself*, regardless of where you stand politically. I very much encourage you to keep this fundamental fact in mind throughout your college career.

YOUR SCHOOL'S GENERAL EDUCATION CURRICULUM

Your college or university most likely expects you to begin working on these cognitive abilities through its general education curriculum (its "GE curriculum"), an important part of your graduation requirements. Much of your first year (and beyond) will probably be devoted to entry-level courses, which are designed to introduce you to a wide range of areas of knowledge.[11]

---

[11] A small number of schools don't have a required GE curriculum. Instead, they place a premium on academic advising to help students develop their own individualized course of studies. That can be an excellent educational model for creative, highly motivated students who want set their own direction in college. But if you're attending such a school, it's still to your advantage to incorporate a broad range of fields within your personal curriculum—even including some you might not initially be inclined to explore.

Please resist the temptation to see your GE classes as merely a series of academic hurdles to clear, before moving on to what you "really want to study." Try *not* to say that you're just "getting them out of the way," even though you will hear other people talk like that. Your school's faculty designed your GE curriculum to provide you an academic foundation for the more concentrated studies you'll pursue later in your major—whatever it turns out to be. This firm and wide conceptual base will set you up to do the more in-depth learning expected in your upper-division classes.

Even more importantly, these GE courses should help motivate you to become a *lifelong learner*. At their best, they will stimulate your curiosity about exploring unfamiliar areas of knowledge and give you new ways to make sense of both the world and your own life. So, let them do this for you! (In fact, students are often surprised by what they carry away from a class they initially resisted taking.) By understanding the value of liberal learning, you can approach your G.E. courses with the interest, respect, and appreciation they deserve.

And let me emphasize that you can and should continue to work on these valuable cognitive skills in your more advanced courses as well. Your professors in those upper-level, more specialized classes may not always mention the broader intellectual abilities I've been describing. But you can always continue to develop your writing, for example, or your critical thinking skills. You also can look for ways to relate the specific topics you're studying to other areas you've already encountered and, most importantly, to the "wicked problems" we'll talk about in a few pages. Finally, as Chris's story illustrates, these cognitive skills and abilities will serve you incredibly well, no matter what professional pathways you follow, initially or later on in your life.

CHOOSING YOUR MAJOR

To be sure, I would never dissuade you from selecting a technical or pre-professional major, provided you're genuinely enthusiastic about studying that field. The world certainly needs more scientists, computing specialists, engineers, architects, doctors and nurses, and ethical business leaders, and pursuing majors in these areas can be enormously satisfying. But it's a profound mistake to choose *any* major solely—or even primarily—because it appears to promise future prosperity. In fact, current employment conditions make lousy predictors of future trends, so any such "guarantee" can turn out to be an illusion. Today's "sure path" to a high-paying career can become tomorrow's ticket to unemployment.

For instance, the tech industry was disproportionally hit by layoffs in the early months of 2023. About a decade ago, when students flooded into law schools—often taking on large loans to do so—too many found, when they graduated, that there weren't enough available positions in law firms to go around. Certainly, as I said above, the world will always need computer scientists and attorneys. But choosing a major *solely* on the basis of potential financial return is like investing for retirement by playing the slots. Besides, a solid liberal education will position you to pursue post-graduate study in a wide variety of areas.

A much more promising way to decide on a major is, first of all, *to select a field that sparks your interest*. Studies suggest that students who choose a major based on their interest—rather than some external reason—perform at higher levels, both during college and for years to come. This is no surprise to psychologists, who've long understood that intrinsic motivation eats extrinsic motivation for breakfast. And this is another reason to take your

GE courses seriously. You never know, in advance, which one might capture your attention and point you to a terrific major.

As you begin considering various majors, it's a great idea to check out what graduates from a given department in your college or university have gone on to do. The answers may surprise you. For example, when I taught in the philosophy department at Denison, our majors went on to careers in advertising, business, law, medicine, and even the back office of a professional baseball team. And of course, some pursued graduate study in philosophy and are teaching at colleges or universities today. Many medical schools now actually prefer humanities majors over science majors—all things being equal and provided, of course, that they've completed the necessary science courses along the way. That's because the medical profession has discovered, through research, that humanities majors often turn out to be more successful physicians (that is, they have better patient outcomes), in large part because of their capacity to relate to their patients as human beings.

And there's something new to be aware of today: no matter your major, it's prudent to understand the threats and opportunities increasingly represented by artificial intelligence (AI)—especially large language generative AI programs, such as ChatGPT. You've probably already encountered these programs in high school, and you certainly will be learning more about them in many of your college classes. They will likely become familiar tools, just like calculators did in math classes several decades ago. In fact, because this technology is so revolutionary—and so widely applicable—some colleges have begun talking about it during their new-student orientation. Properly used, generative AI represents one more way to enhance your learning and to improve your effectiveness as a working professional.

At the same time, it's a very good bet that AI systems will disrupt the work world you'll have to navigate—probably in ways we can only begin to anticipate. Specifically, they threaten to replace any number of people (including college graduates) who previously *thought* their jobs were secure. As Claire Cain Miller and Courtney Cox report:

> The jobs most exposed to automation now are office jobs, those that require more cognitive skills, creativity and high levels of education. The workers affected are likelier to be highly paid, and slightly likelier to be women, a variety of research has found.[12]

We should always regard predictions of the future (including my own!) with a healthy degree of skepticism. But a great deal of evidence now suggests that changes brought on by the rapidly developing field of AI will reverberate across a wide range of workplaces, even if we can't know precisely what form these changes will take.

For these reasons, it becomes even *more* important to equip your intellectual toolkit with skills less likely to be replicated—and replaced—by this technology. As *New York Times* columnist David Brooks writes:

> A.I. will force us humans to double down on *those talents and skills that only humans possess.* The most important thing about A.I. may be that it shows us what it can't do, and so reveals

---

12   Claire Cain Miller and Courtney Cox, "In Reversal Because of A.I., Office Jobs are Now More at Risk," *New York Times*, August 24, 2023, https://www.nytimes.com/2023/08/24/upshot/artificial-intelligence-jobs.html.

who we are and what we have to offer [empha-
sis added].[13]

So, what abilities are *least* likely to be replicated in future AI systems? Among those special capacities, Brooks lists "a distinct personal voice," "presentation skills," "a childlike talent for creativity,"
"unusual worldviews," and "empathy." We don't have the space for
a more in-depth discussion of this topic, but the abilities Brooks
references are precisely the ones best developed through the kind
of liberal arts courses I've been talking about (especially in the
humanities). Yet another reason to make sure to include a broad
selection of liberal arts classes in your personal course of studies.
(We'll have more to say about AI in Chapter 7.)

You may have noticed that what I've been advising collides
head-on with what you've heard over and over: "Make sure you
study a concrete, practical subject in college that will set you up
for a well-paying job following graduation." This conventional
wisdom, though well intentioned, is based upon a misleading
picture of the rapidly evolving work world you'll encounter when
you finish your formal education. In fact, the *narrower* a field of
study, the *shorter* its useful life is likely to be. So, don't be afraid
to pursue a major that excites your passion and complement it by
seeking a broad liberal arts education.

So far, I've been focusing on how to prepare most effectively
for the professional world you'll encounter after graduation. It
turns out, however, that there are even more telling *intrinsic reasons*—beyond advancing your professional career (as important

---

13   David Brooks, "In the Age of A.I., Major in Being Human," *New York Times*,
      February 2, 2023, https://www.nytimes.com/2023/02/02/opinion/ai-human-
      education.html. See also Farhad Manjoo, "A Creator (Me) Made a Masterpiece
      with A.I.," *New York Times*, August 25, 2023, https://www.nytimes.com/
      2023/08/25/opinion/ai-art-intellectual-property.html.

as that is!)—for valuing the kind of liberal learning we've been discussing. Some of these factors relate to the way a broad liberal education can enrich your personal life by helping you appreciate the joy to be found by an appreciation of art, music, theater, literature, and so on. These dimensions of your life will likely become even more important to you as years go by. (I hope you already realize this, but if not, please trust me for now.) They also can help you be a better parent, should you choose that personal direction. Gaining knowledge in these areas increases your likelihood of becoming a more thoughtful and personally fulfilled human being. Life offers no guarantees, but the odds are in favor of this outcome.

In sum, all the things we've been discussing should encourage you to resist any pressure to choose a major that may set you up for just your *first* job or for any other external reason. Instead, choose a field that genuinely inspires your enthusiasm and also promises to contribute to the flexible intellectual toolkit you'll need across your career(s) and, indeed, throughout your life!

WHAT THE WORLD WILL ASK OF YOU

> *Democracy has to be born anew every generation,*
> *and education is its midwife.*
> —*John Dewey*

There are other significant reasons to pursue liberal learning that relate to the urgent social questions confronting all of us—not the least of which are the fate of our planet and the future of our political order. This takes us to the second part of our conversation, to the larger *social values* inherent in a college education.

Today there are more living college and university graduates, both in the United States and around the world, than at any time in history. And yet, it often seems we're further from being able to settle our cultural and political differences—or even have a civil conversation about them—than ever before. Why should this matter to you? Because an essential purpose of any college education is to foster the skills and habits of mind that will help you not only *navigate* the world but also *improve* it. To understand our physical and social environments and help make them better tomorrow than they are today. To leave the world a better place, both for you and for generations to follow.

As we've been discussing, over the next four years, you'll prepare to build a career and construct a life that is satisfying in many ways. These important *personal values*—or *private goods*—associated with a college education are easy to understand because they affect you directly as an individual. But there's a complementary, historically significant, and too-often-overlooked value that I'll now ask you to consider. Your college education also serves a crucial *social purpose* and represents an enormously important *social good*.

I've argued that the educational objectives central to the concept of *liberal learning* are not political in themselves. But they do relate directly to the essential values and attributes of *democratic citizenship*—things that make a democratic republic a viable form of government. In other words, there is a deep connection between a well-functioning democracy and liberal education—a relationship that has shaped both the educational goals and courses of study in colleges and universities in the United States throughout its history.

In our young republic's formative days, political leaders largely honored James Madison's remark that "the advancement and diffusion of knowledge...is the only guardian of true liberty." Accordingly, they made provisions for public schools and established colleges. Those early schools—Harvard, William and Mary, Yale, Princeton, and Penn—were founded in the 1600s and 1700s as small, religious colleges with the primary purpose of training men (primarily white men with sufficient financial means back then) for lives of civic engagement and leadership in business, the military, politics, and the ministry.

Student populations at colleges and universities have become significantly more diverse over the years, making them a much better reflection of our nation and the world at large. And, as you would expect, college curricula and programs also have evolved considerably since those early days—to encompass today's broader and more inclusive perspectives on sociology, history, politics, literature, and most other fields. But properly understood, a liberal education still provides the appropriate preparation—in fact, the *necessary* preparation—for *free persons* whose task is *to govern themselves* in a democratic republic.

Unfortunately, too many contemporary political, business, and even higher education leaders have embraced the idea that today's college education is *solely* a private good. Our society has pretty much lost the sense of a college education as a social good. But to heal our politically imperiled and divided nation, we need to reclaim the idea that a college education is not only a *private* but also a *public good*. Specifically, colleges and universities bear a special responsibility to prepare graduates who can help us move past our current social and political disconnects. This educational objective is every bit as important as preparing you to lead a successful professional life and a fulfilling personal one.

At a moment when the very concepts of *truth* and *facts* have come under withering partisan attack, the world absolutely needs *your* help to elevate our public discourse and political life as a space in which facts (as opposed to "alternative facts") and good arguments can overcome groundless assertions, invalid or unsound arguments, and even outright lies. A major part of this work will be learning how to talk with—and *listen* to—people you don't necessarily agree with politically. To do so, it will be helpful to embrace the basic question: "What would it take to change your mind?" But another part of that work is even more fundamental: helping to rebuild our shared foundations of social agreement and effective public discourse.

We can capture all this in a single sentence: *Beginning with your time in college, I'm challenging you to make a lifelong commitment to becoming an informed, responsible, and caring citizen.*[14] But it's not just me saying this. The pressing needs of our society—and our entire planet—provide ample reason for you to take up this cause. And if *you*, as a college-educated person, don't do it, who will?

Let's talk more about what's at issue here.

WICKED PROBLEMS

The world into which you'll graduate presents all of us with a full slate of challenges—one of which we've recently lived through: the COVID-19 pandemic. It would be difficult to overstate the extent to which this virus disrupted your life, your family's life, and, in fact, all our lives. It radically altered the ways we interact. It threw a monkey wrench into the economy. And no doubt it fouled up your own educational experience beyond all recognition. It also changed college teaching and learning in untold ways. It now seems

---

[14] This phrase comes from the mission statement of Skidmore College. Most colleges and universities include a similar commitment among their stated educational objectives. In short, your school most likely expects you to care about these important topics too.

that we'll be living with COVID-19 for the foreseeable future (like the flu). Long after the initial disturbances of the pandemic have receded in the rear-view mirror, we'll still be sorting out its broad, lingering impacts on both education and society at large.

So, good for you for having survived it! As you begin your college career, I sincerely hope you've regained your academic momentum. If not, you may have to do some extra work to catch up. But when you do, your future self will thank you for making that effort. You also may be dealing with some COVID-related mental health challenges, a topic we'll return to later on (in Chapter 5). But the good news is that—with effective COVID vaccines and boosters designed to deal with emerging variants, along with now familiar public health protocols (e.g., masking, social distancing, and so on), and a better medical understanding of how to contain and deal with the illness when it's contracted— life on a college or university campus once again feels much more like it formerly did. Along with the rest of society, colleges and universities have finally returned to something closer to "normal."

Despite the profound consequences of the pandemic, however, let me suggest that other pressing issues will be even more significant in the long run. Here's just a sample of these other wicked problems we collectively face today and that will continue to affect your life in years to come:

- global climate change, which threatens the future of everyone on the planet in multiple ways– including "our economy, health, well-being, security, and quality of life"[15]

---

[15] "The Importance of Measuring the Fiscal and Economic Costs of Climate Change," by Candace Vahlsing and C Zach Liscow, a report from the Office of Management and Budget issued by The White House (14 March 2023): https:// www.whitehouse.gov/omb/briefing-room/2023/03/14/the-importance-of-measuring-the-fiscal-and-economic-costs-of-climate-change/#:~:text= Climate%20risks%20could%20affect%20the,spur%20the%20transition% 20to%20clean.

- a deep erosion of faith and trust in our political and social institutions—and in too many cases, an outright attack on democracy—coupled with diminished optimism about what the future will bring
- the loss of a common ground of commitment to constitutional and democratic institutions and processes, coupled with an absence of agreed-upon facts as a basis for public deliberation about political decisions
- the willingness of a growing segment of both US and international populations to regard violence as an acceptable form of political expression
- the pressing need to regulate and reimagine the Internet and social media to make them more likely to serve as vehicles for accessing useful information rather than sources of disinformation and nonsense—sometimes dangerous nonsense
- an escalating epidemic of violence involving firearms in our nation
- the ongoing struggle to achieve full economic, racial, and social justice at home and abroad
- the need to assist large segments of the population that have experienced economic disruption because of shifting international economic patterns and domestic political decisions about "globalization" and other dimensions of the economy
- a second industrial revolution, which already has begun, based on expanding and likely disruptive applications of artificial intelligence and robotics across virtually all phases of our lives—a technology that carries exciting promise but also the possibility of significant risk

- the social and political steps that need to be taken to prepare for and, where possible, to prevent future pandemics
- and many others

My use of the phrase "wicked problems" to describe these issues isn't an artifact of having lived for some time in the Northeast; it's actually a technical term that's increasingly being used in these conversations. If you haven't come across it already, you're likely to run into it in your college coursework. It refers to large, unstructured problems that cannot be resolved by relying upon just one area of knowledge or a single (linear) mode of thought. These problems occur in "wicked learning domains," which are quite different from "kind domains."

Kind learning domains are largely defined by clear rules. They tend to provide immediate feedback, which allows you to improve your performance through deliberate practice. Think about working to increase your free-throw-shooting percentage in basketball, learning to play a musical instrument, becoming a better chess player, or improving your competence in geometry or algebra. Even though these learning tasks may not be easy, it's pretty clear what you have to do to master those skills—or, more generally, to solve a problem in such a "kind" context.

By contrast, wicked learning domains lack these clarifying features. As I said above, they are largely *unstructured*; they come with few (if any) effective guidelines; and when you're working in such an environment, it can be difficult to know when or *if* you're making progress toward a solution. Author David Epstein puts it this way:

> In wicked domains, the rules of the game are often unclear or incomplete, there may or may not be repetitive patterns and they may not be

obvious, and feedback is often delayed, inaccurate, or both.[16]

In wicked domains, gaining more experience doing the same thing over and over can actually lead to *worse* performance by reinforcing old patterns of behavior that simply aren't helpful in solving new problems. Successful problem-solving in a wicked domain requires *creative imagination* and the ability to draw upon new ideas, analogies, or information from sometimes seemingly unrelated areas.

Climate change is a prime example of a wicked problem— one that has drawn the particular attention of many current high school and college students.[17] Despite what some politicians would have us believe, you certainly know that climate change is not a hoax. It's all too real. Unprecedented heatwaves, increasingly intense hurricanes, rainstorms, tornados, drought, wildfires, and flooding, represent just some of the most evident consequences of rising global temperatures. Here are some specifics:

- July 2023 was the hottest month ever recorded worldwide, and ocean temperatures in Florida's east coast topped 100° Fahrenheit (basically, what you'd find in a hot tub).
- Smoke from massive Canadian wildfires in spring and summer 2023 affected wide swaths of the US—in some cases forcing temporary shut-downs of airport operations.

---

16 Epstein provides a very clear summary of these concepts in Chapter 1 of *Range*, p. 21; please see Additional Resources.
17 David Gelles, "With TikTok and Lawsuits, Gen Z Takes on Climate Change," *New York Times*, August 19, 2023, https://www.nytimes.com/2023/08/19/climate/young-climate-activists.html?smid=nytcore-ios-share&referringSource=articleShare.

- The devastating wildfire in Maui in August 2023 caused tragic losses of life and property.

I'm sure you could easily come up with other examples of your own.

Addressing both the causes and the far-reaching environmental consequences of climate change is not a task with a straight-line, obvious solution. It requires us to draw upon multiple perspectives: scientific and technological, political and governmental, economic and business, ethical and religious, cultural and social, among others. Above all, for both individuals and nations, continuing to behave in ways that created the problem in the first place clearly will not resolve it.

And as you're no doubt aware, the world is running out of time to address this crisis. At the time of writing, the most recent United Nations climate report states that "earth is likely to cross a critical threshold for global warming within the next decade, and nations will need to make an immediate and drastic shift away from fossil fuels to prevent the planet from heating dangerously beyond that level."[18] These warnings are not new, but continuing research is raising awareness of the rapidly closing window for action and is lending new urgency to the issue.

At the same time, however, taking on the climate crisis will create any number of remarkable *opportunities*. Here's just a sample:

- innovative ways to provide food and water for the growing global population

---

[18] Brad Plumer, "World Has Less Than a Decade to Stop Catastrophic Warming, U.N. Panel Says," *New York Times*, March 20, 2023, https://www.nytimes.com/2023/03/20/climate/global-warming-ipcc-earth.html.

- large and small projects to make the world more sustainable and equitable—especially in energy production, distribution, and use
- novel possibilities to reimagine how societies function and how nations of the world interact and cooperate

These and many other aspects of the response to climate change promise to create new industries with their own jobs and careers. Wicked problems, generally, combine this mix of challenges and possibilities; we just have to identify the opportunities and learn how to make them real.

THE ASSAULT ON DEMOCRACY

The way... we seek is that condition of... being at home in the world, which is called love, and which we term democracy.
—*Ralph Ellison*

Another enormous wicked social problem presently confronting all of us these past few years—perhaps the most significant one of all—is an unprecedented assault on democratic political institutions, both at home and abroad.

Increasingly, foreign autocrats in countries such as Russia, Hungary, Belarus, China, Iran, and North Korea, among others are consolidating their political power and threatening their neighbors. These autocrats maintain that contemporary Western democracies, including the United States, are simply not up to the challenges of the contemporary world. Democracies, they say, are too slow, too divided, and too lacking in shared social values to effectively address threats, make workable long-range plans, and then implement them. *Are they right?*

Russian President Vladimir Putin's cynical and unprovoked invasion of the independent neighboring democratic nation of Ukraine and the response from the US, NATO, and countries around the world have made it clear that standing up for democracy internationally carries economic costs and political challenges for us all. But it is an enormously important cause with implications that extend far beyond this one conflict. Dr. Madeleine Albright, US Secretary of State from 1997 to 2001, offered this comment in an op-ed:

> Ukraine is entitled to its sovereignty, no matter who its neighbors happen to be. In the modern era, great countries accept that, and so must Mr. Putin. This is the message undergirding recent Western diplomacy. It defines the difference between a world governed by the rule of law and one answerable to no rules at all.[19]

Along with our international allies, the US now faces two questions: First, are we are prepared to continue standing up for these long-established principles of international order? And second, are we willing to bear the costs that come with doing so?

Closer to home, we face our own troubling political issues. When US Supreme Court Justice Stephen Breyer spoke at the White House to announce his retirement, he commented that both George Washington and Abraham Lincoln regarded the American democratic republic as an *experiment*—one that most seventeenth-, eighteenth-, and nineteenth-century Europeans expected to *fail*. Breyer continued,

---

[19] Madeleine Albright, "Putin Is Making a Historic Mistake," *New York Times*, February 23, 2022, https://www.nytimes.com/2022/02/23/opinion/putin-ukraine.html.

And…I want you—and I'm talking to the students now—I…want you to pick…this up. It's an experiment that's still going on. And I'll tell you something: you know who will see whether that experiment works? It's you, my friend. It's you, [Mr. and Ms.] high school student. It's you, [Mr. and Ms.] college student. It's you, [Mr. and Ms.] law school student. It's us, but it's you. It's that next generation and the one after that. My grandchildren and their children. They'll determine whether the experiment still works. And of course, I'm an optimist, and I'm pretty sure it will.[20]

Can we prove the critics of democracy to be *wrong* and prove Justice Breyer *right*? For now, the jury is still out.

But the stakes could not be higher. Reflecting on our current domestic political situation, former US President Jimmy Carter wrote:

> I now fear that what we have fought so hard to achieve globally—the right to free and fair elections, unhindered by strongman politicians who seek nothing more than to grow their own power—has become dangerously fragile at home…
>
> Our great nation now teeters on the brink of a widening abyss. Without immediate action, we

---

20   NPR Staff, "Read Justice Breyer's remarks on retiring and his hope in the American 'experiment,'" NPR, January 27, 2022, https://www.npr.org/2022/01/27/1076162088/read-stephen-breyer-retirement-supreme-court.

> are at genuine risk of civil conflict and losing our precious democracy. Americans must set aside their differences and work together before it is too late.[21]

Increasingly, populations in both our country and other advanced democracies have become alarmingly divided, not just over political perspectives but even, as I've noted above, over conflicting views about what counts as an *objective fact*. This political tribalism makes it increasingly difficult not just to develop political solutions to problems but even to hold elections that are regarded as legitimate by a majority of citizens.

Any democracy will face tremendous difficulties in achieving consensus if its citizens cannot agree on a shared ground of reliable data and ways of resolving factual disputes—a *common social reality*—as the starting point for their political deliberations. Beyond this, a functioning democracy also requires a commitment to the equality of all its citizens; affirmation of the rule of law, which must be applied equally to all citizens; protections for freedom of thought, including religious ideas and speech; a free and independent press; a strong and independent judiciary; and an assurance that all eligible voters can, in fact, vote and that their votes will be counted. It needs to provide "space" for difficult conversations and vigorous public debates that address important issues and don't reduce to personal attacks. This list is not exhaustive. But these are basically the rights enshrined in the US Declaration of Independence and the Constitution's Bill of Rights.

---

[21]   Jimmy Carter, "Jimmy Carter: I Fear for Our Democracy," *New York Times*, January 5, 2022, https://www.nytimes.com/2022/01/05/opinion/jan-6-jimmy-carter.html?referringSource=articleShare.

One can argue that, by any stretch of the imagination, these ideals still remain *aspirational* principles—that they have not yet been fully realized in our country. Indeed, they aren't fully embraced by all our citizens. A recent national survey taken by the University of Chicago Project on Security and Threats found increasing support for political violence (on both the right and the left), significant beliefs among some populations that our political institutions are "corrupt," and continuing sharp divergences among different groups about the legitimacy of the 2020 general election.

At the same time and more hopefully, the survey found "support for bipartisan solutions to political violence" among "77 percent of American adults—the equivalent of 200 million people." The authors conclude that:

> This indicates a vast, if untapped, potential to mobilize widespread opposition to political violence against democratic institutions and unify Americans around the commitment to a peaceful democracy.[22]

As a democratic republic, the US clearly remains a work in progress—with both troubling and more encouraging trends existing side-by-side.

---

[22] Robert A. Pape, "July 2023 Survey Report: Tracking Deep Distrust of Democratic Institutions, Conspiracy Beliefs, and Support for Political Violence Among Americans," Chicago Project on Security and Threats, July 10, 2023, https://cpost.uchicago.edu/publications/july_2023_survey_report_tracking_deep_distrust_of_democratic_institutions_conspiracy_beliefs_and_support_for_political_violenc_among_americans/.

WHAT DO YOU THINK ABOUT DEMOCRACY?

Democracy is the worst form of government—except for all the others that have been tried, from time to time.
—Winston Churchill

Current college students tend to be significantly more skeptical about the value of *democracy* itself, as a form of government, than previous generations. Though I strongly agree with Winston Churchill's remark, there's not room here for me to offer a comprehensive defense of democracy against its contemporary critics. Moreover, it's both fair and important to acknowledge the historical acts of the United States that resulted from political decisions supported by many citizens, and of which we should not and cannot be proud.

Examples start with the institution of slavery in our nation's early years, tacitly accepted in the Constitution, and supported by law until the Civil War, the Emancipation Proclamation, and the Thirteenth Amendment to the Constitution (ratified on December 6, 1885); the genocidal conquest of Native Americans to open up land for European settlers; continuing violence towards Black citizens in the post–Civil War Jim Crow era and through today; support of certain brutal foreign dictatorships; decisions increasing the "globalization" of our economy that had the effect of economically displacing millions of previously high-paying jobs; and more.

At the same time, it's equally important to acknowledge the progress our country has made in so many areas, such as civil rights, women's rights, LGBTQ+ rights, providing social safety nets, environmental protection, and so on. True, these gains can be fragile, and more work is called for in *each* of these areas. Today, for example, voting rights and LGBTQ+ rights are under attack in many states. But it remains an empirical fact that the historical record includes *both* failures and successes. In order to arrive at an accurate historical understanding of the United States, we have to be able to hold both sides of that picture in mind.

The resulting question is this: *How can we best understand— and learn from—our past?* I submit that those who wish to close off fields of inquiry for students, ban books from high school and community libraries, and restrict the range of subjects that can be treated in primary, secondary, and college courses are *not* helping us answer this question. If we fail to honestly interrogate and learn from our past, we cannot move beyond it in the future. Those who would limit *your* rights—as a student—to study controversial or so-called "divisive" ideas in college are attempting to restrict *your* freedom of inquiry and expression.

Here's a second question: Would you prefer to live in a world in which the rights referenced above and other legal protections central to democracy were in force, or one in which they were routinely violated? And if the former, here's yet a third question: What role are you willing to play in strengthening these rights and conditions in the future—and so moving us forward toward establishing the "more perfect union" referenced in the Preamble to the US Constitution?

When you enter the post-college, professional, and citizenship phase of your life, you'll have more say in answering these questions—and in helping our society decide how to deal with the other wicked problems referenced above—than you ever did before. Moreover, as Justice Breyer remarked, you'll be dealing with them a lot longer than my generation and, for that matter, your parents' generation.

Earning your college degree will increase the chances that, at some later point, you will gain a position of authority and influence in either the private or public sector. But you don't need to become a political or business leader to make a difference. Each of us can vote responsibly—that is, by taking care to become informed about the candidates who are running and the issues to be decided. Each of us can participate thoughtfully in the informal political conversations among private citizens that are the lifeblood of any democracy. We can support local, state, and national organizations that strengthen civil society. In short, we can care about how our city, state, and nation are run. This all means that learning to grapple with perplexing and pressing wicked problems with an open mind should be central to your college experience because these are the issues that our democratic republic so urgently needs to address.

To repeat my earlier point: *The world absolutely will call upon you to help deal with these challenging issues.* To be part of the solution, you'll need to be both well-educated and well-informed. Above all, you'll need to *care*, not just about your personal and professional life—as important as they certainly will be to you— but also about the lives of your fellow citizens: in your city or town, in your state, in the nation, and across this small planet we all share. In his "Letter from a Birmingham Jail," Dr. Martin Luther King Jr. eloquently commented that:

> We are caught in an *inescapable network of mutuality*, tied in a single garment of destiny. Whatever affects one directly, affects all indirectly. This is the interrelated structure of reality [emphasis added].[23]

---

[23] Martin Luther King Jr., "Letter from Birmingham Jail," Bill of Rights Institute, April 16, 1963, https://billofrightsinstitute.org/primary-sources/letter-from-birmingham-jail.

Dr. King's message is that each of us needs to be concerned about the broader human community because we are all bound together within it—because we share a common fate.

To participate meaningfully in the work that arises from this attitude of care, you'll need to refine and strengthen that intellectual toolkit I've already talked about so much. Let's say a bit more about how these cognitive abilities relate to citizenship in a democratic republic.

INFORMATION, TRUTH, AND CITIZENSHIP

Anyone who can make you believe absurdities
can make you commit atrocities.
—*Voltaire*

To live in a shared social reality, informed, responsible, caring citizens require access to reliable sources of information. Today, in the era of the Internet and social media, this is much easier said than done. To paraphrase E. O. Wilson, we are awash in an ocean of disinformation and unreliable claims about almost everything. Moreover, according to Brandolini's Law,[24] the energy required to refute nonsense (he actually used the word "bullshit") is an order of magnitude greater than the energy involved in producing it. Anyone can easily post a crazy conspiracy theory on the web—something with no basis in fact—and it can spread quickly. By contrast, it takes considerable work to analyze the claim, fact-check it, and publish the results. By that point, the original post

---

[24] This principle is named after Alberto Brandolini, an Italian computer programmer who first articulated this in 2013. To learn more, see Itamar Shatz, "Brandolini's Law: The Bullshit Asymmetry Principle," *Effectiviology*, accessed November 17, 2023, https://effectiviology.com/brandolinis-law/.

may be so widely circulated, repeated, "liked," and believed that it's incredibly difficult for the truth to overtake it and diminish its influence.

So, just how is it possible to begin sorting through it all—to find grounds for reasonable belief and become that informed, responsible citizen I've been talking about? To start, we need to accept that being well informed about current events doesn't just happen. It takes purpose and effort on all our parts. It's especially important to seek out reliable sources of information and not just depend on what you happen to run across in social media. In doing this, it's enormously helpful to know how social information is created, compiled, and curated in news media sources and on the Internet. For instance, you can ask whether a particular news source is clear about its news-gathering policies. [25] Does it own up to errors and publish retractions when it's gotten something wrong? How does it treat a reporter who falsifies data or otherwise lies about what they are writing?[26]

Though this will sound like an old-fashioned suggestion, it's a really good idea to read (at least some part of) a major newspaper every day. Many schools make hard copies of newspapers available on campus free of charge, and they're certainly in the library. But of course you can also access these sources online. Just five minutes a day spent checking out the British Broadcasting Corporation (BBC) world news broadcast on your local public radio station (you can easily do this online too) can give you

---

[25]   *The New York Times*, for example, publishes its policies about, e.g., how it uses anonymous sources. See, "Why does *The New York Times* use anonymous sources, https://www.nytimes.com/article/why-new-york-times-anonymous-sources.html. This sort of transparency is one indication that a news source is reliable.

[26]   For example, the *New York Times*, along with other reputable newspapers and television news networks, have fired reporters and commentators for these reasons. .

an international perspective not readily available from domestic news sources.

If you choose to get most of your information about the world from social media, as more and more people do today, how well are you able to distinguish slick-looking sources that promote unproven or outright false claims from those that are more reputable and dependable? Contrary to science, responsible newspapers, and other *reliable* sources of information, all too many regions of the Internet and social media contain *no* internal mechanisms for correcting errors of fact.

As you probably also know, social media companies design and deploy algorithms to direct your attention to additional stories that reinforce what you've already read. Moreover, large numbers of likes or retweets do not increase the probability that a statement is true. In fact, because social media algorithms also amplify, reinforce, and propagate more radical and outrageous assertions—as opposed to more measured or less incendiary ones—the fact that a particular statement is trending probably indicates that it needs to be further interrogated, not that it should simply be accepted at face value.

Increasing numbers of primary and secondary schools now offer programs in information literacy or media literacy that explore the topics we've been discussing. If you're fortunate, you've already benefitted from one.[27] If not, you can look for opportunities to deepen your media understanding in college, where such programs are becoming more widely available. In fact, more colleges and universities are now including an information literacy component in their GE requirements.

---

[27] For example, see John Henley, "How Finland starts its fight against fake news in primary schools," *The Guardian*, January 29, 2023, https://www.theguardian.com/world/2020/jan/28/fact-from-fiction-finlands-new-lessons-in-combating-fake-news.

Why does all this matter? Unfortunately, history demonstrates the power of Voltaire's remark quoted above: believing empirical claims that have no relation to objective reality can be the first step on a slippery slope towards allowing others to commit heinous acts or even doing so yourself—including both crimes against democracy and crimes against humanity.

To cite just one historical example, Hitler's rise to political power in Germany in the 1930s began with and was, to a significant extent, driven by what even back then was called "The Big Lie": the idea that German Jews were somehow responsible for Germany's defeat in World War I. This was not at all true, of course. But it didn't matter. The fact that too many German citizens allowed themselves to believe it—or chose to remain silent when others repeated it—contributed to the ascent of the Nazi party, helped to fuel its virulent antisemitism, and led directly to World War II and the Holocaust.

We should remind ourselves that the Nazis came to power initially by winning elections in the Weimar Republic, which was a democracy until 1933, when they turned it into a dictatorship. It's also worth remembering that, once they had taken power, the Nazis immediately set out to control all newspapers and other sources of public information. They also set out to ban any books that challenged their political ideology or encouraged people to think critically. In fact, they frequently held well-attended public book-burnings. Tragically, in addition to Nazi political and civic leaders and thugs in their street mobs, far too many faculty members, administrators, and students in German schools and universities went along with this program.

We also desperately need to recapture the distinction between having the *right* to one's own opinion—a *political right* all citizens in a democracy share and should continually affirm—and holding a *justified, well-supported* opinion. There is a real difference. Having the constitutionally based *right* to believe whatever you choose does *not*, in itself, make your beliefs well founded, justified, or true. As the American founding father John Adams famously remarked, "Facts are stubborn things; and whatever may be our wishes, our inclinations, or the dictates of our passion, they cannot alter the state of facts and evidence." It's helpful to remember this, especially when you encounter an outrageous claim on social media, elsewhere on the Internet, or even from one of your friends. Just saying something—whether stating it only once or repeating it over and over—does *not* make it true. If it's a claim about the world, there needs to be solid, reliable evidence to back it up.

Once again, this discussion takes us back to the components of liberal learning. To access the information necessary for effective citizenship, you'll need to understand how reputable statements about the world—reliable empirical claims—are grounded in observation and data; how to discern good arguments from bad ones (and from those that may be indeterminate or ambiguous); how to distinguish absurdities from statements that deserve further consideration; and how all these distinctions should factor into public policy discussions and decisions. A good portion of your time in college should be devoted to learning how to do the absolutely crucial work of testing arguments for *validity* and *soundness*. An argument that follows the rules of good reasoning is valid; an argument that is valid and is also based on true assumptions is sound. But ensuring that your beliefs are grounded in facts and supported by solid reasoning is not always easy to do. In fact, it usually takes a good deal of effort.

In sum, the cognitive skills that are fostered by a liberal education figure prominently in your preparation to become a contributing adult citizen of our twenty-first-century democratic republic. You may or may not be thinking much about such things at the moment, but I urge you to at least tuck these ideas away for future reference. They are important to your personal life, to your professional success, to the future of our political system, to your children (if you choose to have any), and ultimately to the fate of the world.

Your college or university should do its own part in helping you appreciate the enduring benefits of the learning outcomes highlighted above. But sadly, not every school will do this well. That's why it's so important for *you* to be able to make these choices yourself—to ensure that, in addition to gaining in-depth knowledge within your major, you also emerge from college with a broad liberal education that will enable you to construct a life that is both satisfying and socially responsible.

SUMMING UP—CHAPTER ONE

- Your college education should prepare you for a productive and self-fulfilling life in a rapidly evolving world. This is the *personal good* it represents for you. To attain it, you'll need a flexible intellectual toolkit: a broad liberal education that enhances your ability to think for yourself, the capacity to change your mind when necessary, and an inclination to be a lifelong learner. Your school's general education curriculum will launch you on this journey.

- Choose a major that sparks your interest so you can become an engaged student in that field. Your in-depth work here will combine with your general education to provide a foundation for acquiring the more specialized skills and knowledge you'll need later on.

- Your liberal education also prepares you to be a free citizen of a democracy—the *social good* represented in a college education.
- The world will call upon you—as an informed, responsible, and caring citizen—to help resolve the wicked problems all of us are facing.
- One enormous wicked social problem—perhaps the most significant one of all—is an unprecedented assault on democratic political institutions, both at home and abroad.
- To be part of the solution, you will need to be well informed about current issues, which will take a commitment on your part. Specifically, you'll need to understand how claims about the world—empirical claims—should be grounded in data and fact, as well as why some sources of information are more reliable than others. You'll need to actively seek out those reliable sources of information.

How can you best approach your college years to accomplish both the high-sounding general goals we've been discussing and your more immediate personal ones? In the following eight chapters of this book, we'll talk about all this in more detail.

PART TWO

EIGHT STEPS TO A HIGHLY SUCCESSFUL LIFE, IN COLLEGE AND BEYOND

CHAPTER 2
EMBRACE YOUR NEW FREEDOM

College is where you get to test-drive your new adult self.
—*Thomas Tisch*

L et's continue our conversation by thinking not about the start of your undergraduate years but about the closing scene of that movie: your college commencement. Since you've most likely just graduated from high school, the last thing on your mind right now is that next big ceremonial event seemingly far off in the future. But please believe me: your years as an undergraduate will pass far more quickly than you can possibly imagine. If your experience is at all typical, your time in college will seem to fly by much faster than in high school!

So, let me ask you to pause for a moment—maybe even close your eyes—and conjure up an image of *you*, four short years from now (plus or minus), walking across the stage at your college commencement. How will you look, as a new college graduate? What will your family members and friends think about you? Above all, how will *you* feel about your undergraduate career? Will you approach your graduation with justifiable pride because you've taken full advantage of everything college offered to you? Or will you carry a nagging sense of regret across that stage because of opportunities you've squandered, which will never (*never!*) come your way again?

The difference between feeling terrific about what you've accomplished and regretting what you've failed to do, in one of the most significant periods in your life, will largely be a function of your mindset and what you were prepared to do to make your college experience as successful as you're dreaming it will be. All that begins today!

TAKING CHARGE

Here's the first thing to realize about your new college life: you are now fully in charge of you! Let's talk about how to understand and embrace this new reality.

Over the past few years, as you've transitioned from adolescence to the threshold of the adult world, you've experienced ever-greater degrees of *freedom*. But beginning now, this process will accelerate. You're about to make a quantum leap to a whole new level of autonomy, far beyond anything you've known before. No one will tell you when to go to sleep at night or when to get up in the morning, when to go to class, when to study, or when to start researching that paper that isn't due for two weeks. And that's just for starters. To repeat: *You are now fully in charge of you!*

Why is this so important?

Your success in college—and later on in life—will depend on many factors, some of which will be beyond your control. Even so, in four years, as you look back from the vantage point of your next commencement, your success or failure as a college student will have been most strongly influenced by *how well you handled your new level of personal freedom*. This might sound simplistic. But over and over, students I've known have confirmed it. So, it's crucial, from your very first days on campus, to think clearly about what this new level of freedom means to you.

TWO WAYS TO THINK ABOUT FREEDOM

> *Freedom is not regression from integration and determinacy but realization of the higher forms of relatedness. Freedom is self-regulation, self-regulation more difficult and more exacting than the intrigues of a tyrant.... A Marathon runner is more free than a vagabond, and a cosmonaut than a sage in the state of levitation. Otherwise it would be more consistent to bark than write poems and to live in a leprosery than in San Francisco. Or Prague.*
> —*Miroslav Holub*[28]

Surprisingly perhaps, the concept of *freedom, autonomy,* or *self-determination* (we can use these words interchangeably) is not always well understood—even by people who talk about it a lot. Let's begin to unpack this idea by considering a bit of etymology: the history of the word "autonomy." It combines two Ancient Greek roots: "auto," meaning self, and "nomos," meaning law or rule. In short, autonomous persons can determine, for themselves, the laws (or rules or regulations) that govern their behavior. Clear enough. Right? But there are, in fact, *two* different ways to understand what this notion of self-regulation means: a negative and a positive interpretation. Both are important, and a full

---

[28] Miroslav Holub, "Although," poem, in *Intensive Care: Selected and New Poems,* trans. George Theiner, ed. David Young (Oberlin, OH: Oberlin College Press, 1996).

understanding of your new freedom is incomplete without taking each of them into account.

The *negative interpretation of freedom* is actually pretty easy to grasp and apply in your life. In fact, it's so easy that even children do it instinctively. It means *the absence of external direction, constraints, or control over what you might choose to do or not do.*

In political terms, people who are worried about excessive governmental control over their decisions and actions are primarily concerned with this negative sense of autonomy. During the pandemic, for example, it came into play in political disputes over COVID-related masking or vaccine mandates. Folks who resisted governmental directives to wear a mask or get vaccinated because they saw these requirements as restricting their individual choices were focused on the negative interpretation of freedom. They didn't want anyone telling them what they had to do regarding the pandemic. And any consequences of their decisions and actions for their community or public health, in general, were simply not part of the equation for them.

This negative interpretation of freedom is significant, though it's arguably a more pressing concern for people living under authoritarian, repressive governments than it should be for citizens of well-functioning representative democracies. It's played a major role in revolutions against tyrannical governments—including, for example, the American Revolution, along with many others. And, as recent experience demonstrates, it remains actively in play in our public discussions today.

In your own case, you've lived with external direction, guidance, and constraints for your whole life: from your parents, your teachers, religious leaders, coaches, and many others. But as I've acknowledged above, their influence in your life has been diminishing in recent years. So, you've already experienced the kind of increased negative freedom or autonomy that comes from a reduction of outside control over your personal decision-making.

In your new college life, all of sudden, you'll have far fewer external restrictions on your choices than ever before, and it's tempting to focus primarily on this negative aspect of freedom. You could exercise your ability to do whatever you want—to act on whatever impulses occur to you. At the extreme, when they confront this new reality, some students throw out *all* the rules. They go crazy. Some even try to live out what they've seen in the genre of popular college movies, such as *Animal House*. (Spoiler Alert #1: In real life—as opposed to the movies—this does not end well!)

If you have younger siblings, you've no doubt seen a version of this behavior when they've tried to get their way by throwing a temper tantrum. They were just trying to increase their negative freedom by pushing back (hard!) against someone or something that was blocking whatever they wanted to do. In fact, if you think about it, *infants* represent the logical extreme of negative autonomy: they cry when they're hungry, tired, or need a diaper change; they're unburdened with any sense of responsibility toward anyone else. They expect all their desires to be satisfied *right away*. And they are *never* prepared to suffer alone!

I suspect that none of us would set as our life's goal being able to act like a baby. But if you think of your college experience *only* in terms of the restrictions that no longer apply, you will be limiting yourself to this incomplete, negative understanding of freedom. Worst of all, as we'll see, you will be missing a major dimension of what it means to be a fully autonomous, self-regulating, mature, and responsible adult.

By contrast, the *positive interpretation of freedom* is a bit more complicated. It's more difficult to comprehend and even more challenging to practice. But this understanding of autonomy is also the one most appropriate to a mature adult. The positive notion of autonomy or freedom is *not* defined as the absence of external constraints or direction, but rather as the *presence of active, internal self-regulation or self-determination*. This may seem like a very subtle distinction—perhaps one that doesn't really make much of a difference. But it does.

As the poet Miroslav Holub writes in the above-quoted lines, this kind of self-regulation turns out to be "more difficult and more exacting than the intrigues of a tyrant." It's more difficult because it places the burden squarely on *you* to determine what you want to accomplish and then do it. In this context, success is determined *not* by the absence of restrictions on what you do, but rather *by how well you succeed in meeting the goals you set out to achieve.*

In addition, this positive interpretation of freedom inherently involves those "higher forms of relatedness" with others in a human community that Holub also references. The nineteenth-century British writer T. H. Green captures both ideas in one sentence:

> When we speak of freedom as something to be
> so highly prized, we mean a positive power or
> capacity of doing or enjoying *something worth
> doing or enjoying,* and that...we do or enjoy *in
> common with others* [emphasis added].[29]

This interpretation of freedom does turn out to be more complicated and demanding than the other one.

---

[29]   Thomas Hill Green, *Liberal Legislation and the Freedom of Contract: A Lecture* (Oxford: Slatery & Rose, 1881).

There actually are three ideas in play here. First, applying the positive concept of autonomy in your own life requires you to make your own value-judgments. It means deciding for yourself what is most worth doing among the complex array of possibilities that are always available to you—the wide range of things you *could* decide to do (or not do), at any given moment. Second, it means actively regulating your own behavior to carry out your decisions. Third, it means attending to your relationships with and responsibilities to the other members of your community—as opposed to thinking only about your own rights, goals, and desires.

Let's revisit one of Holub's examples to talk more concretely about what all this amounts to. Most people would agree that becoming an astronaut is a worthy goal. And they know it requires dedication, determination, study, training, sacrifice...in short, a great deal of intense and sustained individual work. But this project also depends upon a highly developed web of social relationships. Many people must do their part as members of an enormous team to send an astronaut into space: from doing the basic science and engineering, to constructing the launch vehicle and command capsule, staffing Mission Control, and so on.[30] It's simply not possible to realize the goal of becoming an astronaut if you're living a solitary, unfettered, and undisciplined existence— just doing whatever strikes your fancy. In fact, it's not possible even to *imagine* such a complex project under those conditions. To say this another way, becoming an astronaut is a great example of someone's realizing their positive freedom by structuring their life to take advantage of possibilities only available in a highly

---

[30] For a vivid illustration of what all this means, you might check out *The Right Stuff, Apollo 13,* or *Hidden Figures,* three well made, fact-based, and entertaining movies about the US space program.

developed human community. Now think about how proud of their accomplishments every astronaut was at the conclusion of their mission. Embracing your positive freedom opens up possibilities for achievement—and the *happiness* that accompanies it—that are otherwise unattainable.

To cite a more down-to-earth example: nothing quite compares with the euphoria that comes from finishing your first Marathon (I speak from experience). And yet that goal only becomes attainable if you are willing to regulate your behavior by consistently investing countless hours, over many weeks and months, running the necessary miles in training. Yet, as Holub comments, the self-discipline required to put in all those miles makes you *free* to do something—gives you the *capacity* to do something—that otherwise would be impossible: in this case, to run 26.2 miles. But you don't have to be a serious runner to grasp the general point. Positive freedom represents the payoff— the return on investment—for putting in the time and energy required to accomplish a goal *you* have decided is worthy of your effort.

Why am I spending so much time on this discussion?

Here's the punchline: *this transitional moment in your life represents a terrific opportunity to move beyond an incomplete and less mature grasp of autonomy—the negative interpretation (freedom from)—by adding to it the next level of understanding: the positive interpretation of this important concept (freedom for). Embracing your positive freedom turns out to be the necessary precondition to significant achievement.*

Applying this positive interpretation of autonomy in the context of your new college life—fully embracing your new freedom—means taking charge of your education by setting your own goals and structuring your life to accomplish them. It also means acknowledging your responsibilities to both your new college community and the larger human society, each of which plays an integral role in making your new opportunities available to you. (We'll return to this second idea in Chapter 8.)

Speaking to an assembly of college students, author Adrienne Rich suggested a vivid way to understand what it means to take charge of your education:

> The first thing...is that you cannot afford to think of being here to *receive* an education: you will do much better to think of being here *to claim one*. One of the dictionary definitions of the verb "to claim" is: to take as the rightful owner...
>
> "To receive" is to come into possession of; to act as a receptacle or container for; to accept as authoritative or true. *The difference is... between acting and being acted upon* [emphasis added]....[31]

In sum, to take charge of your college life—to *claim* your education, as Rich says—is to actively and intentionally embrace the academic opportunities and all the other resources at hand to achieve your personal goals. You've now been promoted to the position of chief executive officer (CEO) of *yourself*—with ultimate responsibility for the choices you will make every minute of every day. Understanding this new reality is the first step toward embracing your new freedom and realizing possibilities for your life you might never before have imagined.

---

[31] Adrienne Rich, "Claiming an Education," Speech delivered at the convocation of Douglass College, 1977, https://net-workingworlds.weebly.com/uploads/1/5/1/5/15155460/rich-claiming_an_education-1.pdf.

SUMMING UP—CHAPTER 2

- You're now fully in charge of *you*—you are the CEO of your new college life.
- The first step in taking charge of your college career is to understand the difference between the negative and positive interpretations of *freedom* or *autonomy*. The *negative interpretation* is all about *minimizing external constraints* on your actions. By contrast, the *positive interpretation* is about *intentionally taking on internal constraints*—self-regulation—to achieve a goal you have chosen to pursue.
- Embrace your new positive freedom by actively claiming your education and owning the decisions you will make in setting and *attaining* your personal goals.

Okay. But just what does all this mean for your life in college? What are the initial steps to embrace your new freedom, and the next ones after that? We'll take up these questions in the following chapter.

CHAPTER 3

MAKE NO SMALL PLANS

Make no little plans; they have no magic to stir
[the] blood and probably... will not be realized.
Make big plans; aim high in hope and work.
—*Daniel Burnham*

T he devastating Chicago Fire of 1871 destroyed approximately 17,000 homes, businesses, and other structures—about one-third of the city. Architect Daniel Burnham played a major part in the rebuilding that followed that catastrophe. Among other things, he led the planning for the 1893 World's Columbian Exposition, which brought Chicago to the attention of the world. He then co-authored the 1909 *Plan of Chicago*. His urban designs shaped the city we know today; their outlines are still visible in its streets and buildings. In short, Burnham knew first-hand about making big plans. [32]

MAKING YOUR OWN BIG PLANS

The problem human beings face is not that we aim too high and fail, but that we aim too low and succeed.
—Michelangelo

My next challenge to you is to apply Burnham's good advice in your own life: *Make no small plans. Set your sights on a goal that inspires you! Create your own soaring personal dream.* You are the architect of your own future, with a limitless horizon—or, to change the metaphor, a blank canvas—before you! So, use your creative imagination to envision possibilities that you might never have allowed yourself to seriously consider before. Give yourself the benefit of *audacity*—this isn't the time to go small. As skiers, snowboarders, and skateboarders say, "go big or go home!" Ask yourself this question: *What would I do if I knew I could not fail?* Then set out to do it!

You may be thinking, "easier said than done." True enough. None of this is simple. Formulating your "no small plans"—creating a blueprint of your future—and then making your plans a reality will require discipline (again, positive freedom as self-regulation), commitment, confidence, determination, focus, grit, resilience, lots of hard work, and a measure of luck, along with a good measure of creative imagination. Not everyone can tap into

---

[32] A very readable book that deals with Burnham's work and many other events associated with the 1893 Columbia Exposition—some of them quite surprising—is *The Devil in the White City: Murder, Magic, and Madness at the Fair That Changed America*, by Erik Larson (New York: Knopf Doubleday, 2003). Burnham apparently borrowed his sentence from Machiavelli.

those personal characteristics—much less good fortune—on demand.[33] This is especially true early in your college career when your surroundings may seem so unfamiliar. But if you follow some simple steps, outlined below, the dream that appears out-of-reach on your first day of college will be in your grasp by the time you graduate.

Before we go any further, however, let me also say this: *please do not feel any pressure to* finalize *all of your big plans right away.* College can be stressful and chaotic at first, and some students who crave stability feel they have to choose a particular academic path on day one. Try not to be seduced by that kind of thinking. In fact, *many* students start out unsure of where they want to go, both as a major in college and in a job afterwards.

Others start out with firm plans and then change their minds later on. Still others know right away from their first day what they want to do and stick with it. But whatever description applies to you, you're *normal*! And even if you do have clear ideas about your future—or if you had to apply to a particular academic department or program to gain admission to your university—always remain open to changing your direction later on. Many successful people did just that, and in the end were very glad they

---

[33] On the other hand, many people over the ages have repeated a version of a quotation often credited (probably inaccurately) to Thomas Jefferson: "I am a great believer in luck, and I find the harder I work, the more I have of it." More recently, business writers Jim Collins and Morten T. Hansen have systematically examined the role of luck in the lives of successful business leaders. Their conclusion: these people do not experience more (good) fortunate events than anyone else, but they tend to respond more aggressively to them by "throwing [themselves] at the luck event with ferocious intensity, disrupting [their lives] and not letting up." This can represent a formula for success in any circumstances. See Jim Collins and Morten T. Hansen, "What's Luck Got to Do With It?" *New York Times,* October 29, 2021, https://www.nytimes.com/2011/10/30/business/luck-is-just-the-spark-for-business-giants.html.

did! So, consider your "no small plans" to be a work in progress—one that will evolve over time.

BEGINNING WITH YOU—YOUR PERSONAL MISSION STATEMENT

The start of your college career is a great moment to have a grown-up conversation with yourself about what really matters in your life: your core values. What do you care about most deeply? As you picture your future, what do you see? How would you most like your life to take shape? What kind of mark do you want to make on the world? These can be pretty heavy questions, and we'll return to them in later chapters. But for now, let me suggest a way to begin getting a handle on them.

Your college or university has a mission statement. (I've already referenced Skidmore's mission statement in Chapter 1.) Most businesses and other organizations do as well. A mission statement is a succinct expression of an organization's main purpose—a brief statement of just why it exists and what it is trying to do. At their best, mission statements can be put up on a wall to remind people of why they are working there. Your school's mission statement should give you an idea of why you've chosen to attend your college or university, as opposed to some other one. If you haven't already run into it, why not take a minute to Google your school's mission statement, to see just how it describes its guiding educational goals?

Here are some examples of mission statements from the business and non-profit world:

- **Apple**: Bringing the best user experience to our customers through innovative hardware, software, and services.
- **The United Nations**: The maintenance of international peace and security, the promotion of the well-being of

the peoples of the world, and international cooperation to these ends.

- **Habitat for Humanity**: Habitat works toward our vision by building strength, stability and self-reliance in partnership with families in need of decent and affordable housing.
- **The Macarthur Foundation**: The world is more just when actions are moral, rational, equitable, and fair—and when barriers are removed to provide equitable access, treatment, consideration, and opportunity.
- **The Wounded Warrior Project**: To honor and empower Wounded Warriors who incurred a physical or mental injury, illnesses, or wound, co-incident to your military service on or after September 11, 2001.

Of course, each of these organizations has much more to say about itself—about its broader vision, its values, what it wants to accomplish, and how it plans to do so. But these succinct summary statements get those larger conversations going. They also provide a touch-point for the subsequent decision-making that guides their operations.

So, what about you? What's *your* primary reason for existing—your purpose in life? Again, that's a pretty heady question! Most people haven't thought about it, much less written it down. And if you don't really have an answer right now, that's fine. It can take time to figure out just who you are and what you most want to do with your life. But now is a great time to begin thinking about these things in earnest—to begin working on your own personal mission statement.

Here are a few examples of personal mission statements from some people you'll probably recognize, which might prompt some ideas of your own:

- **Walt Disney**: To make people happy.
- **Richard Branson (founder of Virgin Group)**: To have fun in my journey through life and learn from my mistakes.
- **Maya Angelou**: Not merely to survive, but to thrive; and to do so with some passion, some humor, and some style.
- **Oprah Winfrey**: To be a teacher. And to be known for inspiring my students to be more than they thought they could be.
- **Mahatma Gandhi**: I shall not fear anyone on Earth. I shall fear only God. I shall not bear ill will toward anyone. I shall not submit to injustice from anyone. I shall conquer untruth by truth. And in resisting untruth, I shall put up with all suffering.
- **Greta Thunberg**: I have learned you are never too small to make a difference.

To be precise, Greta Thunberg did not call the quoted sentence her "mission statement," but it captures a guiding value in her life, which she has dedicated to addressing global climate change. The other people quoted above were probably older than you when they wrote those lines. But even just starting to think about a statement of your own is an excellent first move toward making your "no small plans."

So, as you begin considering what you most want to get out of your time at college and where you want your education to take you, step back and see if there's a concise way to summarize your thinking. There's no pressure here. No rush. Even if you change your mind as you go along, thinking about these things can help focus your attention. And if, at some point, you do take a stab at jotting down a first draft of your own personal mission statement, you'll have created something more valuable than you might realize. You can turn to it when you're facing a tough decision. You can ask, "How does each of the options I'm considering fit with my personal mission?" Doing this won't automatically resolve all of your questions. But it can help clarify what to do next.

NEXT STEPS

A good next step in planning is to survey your school's curriculum, the array of courses from which you get to select. Then, as you begin your coursework, perhaps a class that grabs your attention will point you to a major or even a career direction you never considered before. That's one reason why it's a great idea to sample a broad range of subjects in your first year—in those GE courses I spoke about in Chapter 1. Pay special attention to topics that pique your interest. Are there any that seem particularly relevant to your initial ideas about your personal mission and your emerging "no small plans?" What about the cocurricular options (student clubs and organizations) at your new school? Is there one that strikes you as especially engaging? Might it give you some ideas to help shape your plans?

Regardless of what you now imagine for your future, *set yourself the goal of beginning now to formulate your "no small plans" for your college years and beyond*. Charting—and then *following*—your path through the curricular and cocurricular options of your college to achieve your ultimate goals is some of the most important work you'll do for the next few years.

Above all, as I've said, *don't* be afraid to change your mind as you go along. What seemed like a grand plan in your first months of college may well give way to other, *better* ideas later on. That's why most colleges and universities give you several semesters or quarters before you have to declare a major. If you can, it's a very good idea to take one or two years before making that decision. I realize that's not always possible since some programs require an earlier commitment. For example, if you're seriously considering a health profession or a science major, you will probably need to begin taking foundational courses pretty early on. But even in these academic arenas, don't be afraid to revise your "no small plans" if you find your interests moving in another direction.

No matter where you're heading, it's important to aim high from the very start. Here's an example of someone who did just that and who also developed her plans as she went along.

A story of making "no small plans": Jocelyn

Jocelyn came to Skidmore with a strong interest in music, both as a singer and as someone fascinated by the history of music. She performed around campus, and she graduated as a self-determined Ethnomusicology major.[34]

Early in her college career, Jocelyn became acquainted with Caffè Lena, an iconic folk music venue in Saratoga Springs, where many great names in the music business got their start (for example, Bernice Johnson Reagon and Don McLean) or performed over the years (for example, Tom Paxton, Bob Dylan, Ian & Sylvia, Arlo Guthrie, Judy Collins, Tom Rush, and Dar Williams).

---

[34] Most colleges and universities offer the opportunity—with a specified process—for you to create a self-determined major if there is not a program in the curriculum that adequately reflects your interests.

For her senior project, Jocelyn explored Caffè Lena's rich store of historical material, which hadn't ever been cataloged. She curated the collection of more than 800 archival audio recordings and 1,500 photographs; in addition, she recorded hundreds of interviews with key people. In all this work, Jocelyn also drew on the unpublished writing of Lena Spencer, who founded the folk music venue and ran it for many years. The result was a comprehensive history of Caffè Lena.

After Jocelyn graduated, this work evolved into a nearly ten-year commitment as she directed the Caffè Lena History Project in association with the Library of Congress and the GRAMMY Foundation. In 2013, she published a multimedia history of Caffè Lena including a book, a box set of recordings, an exhibit, a website, and live performances—*all* to critical acclaim in the *New York Times*, National Public Radio, *People Magazine*, and elsewhere. It earned her the prestigious ASCAP Deems Taylor Award for Multimedia. In 2016, Jocelyn returned full circle to Caffè Lena as a performer to release her own new album, *Heliotrope*, and in 2019 she received her alma mater's Creative Thought Matters award.

Although her engagement with music remained a central focus throughout Jocelyn's college years, her interests have continued to evolve.

Today she is a GRAMMY Award–nominated music producer; a consultant and educator (regularly presenting workshops for organizations including the *New York Times* Summer Academy and Creative Capital); a recording artist under the name Rabasi Joss; and founder of the archival storytelling studio Arbo Radiko (meaning "tree root"), which produces podcasts, music releases, video content, and publications in collaboration with visionary artists, art estates, organizations, brands, and media companies.

***

If you give yourself permission to explore your interests and then turn them into your own "no small plans," you'll never know, in advance, the exciting places where your journey will lead!

YOUR PERSONAL PLANNING PROCESS

As you begin to consider your options, it's really helpful to write down your ideas. You may already have discovered that writing imposes both a discipline and structure on your thinking. It helps to clarify thoughts that otherwise might remain vague or unformed. If you don't already have one, you might start a journal in which you begin to sketch out your "no small plans" and then elaborate upon them over time. One way or another, try out your ideas on paper or on your computer. Some people who are more visually oriented find that drawing is helpful. Take full advantage of whatever method of brainstorming works for you.

Use whatever process best engages your imagination as a way of focusing your attention on both your plans and the steps needed to fulfil them.

A good way of launching this work is to follow author Stephen Covey's advice to "start with the end in mind." Think about working backward from your long-term goal, if you've been able to come up with one, to discover what needs to happen for you to get there. Then go back to where you are at present. Identify the first things you need to do to start that process, then the next steps, and so on. If you continue to work backward and forward in this way, you can break down that large project—one that might at first seem overwhelming—into smaller, manageable pieces. Then you can tackle them one by one.

If even taking these initial steps seems a daunting proposition, try having some fun with it. After all, you're not being graded on this exercise, and there's no right or wrong answer. You might imagine that someone is writing a book with a main character who just happens to be *you*! Think about what the next chapter in that character's life could look like. Jot down some ideas about what that person might be doing post-college. Then think ahead to the next chapters after that. What might that character be up to five or ten years from now? Where would those new episodes be set (in a city, in the country, overseas)? What would they be doing? With whom would they be working? What kind of life might they be leading? What would the pathway to all this look like?

However you choose to formulate your plans, begin by giving yourself permission to think about your life in new and unfamiliar ways. And by the way, those entry-level courses you'll take during your first year are designed to help you do just that—by providing you a fresh set lenses through which to view the world.

FROM PLANNING TO DOING

*The difference between impossible and
possible lies in determination.*
—Tommy Lasorda

Using your creative imagination to begin developing your personal mission statement and "no small plans," especially if you write them down, is a great start. But it's only a start. The next step is to *commit to bringing your "no small plans" from the realm of ideas to reality*. To do this, it's crucial to organize your time, so you can make continuing progress, on a day-to-day basis, toward achieving your inspiring goals.

Odds are you've already found a way to manage your calendar that served you well enough in high school. But to handle your increased autonomy—your newfound (positive) freedom—and a set of new and more complicated demands on your time, you might find it advisable to take your system to the next level. If so, or if you've never really been able to master your schedule in the first place, you might consider the following example:

A story of getting organized: Ryder Carroll

Ryder Carroll's epiphany came when he was a young pre-college student in the 1990s struggling with attention deficit disorder (ADD). He envied his more organized and successful classmates who were better able to focus on their work, and he wanted to be more like them. To accomplish this, he experimented with various ways to use notebooks and journals to help him get on top of his schoolwork and

concentrate on those things he most needed—
and wanted—to do.

In college, he further developed his organizational system, which he came to call "bullet journaling." It enabled him not only to keep track of
his priorities and the details of his life but also to
become more grounded and intentional about
staying focused on his larger goals. In fact, he
describes it as "a mindfulness practice that's disguised as a productivity system."[35]

Ryder began to share his planning method with a
few colleagues and friends who encouraged him
to make it available to an even wider audience.
He did so, first online, then through Ted Talks,
and eventually by publishing a book in 2018—
*The Bullet Journal Method: Track the Past, Order
the Present, Design the Future*.[36] Promoting his
organizational system is now his full-time job,
and many thousands of students (and others)
have benefitted from it.

---

[35]   Zameena Mejia, "How the creator behind the viral bullet journal turned his
own life hack into a full-time business," CNBC, August 2, 2017, https://www.
cnbc.com/2017/08/02/how-the-creator-behind-the-viral-bullet-journal-
turned-his-own-life-hack-into-a-full-time-business.html. By the way, Ryder
Carroll graduated from Skidmore College, where he majored in creative writing
and graphic design. Please see Additional Resources.

[36]   Ryder Carroll, *The Bullet Journal Method: Track the Past, Order the Present,
Design the Future* (New York: Portfolio, 2018).

***

There are countless ways to organize your life; in fact, there's a whole cottage industry that will happily sell you planners, calendars, and apps for your computer or mobile phone. So, there are many other options besides the bullet journal process, though it's certainly one place you might start. As both a system and a practice, it's quite flexible and leaves ample room for individual creativity in adapting it to your personal style and needs. But the most important point is *to commit to finding the best way for you to keep track of your larger, long-term priorities and then the detailed day-to-day tasks you need to accomplish in order to achieve them.* As I said before, making your big plans a reality will take discipline, focus, initiative, hard work, perseverance, and grit.[37] But breaking them down into smaller tasks and then organizing your time to complete them will create your individual pathway toward success.

On a very practical day-to-day level, some students find it helpful to have early morning classes to get them out of bed and going. Others prefer later options. But however your schedule works out, please pay attention to the seemingly trivial breaks that you'll find in your days—for example, one or two hours between classes. It can be appealing to see those times as opportunities to kick back—to sit in the student union over a cup of coffee, hang out with friends, play a video game, or whatever. But it's often a wiser choice to make more purposeful use of those intervals—to take your cup of coffee into the library (assuming it's permitted), review your notes from your previous class, prepare for your next

---

[37]   There's not enough space here to discuss these abilities in the detail they deserve. But if you'd like to explore any of them further, please check out some of the references in Additional Resources.

one, get a start on that upcoming research project, or whatever else you need to do.

Place this suggestion in a larger frame: For a typical twelve-week quarter or a fourteen-week semester, devoting just four of those "break" hours per week to advancing your most important priorities will yield either *forty-eight or fifty-six hours per term*. That's more than a standard work week! Seemingly small, throw-away bits of time can add up to something significant if you use them consistently. This advice might strike you as trivial, but I assure you it's more useful than it might appear. Managing your time efficiently to stay on top of what you need to do is also a terrific way to avoid the stress that comes when you get behind and have to catch up at the last minute.

Here's a more general way to think about how to accomplish what you most want to get done in college: In this book, we talk a lot about freedom, decision-making, and responsibility. But part of the context for this discussion has to be the understanding that much (most?) of what we do in our daily living involves *habits*. Habits are learned patterns of behavior that we "execute" largely *without* consciously thinking about them. Without making decisions. Consider the mechanics of driving a car, typing on a computer, or hitting a tennis ball. When you were first learning these tasks, you had to think consciously about all their separate components. Not an easy assignment! But when you became more accomplished, you no longer had to focus on those details. You could concentrate on your destination, what you wanted to write, or where you wanted the tennis ball to go.

For many centuries, philosophers (beginning with Aristotle[38]) and, more recently, psychologists have recognized the power of habits to shape the actions of individuals and groups

---

[38]   Aristotle lived in ancient Greece from 384 to 322 BCE.

(including entire nations). Everyone knows how difficult it can be to break a "bad" habit (for example, biting your fingernails or smoking). So, the best strategy is to avoid forming bad habits in the first place and to concentrate on developing the "good" ones that help you achieve your goals.

Here's an important clue about how to do this. Psychological research has demonstrated the power of our environment to shape habitual behavior. For example, if you always have cookies or candy lying about in plain sight, you're more likely to eat them. But if your environment makes it more difficult—psychologists refer to this as friction—then you are less likely to do it. So, placing the cookies out of sight and high up in a cabinet (or better yet, not buying them at all!)—*increasing* the friction—makes it less likely that you'll consume them. Conversely, structuring your environment to make it *easier* to do what you want—that is, *decreasing* the friction—makes it more likely that you'll succeed. So, if you want to take a run in the morning, it helps to lay out your running clothes the night before. If you want to study more effectively, seek out environments that support that goal— for example, the library or a quiet study room in your dorm— as opposed to a more public space where you're prone to being interrupted by friends or bothered by distractions (for example, a television program).

Here's the bottom line: To fully embrace your new (positive) freedom, it's most effective, first, to honestly examine your behavior— to find out what makes you more or less likely to do something—and then do your best to *structure your environment* and *establish habitual patterns of action* that are most likely to *increase* the odds of reaching your goals. Instead of fighting the power of habit, put it to use by reinforcing patterns of behavior most conducive to your success.[39]

Sure, there will be other dimensions to your college life as well: perhaps a job, sports, clubs, exercise, a social life...all of which may be important to you. Yes, college should be fun, too—certainly not work all the time. So, go to football games and go crazy along with everyone else—just not *too* crazy! Some extra-curricular or cocurricular activities will become quite meaningful to you. In fact, they might be important to how you define who you are (for example, intercollegiate sports can be this way for many students). They can even lead to future career opportunities.

But just remember that you can't graduate with a degree in basketball, Greek life, the newspaper, or the hiking club. So, start with your course work and any other obligations you may have, and then don't feel you have to layer in every other appealing possibility on top of them. That is, don't put unrealistic pressure on yourself to do *everything*, to fit in and be liked by everyone, be cool, and have lots of time to party. Remaining mindful of your personal mission statement and your "no small plans" can help you make good choices in balancing the different parts of your college life. Above all, keep your eyes on the prize.

---

[39] For a helpful overview of the research underlying these ideas, see Jerome Groopman, "Can Brain Science Help Us Break Bad Habits?" *The New Yorker*, October 21, 2019, https://www.newyorker.com/magazine/2019/10/28/can-brain-science-help-us-break-bad-habits. For a more in-depth treatment of this topic, see James Clear, *Atomic Habits*, in Additional Resources.

YOU'LL FIND LOTS OF FOLKS TO HELP YOU ALONG THE WAY

When you get into all this good planning, always remember that you don't have to go it alone. Your college or university probably provides multiple resources to assist in making your "no small plans" and managing your time. You'll most likely find them through the student affairs office, the career development center, an office of first-year studies, or somewhere else on campus. You can start by checking out these offices to see what's available.

The professionals in your college community are there to help you chart your course—especially if you face challenges that make it difficult for you to see yourself as successful. That's their job! But they also find it satisfying to assist students, and they'll be happy to have you reach out to them. In fact, they will respect you for doing so. And it's a terrific idea to make that connection early in your first semester or quarter. Many graduates wish they'd visited their school's career services office earlier in their college career, for example.

More informally, you can talk with your academic advisor. Talk with a student life staff member or an athletic coach if you're on a team. Talk with professors or teaching assistants. Look for potential mentors among all the people you encounter—including other students. Go ahead and ask the upper-class students you meet for advice. Share your questions and ideas with these people. Let them help you think through those "no small plans" you are creating and suggest some possible steps to realize them. They're all potential resources for you. But you need to take the initiative and reach out to them.

And don't forget that your parents and family members will always be there to support and encourage you as well. Share your plans and dreams with them too. Tell them what you're thinking about. Listen to what they have to say. You may be surprised by what you hear.

OVERCOMING BARRIERS

I understand that making the first move to talk to one of these people can take a bit of courage. Not everyone is comfortable engaging in those conversations. But make no mistake: shy or introverted students can be very successful in college too. If you happen to fit that description, or if you don't think you can fit in, please be assured that there *is* a place at your school for you! You just have to search for it. In time, you'll develop your own circle of new friends, allies, and mentors who are ready to assist you along your way. We'll talk about some additional ways to do all this in Chapter 6. But for now, here's an example to consider:

A story of overcoming obstacles: Amanda Gorman

You've probably heard of Amanda Gorman, the youngest poet ever invited to speak at a Presidential Inauguration. In 2021, she performed her uplifting poem, "The Hill We Climb," at President Biden's Inauguration when she was just twenty-two years old. She also was named the first National Youth Poet Laureate and has received numerous other awards and honors.

Her first book, which took the Inaugural poem as its title, was the only work of poetry ever to debut as an Amazon #1 best seller. By the time she was twenty-five years old, Amanda had published two additional books: a children's book, *Change Sings: A Children's Anthem*, and a second book of poetry inspired by the pandemic, *Call Us What We Carry*. In addition to her writing, Amanda embarked upon a secondary career in the fashion industry.

As I said, you may have already heard at least some of these details. But did you know that Amanda was raised by a single mother in Los Angeles? In an interview on CBS Mornings with co-host Gayle King,[40] she revealed that "when I was growing up...I wasn't just, kind of a really brainy kid, I was a really Black kid, I was a really skinny kid, I was a really small kid. Also, a kid whose voice was kind of distorted by a speech impediment.... So, all of these things kind of made me feel as 'othered,' or too different, you might say. And so, yeah, it really made me feel sometimes on the outside looking in." To cope with her speech impediment, Amanda would search the thesaurus, looking for words that were easier for her to pronounce.

Despite her challenges, Amanda was already thinking about her future. As an elementary student, she decided she would run for President of the United States in 2034; later on, she resolved to read a poem at a Presidential Inauguration.

---

[40] CBS Mornings, "Amanda Gorman on her historic year, her new book and why she still feels like an 'outsider,'" CBS News, December 7, 2021, https://www.cbsnews.com/news/amanda-gorman-new-book-poem-exclusive/.

(Talk about making "no small plans!") Through hard work, persistence, and dedication to her dreams, Amanda attended Harvard, graduating *cum laude*, and is certainly well launched on a brilliant career.

Reflecting on her trajectory, she said, "I think nowadays, with more age behind me, I look back at it and I am so grateful for that experience, because all the things that made me different make me who I am. And they make me great."[41]

Yet for all her accomplishments and ambition, Amanda remains humble and personable. In fact, she still has times when she struggles to come to terms with her success, worrying about whether she can live up to all the expectations her achievements to-date have created. Sometimes, she even experiences "a little bit of imposter syndrome, because I'm such a nerd, such a geek." She says she is "still trying to figure out who Amanda Gorman is." But she also realizes that her project is not just to "find out" who she is but to continue "creating" who she is going to become.

***

My reason for including Amanda Gorman's story here is that, for all her impressive accomplishments, getting to where she is today wasn't at all easy for her. As you've just read, she had to overcome

---

[41]   Ibid.

a number of obstacles. She benefitted from good role models (especially her mother) and supportive teachers. But it was never effortless. Nothing was ever handed to her.

Like Amanda and so many other successful people, you have to create and own *your* goals, discover your own pathway to achieving them, and then follow through to make your "no small plans" come true. The fashion model, actress, Internet entrepreneur, and Princeton grad Brooke Shields once said, "Even if you go to a great college, you still have to work your ass off." She's right!

No doubt you'll face challenges, perhaps even some significant obstacles along the way. Yet we all can be inspired by the examples of so many others who needed to climb steep hills to bring their dreams to reality. It's a helpful exercise to think of people you know personally who fit this description. And you'll learn about and meet others in college. They did it, and you can do it too! So, let them inspire you. Take one step at a time, and soon enough you'll find yourself at the summit of your own personal mountain.

SUMMING UP—CHAPTER 3

- This is precisely the moment to begin making "no small plans" for your college years and your post-college life. Set your sights on a goal that inspires you! Create your own soaring personal dream.
- Understand that your new plans will evolve over time. Don't feel any pressure to finalize your plans immediately, and don't be afraid to change your mind as you go along.

- Planning doesn't have to be all serious work. Try out some fun or creative ways to imagine where your life might go.
- Think about crafting a personal mission statement that expresses your core values and aspirations.
- To move from planning to doing, find a creative way to identify the actions that will enable you to realize your "no small plans." Be intentional about managing your time. Doing this well will lessen stress!
- Don't hesitate to check in with people who can help you develop your plans and strategize about next steps or overcoming obstacles.

At any stage of life, it's pretty easy to become bored—or annoyed!—with advice. Especially at your age, it probably seems that people are always telling you what to do or not do (yes, as in *this* book!). But the truth is that even tiresome recommendations can turn out to be useful. For example, it's obvious that an Indy or NASCAR driver can't win if their car blows an engine. Similarly, if you don't take care of your physical and emotional health, sooner or later *your* engine is going to blow up and you'll be sidelined from *your* race. You won't be able to bring your "no small plans" to reality. We'll talk about how to avoid this in Chapters 4 and 5.

CHAPTER 4
ESSENTIAL EQUIPMENT PART I: YOUR BODY

One important way to take charge of your new college life is to be purposeful about taking care of yourself physically, mentally, emotionally, and spiritually. Before we get into this conversation, however, let me emphasize what we're *not* going to be talking about. We're *not* going to consider *moral* arguments here. That is, I'm *not* going to preach to you to be "good" by being prudent in taking care of yourself. Instead, my objective in this chapter and the next one is to *empower* you by providing science-based information about where your brain and body are at this point on their developmental arc, identifying some potential threats, and suggesting some practical ways to counter those threats. The objective is to keep your essential equipment running in peak condition. That way, it will sustain the important work you'll be taking on over the coming months and years.

Let's start with two facts—two challenges—that shape the context of what we'll talk about in this chapter and the next one.

TWO CHALLENGES YOU FACE TODAY

I am dragged along by a strange new force.
Desire and reason are pulling in different directions.
I see the right way and approve it, but follow the wrong.
—Ovid

The first challenge relates to our historical context. In earlier times, strict social structures—for example, prohibitions against unmarried men and women being alone together without adult supervision—kept many choices out of the hands of young adults. Those cultural guardrails were also reflected in rules on college or university campuses (for example, the requirement to be back in your residence hall by a certain time at night, bans against men and women being together in dorm rooms, etc.). But for the past hundred years or so, those societal norms have been relaxed, and in the last fifty years, many former campus regulations have been eliminated altogether.

These cultural adjustments make our modern life—and your campus life—much less constrained than it would have been in that increasingly-distant past, significantly increasing your negative freedom. But this situation also imposes significant decision-making burdens upon you and your peers. As a modern college student, you'll face a lot of choices that simply were not on the table in earlier times. Many of these directly affect your body, mind, and spirit.

The second challenge relates to the neurological state of your still-developing brain, and there are two aspects to it. First, the parts of your brain that stimulate exploratory and risk-taking behavior have been happily firing away throughout your adolescence and will continue to do so during your college years. But second, the executive, logical, decision-making part of your brain (the prefrontal cortex) will *not* be fully formed and completely coupled to the rest of your neural structures until sometime *after* you graduate—probably between ages twenty-four to twenty-eight.[42]

These developmental realities set you up to be an eager and proficient college learner. Evolution has hard-wired you to be a fearless daredevil. You're primed and ready to investigate the world, experience new things, and acquire knowledge at an incredible pace. But the part of your brain that says, "Maybe you should stop and think a minute before you try...," is not yet fully engaged. Moreover, you don't yet have sufficient life experience for your creative imagination to conjure up all the possible negative consequences of an action you may be contemplating.

The lines from the Roman poet Ovid[43] quoted above remind us that that there's nothing new about the struggle between *desire* and *reason*. It's a perennial feature of the human condition—one hardly restricted to the contemporary world or people in your age group. But even so, the partial neurological disconnect between these two key parts of your brain, combined with the relaxed social constraints, helps to explain why young people face particular risks of getting into trouble. The tension between desire and reason will play out across the topics we'll discuss in this chapter and the next.

Let me also acknowledge that individuals differ enormously in their physical abilities and psychological makeup. Your condition will influence what you need to do to take care of yourself and navigate your college or university campus. But no matter

---

42 Frances E. Jensen and Amy Ellis Nutt, *The Teenage Brain: A Neuroscientist's Survival Guide to Raising Adolescents and Young Adults* (New York: Harper Paperbacks, 2016).

43 Ovid wrote in the first century CE; the quoted lines are from his *Metamorphoses*, trans. Stephanie McCarter (New York, NY: Penguin Classics, 2022).

what your body type and your mental situation, I believe you'll find some useful ideas in the following pages.

GETTING PHYSICAL

> *Your ego's writing checks your body can't cash!*
> —*Top Gun* (1986)

You probably already know how useful it is to get in some physical activity on a regular basis. If you're a serious athlete—especially if you're on a varsity team—you've already checked that box. But even if you're not playing an intercollegiate sport, it's still important to stay physically fit. And there are all kinds of ways you can do so.

Your college offers a wide array of facilities and options. It's like being given a membership in a health club complete with a full staff of personal trainers and instructors. So, think about making a deal with yourself to work out, run, or just take a good walk or hike on a regular basis. (If you have access to a car, it's a great idea *not* to drive everywhere on campus!) You might take a yoga class, swim, or join an intramural team. Or you could try out a new sport through a class. But one way or another, *make a commitment to stay physically active.*

Doing this tends to be easier if you can involve a friend, and it will help your friend too! But whatever works best for you, investing in yourself by building regular physical activity into your schedule will help you feel better all-around—including emotionally. It will also lower your level of stress. And, in the end, it'll help you be a more successful student.

YOU ARE WHAT YOU EAT

Making good decisions about eating is also crucial to maintaining your health and wellbeing. But I won't say too much about this topic because I assume you've already heard plenty from your parents (and others) about the importance of a nutritious diet. Again, if you're an athlete, you should have a pretty solid idea already about the choices you need to make for breakfast, lunch, and dinner to maintain your strength and endurance. But even if you're not a serious athlete, chances are you understand basic principles of balanced nutrition. If you don't, there's certainly a wealth of information available to you at your college or university, on the Internet, and elsewhere.

Fortunately, most campus dining services have upgraded their offerings in recent years to include wholesome and, in many cases, organic, sustainable, and locally-sourced food. Take advantage of those healthy options at your college or university, especially if you're on a meal plan. If you're living off-campus, there may be financial and time pressures that limit your options for food shopping and meal preparation. But selecting fresh items from your local supermarket (or farmer's market) and cooking for yourself usually represent healthier and less expensive alternatives to processed meals or, worse, a steady diet of fast food—as attractive as those options can seem!

Here's one more quick word to the wise: eating a breakfast loaded with simple sugars—sugary cereal, white bread, donuts, and the like—guarantees you a quick sugar high. You'll feel energized almost right away. For a while. Then, probably in mid-morning (just about the time you're in class), those simple sugars will be out of your bloodstream, and your metabolism will crash.

Two things follow. First, you'll feel an energy drain; second, you might experience what's known as "brain fog." Neither of these conditions helps you focus on your academic work. So, a more effective strategy is to include some protein (eggs, bacon, peanut butter, almond butter, etc.) and complex (whole) grains (e.g., oatmeal) in your breakfast—foods that contain nutrients that are released more slowly into your body. This will give you more lasting energy and a longer attention span. I'm certainly *not* saying you never should have a sweet pastry or other sugary treat. True confession: I like having the occasional donut, scone, or muffin as much as anyone. But the key word here is "occasional." If you make nutritionally sound choices *most* of the time, then indulging in an occasional breakfast pastry or dessert shouldn't knock you off your game.

If you happen to be one of so many young people who have struggled with an eating disorder, the demands of adjusting to your new college situation might trigger those issues again. And let's acknowledge that living through the pandemic may have exacerbated that challenge for you as well. But beginning your college career gives you an excellent opportunity to make a fresh start. *If do you find yourself confronting issues around eating, please check out the resources available through your university or college's counseling center.* It's likely that the mental health professionals there have developed programs aimed at helping students with eating-related conditions. They can assist you in taking charge of this part of your life too. And please know that you are not alone in facing these challenges.

SLEEP

How committed are you to getting a good night's sleep? You may not have thought a lot about this topic. And in your college years, it's easy to feel like an invincible superhero—to believe you can dispense with sleep and power through whatever needs to get done, especially when the demands of your schedule get intense. But research shows that too little sleep has a significant negative impact on learning. For example, scientists who investigate sleep have determined that too little sleep either the night before or the night after a study session makes you far more likely to forget what you've learned in both the short and long run.[44]

This means that the time-honored practice of "pulling an all-nighter" to finish a paper or prepare for an exam actually undercuts what you are trying to accomplish—namely, to pass that exam or write an excellent paper, and most of all, to *learn* something you'll remember later on. You probably can't avoid trading sleep for coursework from time to time. But try not to make a habit of it.

Unfortunately, research has demonstrated that it's just not possible to fully make up for sleep lost during the week by staying in bed longer on the weekend. Catching up on sleep on Saturday or Sunday certainly can feel great, but it can't completely erase a sleep-deficit you've built up over the preceding days. Research also suggests that getting too little sleep will make you more likely

---

[44] For an informative summary of the latest research into the positive effects of sleep (and the negative effects of too little sleep), see Matthew Walker, *Why We Sleep: Unlocking the Power of Sleep and Dreams* (New York: Scribner, 2017). Chapter 6 is especially relevant to questions of sleep-related learning.

to snack on high-calorie foods and drinks.[45] So, getting less sleep than you need actually *increases* your chances of putting on the dreaded "freshman fifteen."

To say all this more positively, one of the best things you can do to help yourself succeed in college (and, after that, in life!) is to ensure that you regularly get a full night's sleep. If you're eighteen to twenty-two years old, this probably means at least eight to ten hours. That's just an average, of course. Some people need more sleep; others can get by just fine on less. If you're not already tuned into what your body requires, you might pay attention to how you are feeling on different days, after different sleep-times—to see just what your optimum sleep cycle looks like.

If you just can't get all the sleep you need at night, then you might try grabbing a short afternoon nap whenever possible. Even putting your head down for a few minutes on a table in the library can do a lot for some students. However you manage it, getting enough sleep will make a big difference in how you feel—and how well you achieve your "no small plans." Given the demands of a full-time college schedule and the challenges of either on-campus or off-campus living, getting enough rest can be a lot easier said than done. But for all the above reasons, it's worth doing all you can to *build good sleep habits into your daily schedule.*

---

[45] A recent (at the time of writing) study divided teenaged subjects into groups that got more sleep (9.5 hours/night) and less (6.5 hours/night). Although "[b]oth sets of teens ate approximately the same number of calories per day... the kind of food they chose varied." Basically, the sleep-deprived group ate more junk food—foods high in carbs and added sugars, and they drank "more sugar-sweetened beverages than their counterparts." They also consumed more of their calories between 9:00 p.m. and 1:00 a.m. This study was limited in various ways, but its results are suggestive: getting less-than-optimal amounts of sleep can undermine healthy food choices too. See, Erin Blakemore, "Sleep deprivation related to poor food choices for teens, study says," *Washington Post,* January 16, 2022, https://www.washingtonpost.com/health/how-much-sleep-do-teens-need/2022/01/14/466a0966-7301-11ec-8b0a-bcfab800c430_story.html.

DRUGS—PRESCRIPTION AND OTHERWISE

Please resist the temptation to think that going to college will magically exempt you from continuing with any prescription medication(s) you're presently taking. It won't! Being autonomous and responsible means managing this facet of your life as well. So, before making a change in your meds, check in with your physician or psychologist. And talk with your parents as well. If you make it a team decision—not one you take entirely on your own—it's much more likely to work out how you want it to.

And speaking of drugs, it's extremely difficult to construct those life-changing "no small plans"—and *absolutely impossible* to execute them!—if you're adrift in a fog of alcohol or other recreational drugs. This is true for anyone at any stage of life. But please consider that neurological research has shown that your eighteen-to-twenty-four-year-old brain is at a particularly sensitive stage of its development. Countless studies have demonstrated that your still-maturing neural networks are especially susceptible to both the short-term and long-term effects of nicotine, alcohol, and other drugs—much more so than for someone who is older. For example,

> Recent brain research…suggests that alcohol impacts adolescents differently than…adults. Young people are more vulnerable to the negative effects of alcohol on the hippocampus—the part of the brain that regulates working memory and learning. Consequently, heavy use of alcohol and other drugs during the teen years can result

in lower scores on tests of memory and attention
in one's early to mid-20s.[46]

In the immediate term, this means that too much alcohol on a
Friday night can still undermine your ability to do well on a test
the following Wednesday. You may not be aware of those lingering
effects, but the data show they can be significant, whether you are
conscious of them or not. It also goes without saying that your
long-term memory can be adversely affected as well.

More importantly, people in your age group (as opposed to
us older folks) face a *considerably higher risk that overuse of alcohol or recreational drugs can create a life-long addiction.* Specifically,
once you've rewired your still-developing brain by excessive use
of those substances, it can become incredibly difficult later on
(sometimes next-to-impossible) to reset it back to its pre-addic-
tive state. This is what makes it so hard for people who become
hooked on drugs or alcohol at your stage in life to get clean and
sober again. For example, it's why a young person who's used
tobacco in their teenage years can experience a persistent desire to
smoke (or use snuff or chewing tobacco) throughout their entire
life, even after they've managed to ditch their cigarettes or snuff.

FENTANYL AND OTHER NEW THREATS

In recent years, a new lethal drug threat has appeared—something most of us hadn't even heard about a few years ago: fentanyl. This is likely not a surprise to you, but even so, you might

---

[46]   Clea McNeely and Jayne Blanchard, "Effects of Tobacco, Alcohol and Drugs
on the Developing Adolescent Brain," in *The Teen Years Explained: A Guide
to Healthy Adolescent Development* (Baltimore: Bloomberg School of Public
Health, 2009).

not know these details: Fentanyl is an extremely powerful opioid, "approximately 100 times more potent than morphine and 50 times more potent than heroin."[47] In controlled medical settings, it's a safe and effective analgesic; it's widely used, for example, to provide pain relief in surgery or for hospitalized cancer patients. Outside of medical contexts however, fentanyl becomes deadly. It's so powerful that even a small amount—that is, just a few particles, which literally fit on the point of a pencil—can steal your life or the life of a friend. In short, *one pill definitely can kill!*

Today, we're in the midst of a *fentanyl-related epidemic*. Let me say this as emphatically as I can: *fentanyl is killing people every day, including those in your age group*. The *Washington Post* reports that fentanyl poisoning has become the "leading cause of death for Americans ages 18 to 49"[48]—surpassing car accidents, suicides, and gun violence. In a provisional tally of drug-related deaths in 2021, The Centers for Disease Control and Prevention "calculated the overall number of drug overdoses at 107,622. Two-thirds were due to fentanyl."[49] I hope these numbers grab your attention.

There are many illegal ways to obtain fentanyl, but increasingly it is showing up hidden in recreational drugs, such as cocaine, heroin, ecstasy, molly, and others. Sometimes it's actually

---

[47] "Drug Fact Sheet: Fentanyl," Department of Justice/Drug Enforcement Administration, October 2022, https://www.dea.gov/sites/default/files/2022-12/Fentanyl%202022%20Drug%20Fact%20Sheet.pdf.

[48] For a cautionary tale that illustrates the horrific effects of the current fentanyl epidemic, see Sari Horwitz, Meryl Kornfield, Nick Miroff, and Steven Rich, "Five down in Apt. 307: Mass fentanyl deaths test a Colorado prosecutor," *Washington Post*, December 15, 2022, https://www.washingtonpost.com/investigations/interactive/2022/fentanyl-poisoning-colorado/.

[49] Nick Miroff, Scott Higham, Steven Rich, Salwan Georges, and Erin Patrick O'Connor, "Cause of death: Washington faltered as fentanyl gripped America," *Washington Post*, December 12, 2022, https://www.washingtonpost.com/investigations/interactive/2022/dea-fentanyl-failure/.

disguised as candy. It goes without saying that there's no quality control with street drugs, so buyers never can really know what's in them. But because of its extreme potency, fentanyl is especially deadly.

Recently, at the time of writing, a new category of elicit narcotics has been emerging in street drugs: nitazenes, primarily coming from China. These "novel opioids"

> can be many times more powerful than fentanyl and can complicate overdose revivals and addiction treatment. Even as elicit fentanyl manufactured in Mexico remains by far the chief catalyst for overdose deaths in the United States, the increasing presence of nitazenes adds another layer of health concerns as users often have no inkling they are consuming those opioids.[50]

So, let's be clear: the widespread presence of fentanyl and other narcotics in illegal substances has turned using recreational drugs of unknown origin into a dangerous form of Russian roulette, even more than it was in the past. And one more thing. Be assured that the people responsible for synthesizing and supplying illegal drugs—from foreign drug cartels to street distributers—don't care one whit about *your* welfare. I'm sorry for all the bad news, but it's important information for you to have.

---

[50] David Ovalle, "On the streets, opioids sometimes more potent than fentanyl: nitazenes," *Washington Post*, December 10, 2023, https://www.washingtonpost.com/health/2023/12/10/nitazenes-opioid-stronger-than-fentanyl/?utm_campaign=wp_post_most&utm_medium=email&utm_source=newsletter&wpisrc=nl_most.

DRINKING AND BINGE DRINKING

Another unfortunate truth is that when you go to college, you're likely to enter an environment where it's very easy to drink. We're not talking about your college or university's official policy, of course. All schools have to follow applicable local and state laws, which require them to prohibit on-campus underage drinking and do their best to regulate the availability of alcohol for students twenty-one years and older. Most schools have developed alcohol education programs, drug-and-alcohol-free (sometimes called "substance-free") residence halls or floors, and alcohol-free events. A minority of them—usually religious-affiliated schools—prohibit drinking on campus altogether. So, your college or university administrators are definitely concerned about campus alcohol consumption and are working hard to do something about its role in your campus culture. It's also helpful to keep in mind that studies show that students tend to *overestimate* the amount of drinking that goes on—that it, what *everyone else* is doing.

But let's be real: Even more than in high school, the *unofficial* student culture on most college and university campuses not only makes alcohol readily available for anyone (including underage students) but actually *encourages* and even *celebrates* drinking, including binge drinking (which we'll say more about in a minute). And, as you're certainly aware, there are many influences in popular culture that do this as well—from music videos to movies to advertisements for beer and liquor and beyond. In short, we're inundated in cultural inducements to drink...and to drink a lot. Many of these messages expressly target college students.

It's no secret why people enjoy consuming alcohol. They like the way it makes them feel. And in our culture, drinking frequently seems a necessary part of socializing. Some people decide not to drink, of course. (More of your peers than you might realize will make this choice.) Some drink responsibly and stay out of trouble. But others do not just drink socially; they intentionally drink to become drunk, even to the point of blacking out. It's up to you to decide where you fit in to this picture.

A good deal of research has looked into the patterns and effects of drinking, but recent work has revised some things you've probably heard before. So, in the spirit of providing up-to-date, useful, science-based information, let's ask: What happens in your brain when you take just one or two drinks, when you get drunk, and then if you keep drinking even beyond that point? This discussion draws upon a recent book by Malcolm Gladwell, *Talking To Strangers: What We Should Know About the People We Don't Know.*[51]

The first effects of alcohol show up in the region of your brain we've already mentioned: your prefrontal cortex—the executive part of your brain that regulates attention, rational decision-making, planning, motivation, and learning. Even one drink begins to turn down the functioning of this area, making you "a little dumber, less capable of handling competing, complicated considerations."[52]

Those first few drinks also affect other areas of your brain, *increasing* activity in the limbic system: "the reward centers of the brain, the areas that govern euphoria."[53] At the same time, alcohol begins to suppress the amygdala, which is responsible for assessing environmental threats—for telling you whether you should be cautious or aware of some potential risk. In sum, right from

---

[51] Malcolm Gladwell, *Talking To Strangers: What We Should Know About the People We Don't Know* (New York: Little, Brown and Company, 2019), 215.
[52] Ibid.
[53] Ibid, 215–6.

the start, drinking makes you less able to think clearly or handle complex ideas; you feel happier, but you become less capable of assessing environmental threats. The more your drink, the greater these effects.

The latest thinking about what this all means focuses *less* on the *loss of inhibition*—an idea earlier discussions of drinking tended to emphasize—and *more* about *reducing your capacity to think about the longer-term implications of what you are doing*. As Gladwell puts it, the combined effect on these three key neural centers makes us "myopic"; that is to say, it *narrows* the scope of our thinking:

> We don't have the brainpower to handle more complex, long-term considerations. We're distracted by the unexpected pleasure of the alcohol. Our neurological burglar alarm is turned off. We become altered versions of ourselves, beholden to the moment.[54]

A major consequence of these effects is that we become more likely to be influenced by our immediate surroundings and the social expectations that are most prominent in that environment.

That's why a bunch of loud, aggressive, drunken guys in a bar may get into a fight. It's also why being in a frat party with drinking, loud music, low lighting, and couples grinding on the dance floor can raise everyone's odds of having sex. Obviously, that's a major reason why college students go to those parties. (We'll return to this topic in the next section.) But the main takeaway I want to leave you with is that *in this altered, alcohol-induced state of euphoria, you become far less able to weigh the long-term*

---

[54] Ibid.

consequences of your actions. It's easy to understand what this does for your decision-making.

What happens if you continue to drink to the point where it would be more-than-foolish to get behind the wheel of a car? At this stage of inebriation, your cerebellum—the area that controls motion and balance—also takes a hit. The resulting loss of motor control makes your movements more awkward, and you find it difficult to do things (walking, dancing, riding a bike, driving) that ordinarily wouldn't pose a challenge. That's why most states consider a blood alcohol content (BAC) between 0.04 and 0.08 grams of alcohol per deciliter of blood to produce physical and psychological impairment: "it delays your reaction time, reduces your ability to see clearly, changes your judgment of speed and distances, [and] often makes you...more prone to take chances."[55] This is also why states are so serious about prohibiting driving under the influence, why they impose severe legal and financial penalties, and why there is such an emphasis on having a designated (non-drinking) driver.

When young people drink to these levels of BAC, there are consequences. The National Institute on Alcohol Abuse and Alcoholism (NIAAA), a division of the National Institutes of Health (NIH), reports that "about 1,519 college students ages 18 to 24 die [annually] from alcohol-related unintentional injuries, including motor vehicle crashes." They also estimate that "about 696,000 students ages 18 to 24 are assaulted by another student who has been drinking," and that a majority of sexual assaults in

[55] "Alcohol and Other Drugs," New York State Department of Motor Vehicles, accessed November 21, 2023, https://dmv.ny.gov/about-dmv/chapter-9-alcohol-and-other-drugs.

college involve alcohol or other substances."[56] These statistics, as significant as they are, can sound dry and unconnected to your own life, but we're talking about why getting drunk can lead you to act in ways you might regret later on.

Increasingly however, college students encounter a culture that encourages them to make a habit of drinking even *beyond* this stage of legal intoxication—to engage in binge drinking, which has become a much more common recreational practice in recent years. The NIAAA defines binge drinking as

> a pattern of drinking alcohol that brings blood alcohol concentration (BAC) to 0.08%...or more. For a typical adult, this pattern corresponds to consuming 5 or more drinks (male), or 4 or more drinks (female), in about 2 hours.[57]

This sex-related difference in the number of drinks needed to reach a given BAC reflects the different ways biological males and females process alcohol. On average, men tend to be larger than women, and greater body mass slows down the effects of alcohol. But because females also tend to have a higher proportion of water in their bodies than males and are more likely to drink on an empty stomach, even a female who is approximately the same size as a male will still tend to process alcohol more quickly. This means that a woman who matches a man drink-for-drink will become drunk faster than he will. Because more and more women are starting to "drink like men," adverse health consequences in this population are increasing even faster than for males.

---

[56] "Harmful and Underage College Drinking," National Institute on Alcohol Abuse and Alcoholism, July 2023, https://www.niaaa.nih.gov/publications/brochures-and-fact-sheets/college-drinking.

[57] Ibid.

Binging takes all the previously-noted effects up another level entirely. If you drink a lot of alcohol very quickly it affects your hippocampus. We've already noted that this small region of your brain plays an essential role in memory formation. When your BAC reaches approximately 0.8 percent, your hippocampus starts to shut down; it stops being able to process what you are experiencing into memory. In other words, reaching this level of intoxication cuts you off from the ability to remember just what you were doing while you were drinking.

This is what people mean when they talk about an alcohol-induced blackout. Gladwell describes it this way:

> When you wake up in the morning after a cocktail party and remember meeting someone but you cannot for the life of you remember their name or the story they told you, that's because the two shots of whiskey you drank in quick succession reached your hippocampus. Drink a little more and the gaps get larger—to the point where maybe you remember pieces of the evening but other details can be summoned only with the greatest difficulty.[58]

It's worth noting that there seems to be little connection between those parts of the experience you *do* remember and what you (later) would regard as significant.

To illustrate this point, Gladwell quotes Aaron White of the NIH, an expert on blackouts:

> "What that means is you might, as a female, go to a party and you remember having a drink

---

[58]   Gladwell, *Talking to Strangers*, 216.

downstairs, but you don't remember getting raped. But then you do remember getting in the taxi." At the next [BAC] level of 0.15—the hippocampus simply shuts down entirely. "In the true, pure blackout," White said, "there's just nothing. Nothing to recall." [59]

It's pretty obvious that people who've reached this state of drunkenness can very easily get into trouble—because of what they do or because of what other people do to them—and can lose all capacity to *remember* some or all of what happened to them. That's pretty scary. Our ability to remember what we've done in our lives is a major part of our *personhood*; it's what makes us who we are. To surrender that capacity is to give up a lot.

If all this isn't enough, here's another troubling fact to consider: as NBC, CBS, and other news sources have reported,[60] between 2009 and 2016, rates of *alcohol-related liver disease* have *tripled* among twenty-five-to-thirty-four-year-olds. Your liver is an extremely important organ that we don't talk about very much these days. But it's the second largest one in your body (only your skin is larger), and it performs hundreds of essential functions, for example: helping to regulate blood sugar levels, removing toxins from the blood, producing bile that helps digest fats and vitamins.

Cirrhosis of the liver—scarring of the liver that can lead to failure—has long been associated with heavy drinking. In the past, however, this condition occurred largely in people who were middle-aged or older. But now alcohol-related liver disease

59   Ibid.
60   Linda Carroll, Patrick Martin, and Zinhle Essamuah, "As alcohol-related liver disease rises in the U.S., a clinic takes a new approach to treatment," NBC News, January 8, 2023, https://www.nbcnews.com/health/health-news/alcohol-liver-disease-rising-young-people-especially-women-rcna64484.

is increasingly showing up in younger people; consequently, death rates have been rising for males and *especially* for females. In short, overuse of alcohol in your teens and early twenties can lead to serious physiological problems just a few years later—even if you're not particularly aware of these adverse health effects as they begin to occur.

And there's one final point to consider: if you drink enough in a brief period of time, the alcohol in your blood can shut down other vital systems in your body to the point where you don't just lose consciousness, you *die*. In fact, it can be quite difficult to tell whether your roommate who's passed out on their bed from drinking will be able "to sleep it off" or will never wake up at all. So, if you ever confront a situation in which you're concerned that someone may have consumed enough alcohol to put their life in danger—when they're completely unresponsive—please don't hesitate to seek help. Call your campus safety office or an RA in your residence hall or dial 911—get someone who can provide immediate medical assistance. Schools increasingly have policies protecting you from judicial action if you report someone who just might be too drunk to survive.

Here's an extreme example of how things can go very wrong because of college drinking: Just a few years ago, the family of a twenty-year-old student at a major state university won a $2.9 million legal settlement over their son's wrongful death. Their son was pledging a fraternity in 2021. As part of his initiation at an off-campus location, he reportedly drank approximately one liter of bourbon. His roommate later found him passed out in their apartment. He was taken to a hospital, but even so, he died three days later. As a result, some members of the fraternity faced criminal charges, and the fraternity was permanently banned from the university. Now the family is partnering with the university to use the settlement money in an effort "to eradicate hazing across the country."[61] This is a worthy goal, and I sincerely hope they succeed. But nothing can bring that young man back to life.

So, now you know. That's a lot of information to process. But embracing your new freedom means, in part, comprehending the potential outcomes of different choices you might make. If you remember these facts about alcohol, you'll be better equipped *to understand* and, I sincerely hope, *to manage the risks associated with drinking.* Specifically, you now know what's going on in your body if you or other people drink up to and past the point of becoming drunk.

Please be aware that you're very likely to face social pressures to drink during your first six weeks on campus. Some schools refer to this time as the "danger zone," when all too many sexual assaults and other serious problems—often alcohol-related problems—occur with new students. This can be especially true on campuses that have fraternities and sororities, and I'll return to this topic in Chapter 9. But alcohol-related hazing can occur on sports teams and in other groups as well. So, please be extra alert and aware of your decisions during this risky period. It may also be helpful to know that in recent years underage drinking has *declined* significantly in the United States.[62] So as I mentioned before, fewer of your classmates may be drinking than you might expect.

If you're already struggling with issues related to drug or alcohol use—or if you start to have these problems in college—*please*

---

[61] Susan H. Greenberg, "University Settles Hazing Case With Family of Dead Student," *Inside Higher Education,* January 24, 2023, https://www.insidehighered.com/quicktakes/2023/01/24/university-settles-hazing-case-family-dead-student.

[62] "Underage Drinking in the United States (ages 12 to 20)," the National Institute of Health National Institute on Alcohol Abuses and Alcoholism, updated 2023, https://www.niaaa.nih.gov/alcohols-effects-health/alcohol-topics/alcohol-facts-and-statistics/underage-drinking-united-states-ages-12-20.

look for help in your school's counseling center. It's a good bet that there are programs designed to assist students confronting these problems. (Many campuses sponsor an Alcoholics Anonymous group, for example.) If you are confused or unclear about how to navigate the drinking scene on your campus, look for offices or organizations at your college or university that provide information and offer opportunities just to talk it over. And don't hesitate to bring up this topic with your new friends, many of whom are probably feeling the way you are. But here's the bottom line: *if you find yourself confronting challenges with drugs or alcohol, you don't have to wait until after college to deal with them. Seek out the resources that are there to help.*

And as seductive as it may be, *please resist the temptation to lean on alcohol or drugs as a substitute for building community or as a shortcut to making new friends.* The adult friendships you develop over the next four years will be important to you for the rest of your life! The French author Antoine de Saint-Exupéry described friendship as "the nicest, hardest, riskiest, and most fragile gift of life." Friendships can indeed be risky or fragile (especially at first), but a genuine friendship is an amazing gift! You never know where your college friendships are going to lead, and it's not unusual for them to last a lifetime. So, your new friendships absolutely merit your time, energy, and clear-headed commitment. Value and invest in your relationships with your college friends the same way you value and invest in yourself. They and *you* are worth the effort. *You* are enough. *You do not need drugs or alcohol to help you make those connections.*

SEX

A major part of taking charge of your life as a young adult is coming to terms with your sexuality. Statistically, it's likely that most new college students already have some sexual experience, although the incidence of teenagers engaging in sex seems to be declining. And, as is the case with drinking, we tend to *overestimate* how much sex *other people* are having. Even so, college is often a time when young people explore this important facet of their lives, if not for the first time, then in greater depth. This aspect of anyone's life can be especially challenging to manage. Just like with drinking, college students can experience peer pressure to be more active sexually than they might want to be. But you *always* have a *choice*—either to give in to this pressure or to resist it. You're in charge of this dimension of your life as well.

Again, my purpose here is not to preach. But part of becoming a responsible adult means understanding how easy it is to take advantage of another person sexually—to harm both them and yourself, both physically and emotionally. As with anything else, the important thing is to be clear about your own values, to see how they relate to this dimension of your life, and then be true to them. This means owning both the emotional and the physical implications of your actions. At the most basic level of responsibility, you have two choices: either *avoid sexual activity altogether* (admittedly, an unlikely option for most college students but a real one nevertheless); or *take care to practice responsible safer sex*. The term "safer sex" is preferred today because there can be no absolute guarantees that any preventative measure (other than abstaining) will protect you or your partner 100 percent of the time.

One important reason for practicing safer sex is to avoid contracting or (worse!) passing along a sexually transmitted infection (STI) to your sexual partner. Many STIs are curable, but some are not. For example, there's no cure for genital herpes; once you have it, it's with you the rest of your life. Fortunately, getting HIV is no longer a death sentence, but contracting it commits you to a lifelong treatment regimen to prevent its progressing to AIDS. At the beginning of 2023, the state of Massachusetts reported two (unrelated) cases of drug-resistant gonorrhea.[63] These and other sobering facts about the increasing prevalence of STIs are powerful arguments for always using a condom, regardless of (or in addition to) whatever other forms of birth control might be available.

The second (and most obvious) reason to practice safer sex, for heterosexuals, is to avoid an unplanned and unwanted pregnancy. Employing effective contraception has become even more critical today in our post–*Roe v. Wade* world—regardless of where you stand on the abortion debate. Following the Supreme Court's decision in *Dobbs v. Jackson Women's Health Organization* (in 2022) and depending on the state in which you attend college, you may now have limited options—or even *no* options—for terminating an unplanned pregnancy.

Though the burden of an unwanted pregnancy often falls *unfairly* on a woman more than upon the equally responsible man, my comments here apply to everyone: *Sexual responsibility is an imperative for* all *adults, regardless of gender identity, sexual orientation, religious beliefs, or political opinions.* This means that *each* party to a potential or actual pregnancy needs to take ownership

---

[63] Cara Murez and Robin Foster, "Two Cases of New Drug-Resistant Gonorrhea Strain Reported in Massachusetts," U.S. News, January 20, 2023, https://www.usnews.com/news/health-news/articles/2023-01-20/two-cases-of-new-drug-resistant-gonorrhea-strain-reported-in-massachusetts.

of their decisions as well as the potential or actual consequences of those decisions.

If you find yourself grappling with any of these tough issues, please know, once again, that many (indeed, most!) of your peers are facing similar challenges. As I've been emphasizing, you're not alone in coming to terms with your new freedom. And there are many people in your college or university who you can turn to for good advice, assistance, or even just a supportive conversation. In addition to their counseling and health centers, most campuses have offices or organizations that provide useful information about understanding your sexuality, practicing safer sex, birth control, and so on. Please don't hesitate to take advantage of these resources.

Of course, these brief comments don't even begin to suggest the psychological and emotional complexity of human sexuality. It's one of the deepest and most fraught aspects of human existence, which is why so much has been written about it over the centuries. I'm just reminding you of some basic facts to help inform your decision-making, and I'm asking you to think about your core personal values and how you choose to apply them in this aspect of your life. We'll return to the larger topic of values in Chapter 7.

THE THREAT OF GUN VIOLENCE ON CAMPUS

Your grandparents' (or great grandparents') generation was defined by having survived the Great Depression and World War II, and they gained a tremendous sense of victory and an optimism about the future when they met those challenges. *Your* generation will be defined by how you respond to the wicked problems noted in Chapter 1, many of which you've been living with for your entire life.

The issue of gun-related violence in our society is certainly one of these defining wicked problems. The national Gun Violence Archive, which tracks reports of gun violence in the US, reports 612 mass-shooting incidents (4 or more people injured or killed) by the end of November 2023.[64] It's well-documented that the US is unique in the world—apart from active war zones—in having to report such a high incidence of gun-related violence. Many mass shootings are expressions of various forms of ideological hate (antisemitism, racism, etc.); others are more random, arising from the shooter's personal issues. These motives are frequently intertwined.

As everyone knows, gun-related outrages affect schools at *all* levels. To cite just one example: on February 14, 2018, a lone student gunman armed with a military-style assault rifle killed seventeen innocent people—students, coaches, and teachers—at Florida's Marjory Stoneman Douglas High School. Tragically of course, that was hardly the first or last such event; others have occurred on university campuses. Even if you've never experienced one of these incidents yourself or know someone who has, you're no doubt all too familiar with lockdown and active shooter drills. It's another sad sign of our times that Texas is now using a booklet with images of Winnie the Pooh to teach elementary students how to respond in such a situation. Current headlines remind us that the risk of mass shootings has not receded—if anything, it's continued to increase.

Regardless of where you stand on the Constitution's Second Amendment—which specifies the right to "keep and bear Arms"

---

[64] See the Gun Violence Archive to explore updated statistics on mass shootings as well as other gun violence figures, https://www.gunviolencearchive.org.

(in the context of "a well regulated Militia")—and whether or not you personally are a gun owner, we all should be able to agree that there is no place in our society for mass murder. There will be less consensus on other dimensions of this issue, but let me mention one troubling recent development. It is now possible to purchase a small plastic piece called, among other names, a machine gun conversion device (MCD) or a "switch," which turns a Glock automatic handgun into a fully automatic weapon—making it, in effect, a hand-held machine gun. (It's also possible to purchase online instructions to make one yourself in a 3D printer.) When they are fired, these weapons are "very hard to control,"[65] which makes them even more dangerous, and they are increasingly being implicated in shootings across the country. Of course, they are illegal under federal law, which means that anyone who obtains such a device is, by definition, a criminal.

Our politics divide on the question of how best to prevent gun-related violence. The issue is complicated by the fact that a substantial subpopulation of our citizens today sees gun ownership—or membership in "gun culture"—as fundamental to their self-identity. Accordingly, they view any attempt to enhance gun safety through legal regulations as an attack on them personally, as an unacceptable constraint on their negative freedom. It's also an undeniable fact that the gun lobby exercises powerful influence over many of our political leaders. So, it's easy to feel powerless in the context of this complex reality. But I want to suggest some things to think about and *do* that, I hope, will help you feel more empowered—as a member of your campus community—in the face of these very real challenges.

---

[65] Stephanie Haines and Devan Markham, "What are 'Glock switches'?" The *Hill*, February 23, 2023, https://thehill.com/homenews/3871083-what-are-glock-switches/.

To begin, please keep in mind that a college or university campus remains, statistically, a very safe environment. Even so, it's likely to feel quite different from what you've experienced in primary and secondary school. Higher education institutions are committed to free expression and free access. Like small cities, their physical environments tend to be larger, more spread out, and less controlled than schools you've known in the past. You'll find fewer, if any, metal detectors at doors, for example.

So, what can you do to exercise care and good judgment in response to potential gun-related and other kinds of threats in your new situation? Let me suggest four positive steps to increase your agency with regard to your own safety and that of other community members:

First, just like in any city, every member of a campus community needs to be alert for potential threats and incidents. This doesn't mean you should become paranoid or obsessed about safety, but it does mean keeping your eyes open and exercising reasonable caution. For example, you might consider not having your head buried in your mobile phone all the time, especially when you're walking around campus—just like on any city street.

Second, most colleges and universities have upgraded their security systems and procedures to include more patrols by campus safety officers, better lighting on sidewalks and paths, increased numbers of security cameras and emergency callboxes, interior locks on classroom doors, and so on. It's smart to be aware of the safety procedures your school has put in place—which probably will be covered in materials sent to you before you arrive or discussed as part of new-student orientation. This information will certainly be available on your school's website, where you can easily check it out. So, please pay attention to it.

Next, as part of exercising reasonable caution, it's wise to keep the following guidelines in mind:

- Understand your school's emergency warning system, which will be activated for any kind of potential disruption, including a dangerous storm, an unlawful intruder on campus, an active shooter, or other potential problems that could threaten your safety. *Know what to do if and when that warning system is activated.*

- Many schools now send safety alerts directly to community members as a text, on social media, or through a special app you can download. Assuming your campus has one, *make sure you are signed up for this system and know how it works.*

- It's always a good idea to stay on designated, lighted paths, especially at night, and it's prudent to walk with someone you know if you can. *Familiarize yourself with your campus emergency callboxes—know how they work before you need to use one.*

- One of the most important safety enhancements is electronic key-card access door locks—especially in residence halls. If you live on campus and your building has such a feature (or even if it doesn't), *please resist the temptation to prop open an external door* for any reason. Keeping those entry doors locked may be inconvenient, but it definitely enhances your safety and everyone else's as well. Keeping your personal room's door locked when you're not there is also a very good idea.

- If, tragically, you experience an active-shooter incident on your campus, remember this simple mantra: Run! Hide! Fight! Escaping the area of highest threat should be your first choice. If you are near a safe location, then shelter in place behind a locked or barricaded door. As a last resort, if you have no other option, then use any means at your disposal to disable or disarm the perpetrator. It is my sincere hope that you *never* have to follow this advice, but it could save your life.

You might regard these guidelines in the spirit of pre-flight safety reminders on a commercial airplane: the chance of ever needing them is small, but it's not zero. So, it's prudent to keep this information in the back of your mind.

Fourth, to return to an earlier theme, it's always smart to be alert when you're in public, regardless of where you are. But let me take this suggestion further. When you're walking in a city, security experts advise us all to *trust our instincts*. We've evolved to be highly accomplished perceivers of complex environmental information—including threats. Your brain does much of this work subconsciously, and it can give you a useful heads-up about potential dangers you haven't yet focused on consciously.

Therefore, *if something doesn't feel right to you—a situation or the way someone you don't recognize is acting, even if you can't quite articulate what the problem is—don't ignore it! Pause. Take another look. Try to figure out what's bothering you. Most importantly, if you feel threatened or just uneasy, don't hesitate to* do *something*: change your direction, cross the street, enter a building where there are other people, or talk with a police or campus safety officer if one happens to be around. Don't hesitate to use a campus safety callbox. There's no need to be embarrassed if it turns out that there was nothing amiss. As you've no doubt heard many times: *if you see something*, say *something!* This is all part of embracing your positive freedom as a caring and responsible member of your campus community. Look out for yourself and for others as well.

Finally, resolving our societal problem of gun-related violence will require serious social and political change at virtually all levels—local, state, and national. Especially since the assault at Marjory Stoneman Douglas High School, many younger citizens have taken up this cause. Effecting political change can be a long and frustrating process—making social change can take even longer. But change *is* possible and working to make it happen—regardless of the issue—can bring its own sense of empowerment. We'll return to this topic in Chapter 8.

Let me conclude this admittedly rather grim section by emphasizing what I said at its beginning: Despite these things that we all need to keep in mind, in most instances, *college and university campuses are very safe places.* Though they happen all too often, the events that have prompted these comments, thankfully, are still rare occurrences. We human beings are psychologically prone to overestimate the probability of disturbing negative events. That's why people can have concerns about the safety of air travel following reports of a serious crash—even though the evidence shows that flying is still *much* safer than driving on a highway. Likewise, we should not allow reports of mass shootings and, in particular, school and campus shootings—*as horrific and unacceptable as they truly are*—to make us feel generally unsafe at a college or university.

There can never be any guarantees. Living always involves some level of risk (which we'll talk about in Chapter 6). We just have to acknowledge this fact, act prudently, and carry on. Following the preceding common-sense suggestions will increase your chances of being OK (just like wearing seatbelts in a car). But always place these reminders in the larger context of a life that's focused primarily on other things—preferably, on your "no small plans."

SUMMING UP–CHAPTER 4

- One challenge you'll face, if you are a traditional-age college student, is the need to make a lot of personal decisions that wouldn't have been in your hands in the past. It doesn't help that, in making those choices, your prefrontal cortex (the rational decision-making part of your brain) will probably not be fully engaged until several years *after* you graduate.

- It's a really good idea to take reasonable care of your body: get some exercise, eat nutritional food, and try to get enough sleep on a regular basis to function at peak capacity.

- Overusing alcohol or other drugs presents both short-term and long-term risks for your still-developing brain and your body. Too much alcohol can degrade your academic performance. It also can lead to serious long-term illness (e.g., alcoholism or liver disease) or death—for you or a friend. You'll find many resources on your campus to help you deal with these issues.

- Drinking too much can also expose you to other risks—including committing or becoming a victim of sexual assault. Binge drinking can result in a blackout, in which you may lose most or all memory of what happened.

- Today, *fentanyl* and other powerful, life-threatening opioids can be hiding in virtually any street drug, and a tiny amount can kill you.

- Embrace your new freedom by making responsible choices regarding sex. In our post–*Roe v. Wade* world, your decisions are even more significant than in the past. If you choose to be sexually active, *always practice safer sex* to avoid contracting a sexually transmitted infection (STI) or experiencing an unwanted pregnancy.

- Though your campus is most likely a very safe place to live and work, colleges and universities are not immune from gun violence. So, know your school's safety plans and procedures, and follow common sense guidelines to increase your personal safety. *If you see something, say something.* We share a responsibility to do our part in protecting ourselves and one another.

Now let's talk about the second part of your *essential equipment*: your emotional life, mind, and spirit.

CHAPTER 5

ESSENTIAL EQUIPMENT PART II: YOUR EMOTIONAL LIFE, MIND, AND SPIRIT

I t's no secret that young people often confront psychological challenges—perhaps more today than ever before. As we've discussed, there are many ways in which the world can seem like a hostile place—there are so many potential causes for discomfort, anxiety, and depression. But embracing your new positive freedom means being intentional about taking charge of this aspect of your life as well. So, let's consider some strategies for doing this.

MAKING TIME AND SPACE FOR YOURSEF

> *Time stops only if you stop long enough to hear it passing.*
> *—Rita Dove, "Postlude"*

As you settle into your new college routine, *give yourself permission to take some time to care for your mental health.* You might set aside a couple of hours on a weekend to catch a movie with a couple of new friends. Read a book for pleasure, not because it's required for a course.[66] Listen to some music that speaks to the deepest levels of your spirit and inspires positive emotions. Some people find that doing art—drawing, painting, pottery, whatever—is relaxing and renewing. (If you're a serious artist, you already know about these benefits.) But regardless of how you do it, look for ways to give yourself a break, periodically, from your regular routine and from any pressures you may be facing. If religious or spiritual practice is important to you, your campus will likely afford many ways to continue it during college. There also will be opportunities to explore these traditions if they are unfamiliar to you and you would like to investigate them.

College is the first time many students share a room with someone else. But no matter your prior experience or how much you like your roommate(s), the lack of privacy can be an intense experience. So, *it's okay to go off by yourself from time to time if you feel you need a break*. Think about getting out into nature by taking a hike, visiting a local park, or just sitting for a few minutes on a bench in an attractive part of your campus. You don't need an excuse to do this, and you don't need to justify it to anyone. Just do it!

Additionally, from time to time, *give yourself the gift of silence*. Search for a place on your campus (or elsewhere) that is quiet and brings you a sense of calm—somewhere that allows you to hear that small-but-important inner voice that reflects your authentic self.

Amidst the constant noise of the virtual environment, it's easy to lose touch with that authentic self and with the people

---

[66] I highly recommend Alan Lightman's short book, *In Praise of Wasting Time*, which reflects on how to rediscover and recover our innermost selves and our relationships with others in today's world; please see Additional Resources.

and things that matter most to you. To help rediscover and nurture that part of you that can too easily be displaced today, periodically treat yourself to a time-out from the overwhelming and overheated digital world: Silence your cell phone. Turn off your texting, email, and social media platforms—even if just for a little while. (And if you find this difficult to do, that should tell you something.) If you're so inclined, meditate or do some yoga. Such practices may already be a familiar part of your usual rhythms, or they may represent relatively new experiences for you. One way or the other, make time to remind yourself of who you are when you are not caught up in the constant demands of today's noisy digital onslaught.

Here's another benefit: some of our most *creative* moments come when we've stepped aside from our day-to-day routines and the demands of the outside world. When you've temporarily *stopped* focusing on the problem or question that's been bugging you, it's amazing how many times that elusive answer will pop into your head.

For all these reasons, it's a great idea to periodically *check in with yourself* to see how you're doing and rediscover what your inner voice has to say. Just sitting down and writing or drawing with a pen or pencil for a few minutes a day can itself be a therapeutic act. That's why so many people find it helpful to keep a journal. (And by the way, studies have shown that taking notes on paper during class is a far better way to remember what you've heard than taking notes on a computer or other digital device.) Giving yourself permission to unplug on a regular basis will pay dividends, not just emotionally but physically and intellectually too.

YOU ABSOLUTELY ARE NOT ALONE

Never be ashamed to need help.
—*Marcus Aurelius*

If you really are feeling alone, anxious, or lost—if these feelings persist without going away in a few days, and especially if they start to interfere with your life—*then please don't hesitate to talk to someone about your concerns*: your RA, your academic advisor, someone at the counseling center, a coach, someone in the office of student life, one of your professors, or someone else you are comfortable talking with.

Recent studies have shown that nearly half of contemporary college-age students struggle with anxiety or depression at one point or another.[67] Dealing with the COVID-19 pandemic—especially with remote learning and social isolation—has exacerbated these issues for many students. In fact, the pandemic affected other age groups as well. One national poll found that "50 percent of households reported someone experiencing 'serious problems with depression, anxiety, stress, or serious problems sleeping in the past few months.'"[68] Moreover, if you are an LGBTQ+ student, you may face increased "mental health challenges compared to [your] heterosexual and cisgender peers."[69] Whatever your personal situation, if you feel overwhelmed and

---

[67] See Kristen Bowe, "College Students and Depression: A Guide for Parents," the Mayo Clinic Health System, August 22, 2023, https://www.mayoclinichealthsystem.org/hometown-health/speaking-of-health/college-students-and-depression.

[68] Sarah Wildman, "Self Sufficiency Is Overrated," *New York Times*, November 25, 2021, https://www.nytimes.com/2021/11/25/opinion/self-sufficiency-generosity.html.

[69] Maria Carrasco, "Addressing the Mental Health of LGBTQ+ Students," Inside Higher Education, October 25, 2021, https://www.insidehighered.com/news/2021/10/26/lgbtq-students-face-sizable-mental-health-disparities.

need help, please take advantage of the many resources available at your college or university. (Yes, there's a theme here.) That's why they're there!

It can also help to remind yourself that even highly successful, famous, and seemingly fearless people can confront depression or other psychological challenges. In her latest book, *The Light We Carry: Overcoming in Uncertain Times*,[70] former First Lady Michelle Obama acknowledges that she too struggled with depression triggered by isolation during the COVID-19 pandemic. She writes that she continues to work on her mental health every day.

Here's an example of someone closer to your age group:

A competitive skier's story: Lindsey Vonn

> World-class competitive skier Lindsey Vonn has been described as "the most dedicated and fearless female skier of all time—with 82 World Cup wins, three Olympic medals, and 20 World Cup titles." Yet she now openly talks about dealing with depression for much of her life. Skiing often provided a refuge from her worst feelings, but even while she was competing, there were times when Lindsey struggled with mental health challenges. Medication helped, but she also came to realize that "antidepressants don't magically fix everything. 'I learned that it's up to me…to make sure I'm maintaining good mental health by doing all those things that help me stay

---

[70]   Michelle Obama, *The Light We Carry: Overcoming in Uncertain Times* (New York: Crown, 2022).

positive, like journaling, being with friends, and working out.'"[71]

Now that she's retired from competition, Lindsey has joined other prominent athletes in speaking out about their own mental health challenges—making the point that these issues can afflict anyone, that we need to be proactive in seeking help, and above all, that we must commit to moving our life in a positive direction.

***

In keeping with the theme of self-care, it's important to be clear-headed about what you reasonably can and cannot expect from your school's counseling center. Yes, you should be able to talk with a mental health professional who can assess what you're dealing with and recommend next steps. And ideally, you shouldn't have to wait too long (not more than one or two days—fewer if you feel it's an emergency) for your first appointment. But no college or university, no matter how robust its financial resources, can provide 24/7 access to counseling personnel or long-term one-on-one counseling for every student who comes seeking help. There simply can never be enough counselors at any school to support that level of services.

What your counseling center *can* do, however, is offer a range of programs—group programs, online resources, and yes, in some cases, individual counseling sessions—to help you take

---

[71] Johnny Dood, "Olympic Skiing Legend Lindsey Vonn Says: 'Depression Is Something I Work on Every Day'," *People*, January 6, 2022, https://people.com/sports/skiing-legend-lindsey-vonn-depression-work-on-every-day-memoir-rise/.

charge of your mental and emotional health. Many schools sponsor *peer-support programs*, in which trained students provide help and encouragement to their classmates. These programs can be quite effective and can also serve to connect you, if needed, with the professionals in the counseling center.

Some of the best models have you follow up an initial counseling session with some personal "homework"—steps for you to take to help you begin to address your concerns. Typically, the center will schedule a check-in session a few days or weeks later to see where you are at that point and determine what further actions might be called for. This is actually an empowering process because it reinforces the awareness that *you* are in charge of your mental and emotional health along with the other dimensions of your life. At the same time, it brings in professional assistance, if you need it, to help you reassert control.

After all, your objective is *not* to spend the rest of your college days visiting the counseling center but rather to move towards the kind of independence and self-reliance you'll need when you graduate into the post-college world. None of us should ever be content to live an isolated, lonely existence. We all need networks of friends, loved ones, and colleagues to help us deal with what life throws our way. But each of us also needs to be the captain of our own ship.

AVOIDING SELF-HARM AND CREATING MEANING IN YOUR LIFE

If you're on your own in this life
The days and nights are long
When you think you've had too much
Of this life to hang on.

Well, everybody hurts sometimes
Everybody cries ...
So hold on, hold on
Hold on, hold on, hold on.
—R.E.M., *"Everybody Hurts"*[72]

Before we leave the topic of self-care, let's acknowledge that, sadly, incidences of self-harm and suicide are increasing among adolescents and young adults. In 2006, suicide was the *third* leading cause of death for young people—representing 11 percent of fatalities, behind accidents (48 percent—the vast majority of which were automobile accidents) and homicides (13 percent).[73] Those numbers were troubling enough. But by 2019, intentional self-harm or suicide had become "the *second* [emphasis mine] leading cause of death among teenagers aged 15 to 19 years in the United States, contributing around 21.5 percent of deaths among [this] age group."[74] Many people believe these numbers represent a national public health emergency. I certainly agree.

Many factors have driven the changes in these numbers, not the least of which is the unfortunate availability on the Internet of information that can be seen as facilitating and even encouraging self-harm. In fact, the increased use of cell phones and social media tracks in a straight line with increases in mental health

---

[72] R.E.M., "Everybody Hurts," track 4 on *Automatic for the People*, Warner Bros, 1992.

[73] Arialdi M. Miniño, "NCHS Data Brief No. 37: Mortality Among Teenagers Aged 12-19 Years: United States, 1999-2006," Centers for Disease Control and Prevention, May 2010, https://www.cdc.gov/nchs/products/databriefs/db37.htm. [Note: These figures vary among racial and ethnic groups.]

[74] John Elfein, "Distribution of the ten leading causes of death among teenagers aged 15 to 19 years in the United States in 2019," *Statista*, June 22, 2023, https://www.statista.com/statistics/1017959/distribution-of-the-10-leading-causes-of-death-among-teenagers/.

challenges for young people. And as we've noted, the pandemic made an already difficult situation even worse.

Here's the important take-away: If you are one of so many young people who have wrestled with significant depression or have felt that your existence has no value, perhaps even to the point of contemplating ending your life, I understand that anything I might say here can sound hollow at best. But even so, *let me urge you to consider how many people in your life—starting with your parents, family members, and friends—love you and who definitely will not be better off if you are gone.*

If you find yourself having serious thoughts about harming yourself, *please, please,* please(!) *summon the courage to seek help wherever you can find it, starting with the resources available on your campus.* As I've said numerous times already, *take the initiative to talk with someone about how you are feeling.* They will respect you for doing so, and they will make their best effort to assist you.

And if you pick up troubling signs in a roommate, friend, or acquaintance—for example, if you hear them say how worthless their life is, if they begin giving away prized possessions or pets, or if they talk about harming themselves—*don't ignore them.* Share your concerns with the person themselves or with an RA, someone in the counseling center, or a faculty member.

> In the United States, you can call the National Suicide Prevention Lifeline at 9-8-8. You also can visit SpeakingOfSuicide (https://www.speakingofsuicide.com/resources/) to find additional assistance.
>
> Outside the United States, this *New York Times* article provides helpful information: https://www.nytimes.com/article/suicide-prevention-helplines.html.

This is another moment when, *if you* see *something, you need to* say *something.*

There are other resources available, too, beyond your college or university, as noted above.

Above all, *please do not give up on yourself* before you have the chance to see just how far you'll grow as a person throughout your time as an undergraduate. Don't throw away the opportunity to meet that new you who, in a few years, will likely be in a very different place. In a column on suffering, David Brooks paraphrases the psychologist Viktor Frankl, who in his acclaimed book *Man's Search for Meaning*, reflected on his personal experience in the Nazi death camps during WWII. There along with so many others, Frankl both witnessed and experienced horrific suffering.

> Frankl argued that we often can't control what happens to us in life, that we can control only how we respond to it. If we respond to terrible circumstances with tenacity, courage, unselfishness and dignity, then we can add a deeper meaning to life. One can win small daily victories over hard circumstances.[75]

If your own situation ever tempts you to lose hope, please do all you can to commit to continuing on your journey. Focus on creating what Frankl calls those "small daily victories" in your own life. One thing that can help is to work on your personal mission statement, your "no small plans," or a larger cause that inspires you. (We'll discuss this more in Chapter 8.)

Please don't deny yourself the opportunity to get to know the more experienced and mature person you will inevitably become over the course of your college years and later in your post-college

---

75   David Brooks, "What Do You Say to the Sufferer?" *New York Times*, December 9, 2021, https://www.nytimes.com/2021/12/09/opinion/sufferer-stranger-pain.html?referringSource=articleShare.

life. Yes, wrestling with personal challenges can require considerable courage, and we'll talk about this important idea more in the next chapter. But in the long run, you will respect yourself for persisting. And your older and wiser self will thank you. *Please remember that every human life—even yours!—is precious and has inestimable value. Every life deserves to be cherished and preserved.*

CIRCUMSTANCES

> *The only happy people I've met are those*
> *who have found some way to serve.*
> *—Richard Rohr*[76]

Yes, life is too often unfair. Just as there can be no guarantees of safety, there can be no guarantees of happiness...for *any* of us. Indeed, the Ancient Greek philosopher Aristotle commented that many factors beyond our control—including random chance—can affect whether we are happy.[77] Shit happens, as we say today. But, as Viktor Frankl urged, *we absolutely can control our response* to situations, however positive or negative they may appear at the moment.

Here's another take on this theme: By the end of his service in the Navy, Admiral William McRaven was responsible for leading all Navy SEALs and other such units in the United States Special Operations Command (USSOCOM). Across his long and successful military career, McRaven encountered his share of adversity. This is what he says about confronting unfair circumstances:

---

[76] Richard Rohr, *Essential Teachings on Love*, (Maryknoll: Orbis Books, 2018), 15–16.

[77] Aristotle wrote about the role of chance in his *Nicomachean Ethics*.

It is easy to blame your lot in life on some out-side force, to stop trying because you believe fate is against you. It is easy to think that where you were raised, how your parents treated you, or what school you went to is all that determines your future. Nothing could be further from the truth. The common people and the great men and women are all defined by how they deal with life's unfairness. Helen Keller, Nelson Mandela, Stephen Hawking, Malala Yousafzai....[78]

No matter what situation we encounter, life always offers us a choice: we can complain about unfairness, surrender to despair, and give up; or we can take responsibility for our actions, refuse to quit, make a plan, and decide what to do next.

Chasing happiness—that is, focusing on being happy and trying to raise the happiness level in your life—usually turns out to be a *losing strategy*. Happiness often proves an elusive target; the more we seek it, the faster it seems to slip away. By contrast, working hard to achieve what you've determined to be a worthy goal, even in the face of significant adversity—that is, focusing on a specific objective that is meaningful to *you*—often produces happiness as a by-product. Helen Keller, who lost both her sight and hearing to illness at a very early age, said, "Life is either a daring adventure or nothing." At virtually any moment, you too can decide to regard your own life as either a problem or "a daring adventure." It really is up to you!

Today, increasing numbers of psychologists are doing research to discover just what makes us happy. One thing they've

---

[78] Admiral William H. McRraven, chap. 4 in *Make Your Bed: Little Things That Can Change Your Life and Maybe the World* (New York: Grand Central Publishing, 2017); please see Additional Resources.

learned is that having more money does *not* necessarily make you happier (unless you start out with so little that you can't even put food on the table). However, having a robust network of positive social relations—one's immediate family, friends, or a group of people who are working to achieve a common cause—is a very good predictor of happiness.[79] And though it's also possible to make affirming connections through social media, our relationships are richer when people physically spend time together. We are *physical* beings, not virtual ones.

The best advice, overall, is *not* to pursue happiness itself but rather to *put your efforts into creating an active life that you share with others you care about and in which you engage in work that is meaningful to you.* In pursing these goals, you make it possible for happiness to find you. It also significantly helps if you look for ways to experience and express gratitude, something else we'll talk about later in Chapter 8.

RIDING YOUR LIFE'S INTENSE WAVES

It may be helpful to think of emotional balance as mastering a surfboard—honoring the ability to take life's gnarliest waves without wiping out, while catching the good ones and riding them all the way to the shore, enjoying the last splash.
—Liz Brody[80]

---

[79] For a brief overview of this research, see David Marchese, "Yale's Happiness Professor Says Anxiety Is Destroying Her Students," *New York Times*, February 18, 2022, https://www.nytimes.com/interactive/2022/02/21/magazine/laurie-santos-interview.html.

[80] Liz Brody, "We all seek emotional balance, but what exactly does that mean?" Oprah.Com, accessed December 4, 2023, https://www.oprah.com/spirit/emotional balance-strategies-lluminari/all.

I'll let you in on one last little secret about the early days of your college career: You're likely to look around and think that all your peers have their act together, that *they*—as opposed to *you*—are perfectly adjusted and dialed in to this new situation. It's rather like being forced to live in a universe defined entirely by other people's highly curated Instagram posts. *But it's just not true!*

Dislocation, disorientation, and discomfort are perfectly normal parts of nearly everyone's college life. Most first-year students will be feeling their way through this transition—some are just better at hiding their unease. And by the way, these comments apply equally to the older students you'll meet. Even though they may *seem* to have everything figured out, I can assure you that they also went through moments of questioning themselves, wondering if *they* were going to make it. On certain days, they may still be wondering! But they overcame their own uncertainties, and you will too—*if* you hang in there.

So, *try not to be taken by surprise if you experience episodes of self-doubt*—either in your academic work or outside the classroom. You are definitely not alone in feeling this way! At some point, most beginning college students question whether they'll be able to deal with all the new challenges they're facing. Perhaps your parents had that experience themselves at an earlier stage of their life. (In fact, it's a great conversation-starter to ask them how they felt when *they* started college or first moved out of their parents' house.) For what it's worth, I experienced a few days of feeling homesick in my own early weeks at college. Fortunately, these feelings passed pretty quickly when I started meeting new friends and becoming immersed in my coursework.

If you're feeling unsure or fighting homesickness, it's likely that you'll be able to work through it as well. So, give yourself the chance to do so. Focus on the goals you've identified and the day-to-day steps toward achieving them. The important thing is to keep at it. And soon enough, *you* will be one of those more experienced upper-division students, and the next group of new arrivals will be looking up to *you* with respect and awe!

Being intentional about taking charge of the physical and psychological aspects of your life in the midst of the troubling times we all have to deal with will give you a great sense of accomplishment. In addition, it will position you to do all the other things that will make your time in college truly successful!

SUMMING UP—CHAPTER 5

- As you create your new college life, set aside some time and space for yourself—ways to give yourself a break from your routine and lower any stress you may be feeling. Check in with yourself from time to time and listen to what your authentic inner voice has to say.
- If you find yourself feeling overwhelmed—especially if these feelings begin to interfere with your work or other important aspects of your life—don't hesitate to access the resources on your campus: the counseling center, other support offices, your academic advisor, peers, or whomever.
- Above all, please seek help if you are tempted to harm yourself in any way—your life has immense value, both to you and to those who love you. You are worth whatever effort it takes to work through your issues.
- Circumstances can be against us in many ways. The most important thing is how we decide to react to them. You always have a choice.

- Your friends and others you meet may seem to have their act together in ways you don't. But understand that most everyone struggles with challenges. Some just do a better job of disguising it.

- Embrace your new-found positive freedom and make the intelligent choices that will empower you to take charge of your new college life—to surf those "gnarliest waves" that will inevitably come your way—and keep you on track to realizing your "no small plans," not on a pathway to regret.

Does taking care of yourself mean leading a risk-free life? Do you have to avoid venturing into any unknown territory, where you can't be sure you'll emerge safely on the other side? Not at all! As I've emphasized, there's no practical way to eliminate risk from your life—or anyone else's. More importantly, every great accomplishment comes with risk, including what *you* want to achieve in your college career. We'll consider what this this means in the next chapter.

CHAPTER 6
TAKE GOOD RISKS

You gain strength, courage, and confidence by every experience
in which you really stop to look fear in the face.
—*Eleanor Roosevelt*

About 2,400 years ago, the Greek philosopher Socrates[81] taught that the first step on the road to wisdom is to "know thyself"—to figure out just who you really are. This project requires not just *knowing* but also *doing*. As we progress through our lives, we compose a personal history that is the sum of our actions. The chapters of that narrative combine to make us who and what we are, defining each of us as unique individuals. The twin tasks of *learning who you are* and *making yourself into the person you'll become* flow together in a thoughtful and purposeful life, and *both require taking good risks*.

---

[81] Socrates lived in Athens, Greece, from 470 to 399 BCE.

EMPTY YOUR TEACUP—CULTIVATE A BEGINNER'S MIND

The Zen Buddhist tradition includes the story of a professor who travels to meet with a renowned teacher. After the professor arrives, he begins telling the teacher what he thinks he's already learned about Zen. The teacher listens patiently. After a while, the teacher offers tea. He begins pouring it into the professor's cup. But when the cup is full, he continues to pour until the tea runs over the sides and down on to the floor. Finally, the professor can't keep from crying out, "Stop! It won't hold any more! It's already too full!" The master replies, "Like this cup you are too full of your own ideas. How can you learn anything new, if you don't first empty your teacup?"[82]

In the Zen tradition, to empty your teacup is to rediscover what is called "beginner's mind." This phrase refers to our mindset when we approach a new subject, task, or anything unfamiliar. We know that we don't know much or maybe anything at all about it. And so, our mind is open to new experiences and ideas. But once we begin to think we've mastered a subject, it becomes more difficult to hear something new—something we don't already believe we know. This story features a professor, but it applies to all of us.

It's very easy for college students to feel that they're already supposed to know a lot, that to display curiosity or ask a question in class is to reveal weakness or to risk being thought of as dumb. But please understand that this is not at all the case. Learning requires an openness to new ideas—a willingness to explore unfamiliar intellectual territory and see what might be there. At a later stage of this process, there will be plenty of time for critical

---

[82]   There are many versions of this story. My telling draws upon Paul Reps, *Zen Flesh, Zen Bones: A Collection of Zen and Pre-Zen Writings* (Garden City, NY: Anchor Books, Doubleday & Company, 1957).

thought—for challenging those new ideas, to determine what's there that might be worthy of being accepted. But we first need to understand them on their own terms.

Are you willing to risk emptying your teacup—to nurture your curiosity, to cultivate a beginner's mind, and to open yourself to learning new things? If you approach your classes with this attitude, you'll earn the respect of your professors and encourage them to take you seriously. You'll also earn the respect of your classmates. Most of all, you'll give yourself the best chance of expanding your intellectual horizons.

You can take Socrates's charge referenced at the beginning of this chapter as an invitation to empty *your* personal teacup—to give up some of your certainty about just who you are and what you think you know for sure. The poet Emily Dickinson wrote, "The soul should always stand ajar," and even a small opening unlocks the door to curiosity, creating an avenue for new ideas to enter.

ONE KEY TO OPENING YOUR MIND

An effective way to unbolt the door to your mind is to realize that we all too easily and far too often get things wrong. Talking about this fact of life, author David Foster Wallace observed that growing up intellectually requires us to abandon:

> The arrogance, blind certainty, and closed-mindedness that's like an imprisonment so complete the prisoner doesn't even know he's locked up. ... This is part of what the liberal arts mantra of "teaching me how to think" is really supposed to mean: to be just a little less arrogant, to have

some "critical awareness" about myself and my
certainties...because a huge percentage of the
stuff that I tend to be automatically certain of is,
it turns out, totally wrong and deluded.[83]

In making this observation, Wallace—who was a celebrated
author of both fiction and nonfiction books, as well as a college
professor of English—has all of history on his side.

None of us can escape this fate; we all are highly *fallible* creatures. We make mistakes all the time, in both small and large
matters. How many past cultures and nations embraced certain
ideas with their whole hearts and minds that we now look upon
with dismay (or contempt)? For example, think about the belief,
which was widely held for thousands of years, that slavery is an
acceptable human practice or the virulent antisemitism that
Nazi Germany (and, unfortunately, too many other countries)
promoted before and during WWII, which directly led to the
Holocaust. Tragically, antisemitism is again on the rise in our
contemporary world. But I'm sure you can easily come up with
your own examples of other stupid and hateful ideas people have
enthusiastically believed over the ages.

Taking the good risks we'll talk about in this chapter may lead
you to revise or even replace some of your previous beliefs. You
might encounter some new ideas that are more solidly grounded
in facts or justified by arguments you've never considered before.
You might even find that some of your long-held, deeply cherished ideas—beliefs that previously seemed quite important to
you, maybe even ones that were central to your identity—are up
for reevaluation.

---

[83]   David Foster Wallace, *This Is Water: Some Thoughts, Delivered on a Significant
Occasion, about Living a Compassionate Life* (New York: Little, Brown and
Company, 2009). Please see Additional Resources.

As Wallace also says, being mindful of the limits on our ability to know provides a check on the very human temptation toward *arrogance*, which is the opposite of the beginner's mind we just talked about. By contrast, acknowledging our *fallibility* makes it much easier to consider alternative perspectives. This is all to say that adopting an attitude of *intellectual humility* is enormously helpful in expanding your intellectual horizons—the main reason for taking those good risks in college. So, let's look at some of the risks that can help you stretch both your mind and spirit.

ASK THE BIG QUESTIONS

> *LUKE: I'm not afraid.*
> *YODA: You will be. You will be!*
> —*Star Wars Episode V—The Empire Strikes Back*

In your undergraduate years, you'll encounter ideas that are different from those you've heard from your high school teachers, clergy, friends, or even your parents. When this happens, you might remind yourself that you did not come to college to keep thinking the way you did in high school, but rather to extend your intellectual horizons and cultivate your ability to think for yourself. You also may become acutely aware of differences between what you're hearing in one course and another. As I wrote in Chapter 1, the disciplines you'll study use their own sets of intellectual tools; they have unique ways of investigating and making sense of the world. They also have their own values, which you'll need to understand and learn how to critically interrogate. In short, you're entering a more complex cognitive realm than you've probably ever encountered before.

As you explore this new landscape—and as you get to know yourself in new ways and think more deeply about the personal story you're composing—it's the perfect time to ask yourself some of the "big questions" that people across many cultures have wrestled with for thousands of years. Here are a few examples, some of which will sound familiar from our previous discussion of your personal mission statement (in Chapter 3):

- What kind of person am I? What values shape my actions? What do I stand for? What am I willing to *fight* for?

- Do I feel good about who I am today? If not, what changes do I need to make? What kind of person do I want to be in the future? In the long run, what will make me proud of my life? What personal legacy do I want to create?

- How do I interact with other people? How *should* I treat them? How do I want them to treat me?

- What kind of natural world do I want to live in and eventually pass along to the next generation? What are my personal responsibilities to help address the planetary environmental issues we face and create a more sustainable world?

- What kind of social world do I want to live in and eventually pass along? What are my personal responsibilities in helping to create a more just and equitable world?

These questions may appear simple at first, but if you allow yourself to engage them seriously, they turn out to be deceptively complex and perhaps a bit intimidating. Yet they are appropriate topics of inquiry for an autonomous, responsible adult. So, try to keep them in mind throughout your college years. Notice when they come up in your classes. Even when they're not explicitly mentioned, look for ways to relate them to what you are studying. And then commit to carrying them with you after you graduate.

And just in case you might be thinking that these "big questions" are too abstract to be relevant to your own life, consider this one:

- How should we define *personhood*? Specifically, at what point does a human fetus *legally* become a *person*?

Now that the Supreme Court has held that US citizens no longer have a constitutional right to abortion, some state legislatures are considering whether to define a human fetus, at any stage of its development, to be a person under the law. Doing so would afford every fetus full legal rights, potentially making *any* abortion—for whatever reason—equivalent to murder. Regardless of your beliefs on the morality of this medical procedure, to be an informed, responsible citizen today, you need to consider such complicated ethical and political questions and understand the implications of resolving them in one way or another. Thinking clearly about these issues will then help you decide how to vote in local, state, and national elections.[84]

Stepping into this uncharted territory of new and unfamiliar ideas can be perplexing and sometimes intimidating. That's fine. Feeling some cognitive disorientation or discomfort is an entirely normal part of going to college. In fact, this experience is one of the surest signs that you're learning and growing as a person. It will serve you well to get used to it—indeed, to embrace

---

[84] For an informative and accessible treatment of the historical and philosophical dimensions of this issue, see Elizabeth Dias, "When Does Life Begin?" *New York Times*, December 31, 2022, https://www.nytimes.com/interactive/2022/12/31/us/human-life-begin.html.

it: *to become comfortable with being uncomfortable*! And remember, most of your classmates are feeling this way as well. So, be brave enough to try out some of the new and perhaps even "dangerous" ideas you will encounter, even when they test some of your most deeply held beliefs.

If a particular conversation (whether inside or outside a classroom) becomes uncomfortable, make up your mind *not* to bail on it but to stay in the room! Don't give up on that discussion, on the people you're talking with, or on yourself. You can handle it! If you hang in there, you *will* get through it! And who knows? Something you say might help your friends consider an idea or point of view they never thought of before. And you might come away with some new insights yourself.

A story of taking good risks: Cynthia Carroll

> Cynthia Blum Carroll came to Skidmore College in the late 1970s intending to major in studio art. To satisfy a GE science requirement, she took a chance by enrolling in a geology course. To her surprise, she found that the subject fascinated her. It led her to other courses in that area and eventually to majoring in geology. She pursued summer opportunities for geological field work, went on to earn a master's degree in geology from the University of Kansas, and then added an MBA from Harvard. At the time, this area attracted very few women, and the companies relying on geology were entirely male-dominated. But Cynthia simply ignored any potential barriers related to her gender.

She began her professional career as a geologist for the Amoco Production Company. Next, she joined Alcan Aluminum Limited, a Canadian company that was one of the largest industrial producers of aluminum in the world. From 1989 to 2006, she held a number of management positions in Alcan, including Chief Executive Officer (CEO) for its Primary Metal Group from 2002 to 2006. Then in 2007, Cynthia was named CEO of Anglo American, which is based in Great Britain and is one of the world's largest international mining and commodities corporations. She became the first non–South African person to hold this position at Anglo American and the first female CEO in the entire industry!

While attending to Anglo American's business interests, Cynthia took a series of good risks by focusing on sustainability and safety throughout the company's worldwide group of mines. One of the first things she did was to close her company's platinum mine in South Africa—the largest in the world—because she found its worker-safety record unacceptable. She kept the mine closed for six months, not allowing it to reopen until she was satisfied that more effective safety measures had been put in place. This decision elevated worker-protection standards, not just for her company but for the entire global mining industry. Cynthia then went on to establish "enterprise zones" around her company's mines, creating future job opportunities for the company's employees when the mines were eventually played out.

Because of Cynthia's efforts, Anglo American became the only commodities company to be formally recognized by the United Nations for the jobs that were created above and beyond its mining business. Furthermore, under her leadership, the company provided medical treatment for HIV/AIDS to more than 100,000 workers and non-workers. She was routinely cited by Forbes and other media outlets as one of the most powerful and influential women in international business.

***

Cynthia Carroll's career demonstrates that your horizons don't need to be limited by other people's preconceptions about what you can and cannot do. She used her liberal arts education to combine business acumen with ethical concerns for environmental sustainability and human rights. But none of this would have happened had she not changed her mind in college about her "no small plans" and taken a chance on a (then) non-traditional major for women—and had she not gone on to embrace those additional good professional risks that certainly paid off both for her and the entire mining and commodities industry.

TAKE SOME GOOD ACADEMIC RISKS

As Cynthia's story illustrates, one of the most important good risks you can take in college is to explore educational experiences that might initially lead you out of your comfort zone but can pay significant dividends in the long run. For example, you might sign up for a course that makes you nervous—one that might challenge you to think in new ways or lead you to examine some of your most cherished beliefs. A course in religious studies, sociology, anthropology, philosophy, or literature might be ideal. You may not change your mind about anything you already believe, but the experience will help you understand and affirm those previous ideas more thoughtfully. If you aren't majoring in one of the sciences, taking at least one or two sciences courses will give you insight into that important area of knowledge.

If it's a viable option for you, consider studying off-campus or abroad for a semester or even a full year. If you can, try to select a location that offers the prospect of genuinely new and different experiences and perspectives. Likewise, check out service-learning and internship opportunities that will connect your studies with practical experiences beyond your classroom.

Why not attend some public lectures on topics that appeal to you, and then try out others that, at first, might seem less interesting? Investigate music, theater, or dance performances; visit an art gallery on your campus. Look for new ways to expand your cultural horizons. You never know which experience might spark a new interest.

Resist the temptation to take "gut" (easy) courses. Your college years offer you the opportunity to hone your work ethic as much as your mind. (And by the way, a solid work ethic will be highly valued by future employers.) Don't shy away from a potentially engaging class that looks difficult, perhaps one taught by a faculty member with a reputation as a tough grader. Even if you end up with a slightly lower grade than you usually get, the experience of being pushed to perform at a higher level will be worth it. Moreover, a faculty member who at first makes you feel a bit uneasy could end up helping you see the world in unexpected and insightful ways. Perhaps someone from another country with an unfamiliar accent will broaden your horizons.

Take responsibility for succeeding in *all* your courses, whether in your major, GE requirements, or electives. This means:

- Commit to *attending every single class session*—even on those days when you might not especially feel like it.
- Keep up with your assigned readings.
- Listen actively to the lectures, take good notes, and review them frequently—not only when you're facing an exam.
- Participate in class discussions—even if this doesn't come easily for you.
- Ask questions when you need to. Your fellow students will probably have similar questions, and they'll respect *you* for speaking up!
- Stay on top of writing assignments—don't wait until the last minute to begin.
- If you feel lost or just have additional questions that you don't want to bring up in class, visit your professor or teaching assistant (TA) during their posted office hours. Ask them to help you make sense of what's confusing you.
- If you still need extra help, ask your professor or TA about finding a tutor.

You might feel a bit tentative about starting those conversations, but keep in mind that these folks chose their professions precisely because they want to help young people learn. Most will be happy to help you! And don't be surprised if a teacher who initially seemed off-putting ends up becoming a mentor and possibly even a lifelong friend.

A second story of good risk-taking: Heather Hurst

Heather Hurst started college as a serious painter and, like Cynthia Carroll, intended to become an art major. But along the way, she took a GE course in anthropology that led to a summer experience researching the ancient Mayan culture in Central America. She fell in love with both this activity and the subject matter. She eventually designed her own self-determined major that combined her new interests in anthropology and archeology with her previous love of art.

Heather began working to recreate, in exact archaeological detail, the murals found on walls inside long-buried Mayan temples, some of which had not seen the light of day for over a thousand years. These paintings represent virtually our only sources of information about that once-flourishing culture. This work became her passion and then her career. It earned her a prestigious MacArthur Foundation "Genius" award, and she used those funds to support graduate studies at Yale.

After completing her PhD and receiving many additional honors for her work, Heather has become a world-renowned scholar and has returned to teach at her alma mater, Skidmore, where she chairs the Department of Anthropology. She recently participated in a research project that discovered and then reported on a formerly unknown Mayan artifact—one that appears to be a calendar fragment dating a century earlier than any previously known example.

***

You'll never know how *any* course might inspire you, or where it may lead. All you can do is take the good risk and find out.

TAKE SOME GOOD PERSONAL AND EMOTIONAL RISKS

It can also be scary to move outside of your *social* comfort zone. But good social risks are just as important for your personal growth as academic risks. Unfortunately, many young Americans lately have been growing up in increasingly homogeneous, non-diverse communities—some of which are now *more* segregated along racial, socioeconomic, religious, ethnic, or political lines than in the past. This means that you may have had relatively few pre-college interactions with people who seem different from you, in whatever way(s) that might be.

In recent decades, most colleges and universities have worked deliberately to diversify both their student populations and those of their faculty and staff members. They understand that a meaningful education cannot be one-dimensional. The increased diversity of backgrounds and life experiences represented within its campus community is one of a school's greatest advantages, and it offers significant opportunities to everyone. We all learn best when we are immersed in settings (both in and out of the classroom) that replicate the numerous perspectives, backgrounds, beliefs, and life experiences of the global community.

Your college or university offers incredible opportunities to meet people you might not be used to hanging out with, whose backgrounds may be quite unlike yours. You no doubt will encounter people who strike you, at least at first, as being too unfamiliar to connect with. It's true that different life experiences can lead to divergent ways of thinking and perceiving the world. Sometimes it requires intentional effort to bridge those gaps. But always remind yourself that *you cannot read another person's story from their face!* This is true whether that person looks like you or not. You have to get to know the particulars of someone's life before you can discover what you can learn from them. And what they might be able to learn from *you!*

A third portrait of good risks: Abdul and Jacob

Abdul spent his early life growing up in a Palestinian refugee camp in Damascus, Syria—one of the most difficult environments imaginable and one that offered few prospects for his future. Fortunately, when he was a teenager, Abdul was able to flee his home country (at great personal risk) and travel to Northern Europe. There he earned a scholarship to study in an outstanding international high school and eventually made his way to the United States for college.

Based on his experiences, Abdul came to Skidmore with strong opinions about Middle Eastern politics, especially regarding the Palestinian-Israeli conflict. Understandably, he was highly critical of the state of Israel's policies. But soon after he arrived on campus, Abdul met Jacob, a Jewish-American first-year student. Abdul had never personally known any Jewish people before. For his part, this was Jacob's first opportunity to have a face-to-face interaction with a Palestinian. And of course, he had his own strong beliefs about Middle Eastern politics.

Right away, Jacob and Abdul started arguing about these political issues. As their conversations continued, they gave each other articles to read from the Council on Foreign Relations or the journal *Foreign Affairs* and looked for other ways to support their positions. But they never gave up on their vigorous discussions.

Jacob and Abdul continued to talk and get to know one another better. And then something interesting and unexpected started to happen. They realized they *liked* one another, and they soon became inseparable. Both also came to see that their own political perspectives had been limited by their particular experiences. As their friendship developed and their respect for one another grew, they began to understand more about each other's point of view. They certainly didn't change all their beliefs, but they modified many of their ideas in significant ways. Most importantly, over time, they each gained a more nuanced perspective on Israel, Palestine, Syria, and ultimately the whole Middle East.

Abdul later commented, "I now have a more complex and comprehensive view of the world because I spent time understanding and living with 'the other.' I think my presence also contributed in the other direction. It helped my fellow students' views of the world become more complex and well-rounded." Abdul and Jacob became roommates for a while, and they remain close friends today. After college, Jacob invited Abdul to his wedding.

As an undergraduate, Abdul worked for a time with the Brookings Institution and then with J-Street, a nonprofit organization whose mission is to bring Israelis and Palestinians closer together. Today he works for Goldman Sachs and is pursuing an MBA at Harvard Business School. He continues to seek ways to heal the divisions of the Middle East and to address issues of social inequality here in the US.

Jacob went on to graduate from the George Washington University Law School and now works as an international trade attorney in Washington, DC. He has built his career—helping companies navigate trade remedies, customs, and other policies affecting the importation of goods—on some of the core interests he developed in college: international affairs, politics, and business. Regarding Abdul, Jacob remarked, "I've never had and likely never will have a friendship as mesmerizing as what we shared in college."

***

This story doesn't just illustrate the enormous personal rewards that can follow from being open to meeting new people and getting to know them beneath the surface level. It also demonstrates the power of something we talked about back in Chapter 1: the ability to change your mind when you come upon new facts or persuasive arguments you've never considered before. Meeting and talking with people whose perspectives on the world differ from your own is one of the best ways to experience the power of considering fresh ideas. It helps you appreciate what I called the fundamental question for a citizen in a democracy: "What would it take to change your mind?" Well-reasoned intellectual flexibility is one of the most important components in your intellectual toolkit, and developing it should be a major goal of your liberal education. It's an ability that will serve you extremely well now and for the rest of your life.

EXPANDING YOUR CIRCLE OF FRIENDS

So, for all kinds of reasons, *it's a terrific idea to seek out ways to connect with people who may initially seem very unlike you.* Find out how their lives relate to yours. Their struggles, hopes, and dreams will probably echo yours in lots of ways—provided you seek out that common ground. There is so much that unites us in our underlying humanity! Try to picture the people you meet as potential friends you just haven't gotten to know yet. This will help you think in new ways about those you encounter—and about *yourself*.

Here are some practical suggestions for expanding your circle of connections:

- Explore some campus cocurricular activities (such as political, religious, or culture-based student organizations) that are not only fun but allow you to interact with folks you might not otherwise have gotten to know.
- Attend an athletic event, club event, or another activity you've never tried before, and talk with people you meet there.
- Look around to see who's in your classes. Take the good risk of introducing yourself to someone you don't know—especially someone whose background might appear different from yours.
- Remind yourself that any person who initially makes you feel uncomfortable still deserves to be valued and respected, just as you deserve to be respected and valued by them. (And who knows? Maybe *you* make *them* feel uncomfortable as well!) Welcome the discovery of a possible new friend.

LEARNING TO LEARN FROM FAILURE

Ever tried. Ever failed. No matter. Try again. Fail again. Fail better.
—*Samuel Becket*

As you embrace all these good risks, not everything you attempt to do will work out as planned. A Chinese proverb says, "Even a good rider is sure to fall someday." And indeed, the only people who never fall off their horses are those who never attempt anything difficult. Our best plans can be disrupted by forces beyond our control or by our own limitations or mistakes. There are numerous ways things can go wrong. Failure is just one more inescapable element of our human condition.

Some people react to this awareness by becoming more cautious; they avoid trying new things. Fear of failure can even become paralyzing, leading you to avoid taking any risks at all. But it's possible—and far preferable—to adopt a different attitude. You can let your curiosity overcome your fears. It's useful to recall something else that Eleanor Roosevelt recommended: "Do one thing every day that scares you." (Notice that she *didn't* say, "Do one thing every day that scares your parents—or your college or university president!") So, always make it a *good* risk, not a *dumb* one in which the potential downside significantly outweighs the potential reward.

Taking this idea further, you can encourage yourself *to appreciate the value of failure*. In fact, many times you'll profit more from trying something that's a stretch and coming up short than from succeeding at an easier task. Scientists, for example, value failed experiments because they help to rule out dead-end hypotheses and often point towards more promising research directions. You can adopt a similar attitude. Please also keep in mind that no matter how important a given misstep may feel during your college years, it's probably *not* a matter of life and death.

But what if it were? Consider these additional thoughts from Admiral McRaven, whom we heard from before (in Chapter 5):

> By 2003, I found myself in combat in Iraq and
> Afghanistan. Now that I was a one-star admiral
> leading troops in a war zone, every decision I

made had its consequences. Over the next several years, I stumbled often. But, for every failure, for every mistake, there were hundreds of successes: hostages rescued, suicide bombers stopped, pirates captured, terrorists killed, and countless lives saved. I realized that [my] past failures had strengthened me, taught me that no one is immune from mistakes. True leaders must learn from their failures, use the lessons to motivate themselves, and not be afraid to try again or make the next tough decision.[85]

If a Navy SEAL combat commander can respond this way to *his* failures—in situations where his life and those of his team members literally were on the line—then surely *you* can commit to learning from the times in college when your plans don't work out.

The trick, as McRaven suggests, is to *treat failure as a teacher*—maybe a harsh and demanding teacher at times, but nevertheless a powerful and effective one. So, when you've tried hard but come up short, pause a moment, take a step back, and ask yourself questions like these:

- What caused the problem?
- What might I have done differently?
- Could I have planned better or thought ahead more clearly?
- Should I have started sooner?
- Could I have worked more diligently, consistently, efficiently, or effectively?

---

[85] McRaven, chap. 6 in *Make Your Bed*.

- What other lessons does this incident present as I look to the future?

Regardless of whether you could have done something different that might have changed the outcome, *accept it, learn from it, and let it go*. You can't rewind the clock. So, after you've gained everything you can from a failed effort, put that episode in the rearview mirror and move forward.

Realize, too, that *you can benefit as much from someone else's missteps as from your own,* and this goes both ways. So, be brave enough to share your mistakes openly with your friends. Talk about where you slipped up and what you've learned as a result. Remember that your peers are experimenting and sometimes failing as well. Ask what *they've* figured out along the way. Tapping into that collective experience will multiply your educational dividends along with those of your friends. Valuing failure also helps *remove any pressure you might feel to be perfect.* Despite what you might see in your friends' social media feeds, none of us is ever perfect—not even our heroes.

In sum, always take your best shot. Challenge yourself to go for the highest level of excellence you can imagine. But don't beat yourself up for falling short of perfection. No human being has *ever* pulled that off. Most importantly, be purposeful about learning from failure. In fact, one suggestive definition of *learning* is *making* new *mistakes.*

PRACTICE PERSERVERNCE

It's hard to beat a person who never gives up.
—*Babe Ruth*

The next key mindset to work on—one that's essential in making the most of the good risks you'll be taking and moving on from the setbacks you'll experience—is to *become* relentless *in pursuing your goals*. Treat each failure as a *temporary* stumbling block, and then decide how you're going to pick yourself up and go forward. Babe Ruth knew what he was talking about: in 1923, when he broke the record for the highest batting average, he also struck out more than any other batter in baseball. It *is* hard to beat someone who never gives up!

During the darkest early days of World War II, when America had not yet entered the conflict and it was not at all clear that Great Britain could hold out against the Blitz or survive an expected German invasion, Prime Minister Winston Churchill visited his old preparatory school to attend an evening prayer service and to speak to the boys. His address included the following words: "*Never give in. Never give in. Never give in!*" His message inspired both the students and staff members who heard it in that most troubling time, and I encourage *you* to take it to heart as well.

Always remember that the most satisfying moments come when you succeed in doing something you initially feared you couldn't accomplish at all—a challenge that might have scared you but you didn't let stop you. *Refuse to be defeated! Keep at it:* "*Try again. Fail again. Fail better.*" *And never ever, ever, ever... give up!*

OVERCOMING FEAR

> *The opposite of fear is love.*
> —Steven Pressfield

Let's acknowledge that, at times, it can be incredibly difficult to do what I've been talking about: to take on a daunting challenge or persevere in the wake of a personal disaster. So, where can you find the courage to overcome your fears, tackle good risks, and move beyond your failures?

The standard advice (going all the way back to Aristotle) is that we "become brave by performing brave acts."[86] In the long run, this is probably the most powerful way to counter a given fear: to prove to yourself that you actually *can* do whatever initially seemed impossible. Yet that suggestion may not sound particularly helpful when you're staring up at a mountain you haven't yet climbed. Just how are you supposed to overcome your fears *before* you've succeeded? Here are three suggestions that might prove useful to you.

First, it can be helpful to realize that most people have to face their own fears and nervousness at some point in their careers. This includes high achievers who've discovered that being nervous or fearful is just an inevitable aspect of what they do. In fact, it can be *helpful*. The champion golfer Jack Nicklaus talked about how he had to feel nervous before a tournament in order to play his best. Even professional Broadway actors can experience stage fright before going on. Bill Russell, one of the all-time great NBA players, routinely felt so anxious before a game that he would throw up in the locker room. Indeed, when his teammates heard him doing it, they were encouraged because they knew he was ready to play his best.

Just before the 2022 Winter Olympics, the *New York Times* ran a series of interviews with superstar skiers and snowboarders. All of them acknowledged that fear is their constant companion: fear of failing to perform up to their own and others' expectations, fear of losing, and certainly fear of injury or even death. They manage their nerves through meticulous preparation for their

---

[86] Aristotle addressed this topic in his *Nicomachean Ethics*.

runs and tricks, by accepting that fear will be there every time they step on to the snow to compete, and by feeding off the adrenaline that it generates.

Eighteen-year-old gold-medalist skier Eileen Gu (who competes in halfpipe, slope style, and big air) commented, "Instead of ignoring fear, we build unique relationships with it by developing a profound sense of self-awareness and making deliberate risk assessments."[87] Other Olympians noted that they try to feel *just the right amount* of fear: "Too much can be debilitating. Too little can be worse."[88] These world-class athletes face extreme challenges most of us can scarcely imagine, but we can still learn from their example. *If you accept that some level of nervousness—or even outright fear in the face of a challenge—is often just part of the deal, you can learn to acknowledge those feelings, embrace them, and turn them into allies to help you perform at your best.*

A second effective way to handle nervousness is to *concentrate your full attention on the task at hand.* The more you can focus on what you're trying to *do*, the less psychological energy will be available to feed your fears, and the less power they will hold over you. To say this in a different way: the more you can immerse yourself in the activity, project, or goal—the more you succeed in directing your attention *outward*—the less time or psychic energy you will have to dwell on feeling afraid. The more practiced you become in making this shift in attention from inside of yourself to outside, the better you will be at sidelining your anxiety.

[87] Eileen Gu, "I Admit It. I'm In Love With Fear," *New York Times* February 7, 2022, https://www.nytimes.com/interactive/2022/sports/olympics/eileen-gu-skiing-fear.html?referringSource=articleShare.

[88] "What Scares the World's Most Daring Olympians," *New York Times* February 7, 2022, https://www.nytimes.com/interactive/2022/sports/olympics/athletes-winter-injuries.html?referringSource=articleShare.

Lastly, from time immemorial, soldiers who survived the cauldron of battle have reported on what sustained them—what gave them the courage to perform under conditions of extraordinary danger. Often it wasn't their allegiance to their country or their cause, as important as these factors certainly are. More significantly, it was the *loyalty* and—as author Steven Pressfield says in the quote at the beginning of this section—the *love* they felt toward their comrades fighting alongside them.

Athletes in team sports that require physical courage (football, ice hockey, lacrosse, field hockey, rugby, and the like) can experience something akin to these feelings. They don't want to let down their teammates, so they push through their fears and do their jobs. The same is true for actors in a play or musicians in an ensemble. They know they must do their part for the performance to succeed, and they don't want to disappoint their fellow performers. In each of these cases, embracing that personal bond helps people find the courage to perform well under pressure. Love for those who are depending on you *is* the opposite of fear.

But even if you've never been a soldier, a varsity athlete, or a performer, you still can translate these insights into your own way of rising to the challenge of trying to do something that's fear-inducing. In an essay that appeared exactly one year after President Biden's Inauguration, Amanda Gorman, whose life story we've already talked about (in Chapter 3), described the anxiety she experienced before reading her inaugural poem, which almost kept her from going through with it at all, and her general sense that we are living in scary times. She writes,

> I am a firm believer that often terror is trying to tell us of a force far greater than despair. In this way, I look at fear not as cowardice but as a call forward, a summons to fight for what we hold

dear. And now more than ever, we have every right to be affected, afflicted, affronted. If you're alive, you're afraid. If you're not afraid, then you're not paying attention. The only thing we have to fear is *having no fear itself*—having no feeling on behalf of whom and what we've lost, whom and what we love. ...

And yes, I am still terrified every day. Yet fear can be love trying its best in the dark. So do not fear your own fear. Own it. Free it. This isn't a liberation I or anyone can give you—it's a power you must look for, learn, love, lead and locate in yourself.[89]

Fear can indeed be "love trying its best in the dark." And a robust love can push that fear just far enough aside to allow you to act.

So, *commit to finding a way to fall in love with the difficult thing you are setting out to do.* Look for something in that challenging class that can engage your imagination—find something to love in the subject matter. Discover something in that tough paper assignment or complicated project that is meaningful to you, then focus on it. Often, falling in love with what you're trying to do requires looking beneath the surface—to find the deeper core where things really begin to get interesting. This is true for any difficult academic subject, learning to play a musical instrument, mastering a fine art, or whatever.

---

[89] Amanda Gorman, "Why I Almost Didn't Read My Poem at the Inauguration," *New York Times,* January 20, 2022, https://www.nytimes.com/2022/01/20/opinion/amanda-gorman-poem-inauguration.html?referringSource=articleShare.

If the challenge is a group project, commit to caring about your teammates. Focus on *their* success, not just on yours, and let those feelings inspire you to action. Work to develop a sense of common purpose and loyalty to the classmates you are doing it with. Concentrate on not letting down your new friends. If you aren't doing a group project, consider pulling together your own team. For example, if you're struggling to pass a course on your own, you might approach some other students in the class and form a study group. Working with peers to master a tough subject—in effect, by teaching it to one another—can have tremendous benefits. From my own experience in the classroom, I can assure you that one of the best ways to learn *any* subject (and possibly even fall in love with it!) is to teach it to someone else.

Beyond dispute, love is one of the most powerful human emotions, if not the most powerful. It can truly vanquish fear by *transferring the focus of your attention from inside yourself, where timidity and fear take root, to outside yourself*—to the people working with you or the objective you're aiming to achieve. So, practice tapping into love. This ability will serve you well, not just in college but for the rest of your life.

SUMMING UP—CHAPTER 6

- As you begin this new phase of your journey to discover who you are and create the person you'll become, it's useful to cultivate a "beginner's mind," an openness to new ideas.
- A powerful way to start is to acknowledge the fallibility you share with every other human being—the fact that we frequently get things wrong. This awareness

encourages an attitude of intellectual humility (an attitude rather lacking in the world today).

- Take some intellectual risks: ask the perennial "big questions" and explore some challenging new ideas that might stretch your intellectual horizons.

- Embrace your new freedom by taking responsibility for succeeding in *all* your courses—do the things that will move you toward that goal.

- Take some personal risks: reach out to people you might not ordinarily get to know and see what they might have to teach you. Expand your circle of new friends.

- Failure is another inevitable aspect of human life; not all our plans work out as we want them to. But you can learn from your failures and refuse to be defeated in advancing your "no small plans." Adopting both those attitudes will serve you well.

- It's not always easy to find the courage required to never ever, ever…give up. One powerful strategy for doing so is to shift your focus from inside—on how *you're* feeling— to outside: to the project you are trying to complete or the goal you are trying to achieve.

- Find something to love about that difficult subject and commit to caring about the people you're working with.

Some of our most difficult challenges concern our relationships with others and our personal values. We'll talk about them next.

CHAPTER 7

DO THE RIGHT THING

Intelligence plus character—that is the goal of true education.
—*Dr. Martin Luther King, Jr.*

S ometimes a choice about what to do can present us with a genuine moral dilemma: a situation in which it's just not clear which course of action represents the ethically right decision. (And, of course, there can be more than two options.) A vexing moral dilemma can resist all attempts to resolve it. Perhaps there just isn't a good solution, and so we're forced to choose the *least bad* option. Let's think further about this kind of ethical complexity.

ETHICAL COMPLEXITY

You may have read the novel *Sophie's Choice* or seen the film by the same name.[90] In *Sophie's Choice*, the main character faces a

---

[90]   *Sophie's Choice*, by William Styron (New York: Random House, 1979), won a National Book Award for fiction. The film (1982) starred Kevin Kline, Peter MacNicol, and Meryl Streep, who won an Academy Award for her performance.

horrifying, and ultimately unresolvable, moral dilemma. She has just been transported to a death camp in World War II with her two young children, a boy and a girl, and a German officer forces her to choose between them—one will live, the other will be sent to die. The only ethically acceptable solution here is to eliminate the source of the dilemma, which meant defeating the Nazis in WWII. But that was not an option in the moment, and the Allies' eventual victory did not bring back Sophie's lost child or the millions of other victims of that war. Fortunately, most of the time we do not find ourselves in this kind of dramatic and unresolvable situation, and it's reasonably evident what we ought to do—provided we are honest about our values.

But sometimes a morally complicated state of affairs presents us with another kind of challenge: *it forces us to hold two competing ideas in balance.* Consider a recent geopolitical situation that has reverberated on many college and university campuses. In October 2023, Hamas fighters from the Gaza Strip, attacked the state of Israel deliberately targeting civilians: murdering babies, teen-agers, and grandparents (along with others), sexually assaulting women, and seizing approximately 240 hostages. Regardless of where you stand with regard to the larger relationship between Israel and the Palestinians, the inhumanity of these actions, which violate international conventions governing warfare, deserves to be condemned in the strongest possible terms.

At the same time, one can reasonably criticize—and, some would say, condemn—the policies the state of Israel historically has enacted towards the Palestinians or its conduct of this ensuing war. This critique emphasizes the large number of civilian casualties that have occurred in Gaza, resulting from Israel's military campaign against Hamas.

It is possible—and, in fact, it is *reasonable*—to hold both attitudes, while acknowledging the tension between them. Reporting from Gaza City during Israel's invasion, the *Washington Post* columnist David Ignatius commented: "It's a war in which we've all looked into the abyss.... This conflict has raised excruciating issues that I can't begin to resolve."[91] The complexities of human existence often require us to take a nuanced view, beyond the easy division of the world into absolute right and absolute wrong. Thus, Nicholas Kristof writes about this situation writ large:

> The first myth is that in the conflict in the Middle East there is right on one side and wrong on the other (even if people disagree about which is which). Life isn't that neat. The tragedy of the Middle East is that this is a clash of *right versus right*. [Emphasis added.] That does not excuse Hamas's massacre and savagery or Israel's leveling of entire neighborhoods in Gaza, but underlying the conflict are certain legitimate aspirations [on both sides] that deserve to be fulfilled.[92]

It can be a major challenge to navigate such fraught situations and decide how to respond. Kristof urges that we begin by acknowledging the humanity present on both sides:

---

91 David Ignatius, "A silent desperation on the slow march out of Gaza City," *Washington Post*, November 12, 2023), https://www.washingtonpost.com/opinions/2023/11/12/gaza-city-humanitarian-corridor-israel-war/.

92 Nicholas Kristof , "What We Get Wrong About Israel and Gaza," the *New York Times*, November 15, 2023, https://www.nytimes.com/2023/11/15/opinion/israel-gaza-facts.html?smid=nytcore-ios-share&referringSource=articleShare.

> Whatever side you are more inclined toward, remember that the other includes desperate human beings merely hoping that their children can live freely and thrive in their own nation. ...

> If you only weep for Israeli children, or only for Palestinian children, you have a problem that goes beyond your tear ducts. Children on both sides have been slaughtered quite recklessly, and fixing this crisis starts with acknowledging a principle so basic it shouldn't need mentioning: All children's lives have equal value, and good people come in all nationalities.

To be informed and ethically sensitive persons, we sometimes are called upon to wrestle with such complex ethical realities. No one ever claimed that being a caring, responsible adult is easy.

And let us be very clear: even if one is passionately opposed to the actions of the State of Israel (which do not necessarily reflect the views of all Jewish people) in regard to the Palestinian people, *that can be no excuse—and absolutely no justification*—for antisemitism, which is a prejudicial attitude directed generally against people of Jewish heritage. Likewise, even if one is passionately opposed to the actions of Hamas (which do not necessarily reflect the views of all Palestinian people), *that can be no excuse— and absolutely no justification*—for Islamophobia, which is a prejudicial attitude generally directed against Muslims, or for general anti-Palestinian attitudes.

STARTING WITH RESPECT

*I respect myself and insist upon it from everybody. And
because I do it, I then respect everybody, too.*
—Maya Angelou

I noted in the previous chapter that this is an appropriate juncture in your life both to acknowledge the complexity of ethical
decision-making and reflect on your own values. To ask: *"What
do I stand for?"* That question is central to the project of living a
principled life, or following Dr. King, *a life of character.* If you can
be clear about what you stand for, then these four simple words—
do the right thing—can guide the greater part of your ethical
decision-making.

In college, your primary task is to focus on your intellectual
and personal development. Colleges and universities are great
places to do this. But they are not always the utopias we'd like
them to be. In fact, they can present us with some pretty tough
ethical challenges. I encourage you to treat these occasions as
opportunities to think about the decisions you face as a responsible adult in more informed and nuanced ways than you might
have done in the past. This is an important aspect of the personal
work that enables you to live a principled life. Let's talk about
what all this might mean.

In the above quotation, author Maya Angelou offers a helpful
starting point. I suggest you follow her lead and *begin your college
days by making a firm commitment to respect both yourself and your
fellow students.* Then, in turn, *expect respect from them.* To respect
a person is to acknowledge their fundamental humanity—the fact
that every human being has intrinsic value or dignity and inherent rights. Including *you!* But of course, we're talking about more
than just thoughts and feelings here. Living a principled life based

on respect requires you to *act* accordingly—for example, to speak up in the face of disrespect, either to you or someone else.

Admittedly, this is not always an easy assignment for anyone—especially for someone at your stage of life, where the opinions of your peers matter so much. In fact, it can seem next-to-impossible to say or do something at odds with a group of your friends. But doing the right thing sometimes means, as Eleanor Roosevelt said, that you must "do the thing you think you cannot do." It may be reassuring to know that your fellow students are wrestling with similar questions and issues, facing their own ethical challenges. But if *you* choose to live a principled life—if you consistently make it a point to *do the right thing*—they will respect you for doing so.

Your school likely has a *student code of conduct*, which sets out its expectations for members of your campus community. It almost certainly includes some form of *honor code*, which expects you to hold *yourself* accountable for following those institutional rules. You'll likely hear about all this during new-student orientation. Different universities and colleges place varying levels of emphasis on these regulations and enforce them in different ways. But please be assured that *every* college or university—including *yours!*—takes its rules of conduct seriously. So, it's a very good idea, early on, to *become familiar with your school's student code of conduct and take it to heart*. Now let's talk about some specific ways to put these ideas into practice.

SEXUAL- AND GENDER-BASED MISCONDUCT

Take sexual- and gender-based misconduct, for instance. Sexual assault—basically, forcing someone to engage in sexual behavior to which they've not given free, informed, open, and full consent—is still far too prevalent, not only in our society but also within our academic institutions. Over the past several decades, this issue has received a great deal of attention from both federal and state governments, by all colleges and universities, and throughout the news media. It's hardly a new problem, and the data show that it remains significant everywhere. But the fact that this issue has a long history doesn't diminish either its importance or its profound impact on the person who is targeted. From what I've seen as a college administrator, I can tell you that such misconduct has enormous power, not only to destroy individual students' lives but even to poison an entire campus.

The simple truth is that these hurtful actions do not have to happen. They result from individual choices. Surely, we all can agree that taking advantage of another person sexually or attacking someone because of their gender or sexual orientation has *no* place anywhere in a civil society, much less on your college or university campus. Therefore, my challenge to you and to all new college students everywhere is to *do your part in making your college or university a place where sexual- and gender-based misconduct and sexual assault do not occur.* Understand that "no" always means *no*! Full stop. And remember (as we saw in Chapter 4), the majority of sexual assaults occur when one or both parties have been drinking, possibly to the point of blacking out, when their recollections of what happened may be uncertain or nonexistent. So, one aspect of avoiding sexual misconduct is managing your own use of alcohol (or other drugs) to remain fully in charge of what *you're* doing—regardless of what's going on around you.

Even though you can't control anyone else's decisions and actions, as I have emphasized throughout this book, *you are in charge of your own.* So, as one of your ways to lead a principled life, *make a personal commitment to never engage in toxic sexual- or gender-related behavior.* Then *refuse to tolerate it among your friends and other peers.* Expect your college or university to strive for *zero* instances of sexual or gender-based misconduct as well. Admittedly, that's a very high bar. But those of us who are privileged to attend a university or college—along with the people who work there—should be willing to take on that assignment. After all, what's the alternative? How much sexual- or gender-based misconduct *is* acceptable? A little? A lot? How much? Again, the answer *should* be *none.* Strive for *zero instances*! *Do the right thing*!

It's important to be clear that the consequences of violating your school's rules relating to sexual- and gender-based misconduct can be serious and far-reaching, with the potential to profoundly affect your post-college life. If you are found responsible for such actions, you can be suspended or expelled, and it's by no means guaranteed that you will be readmitted or able to transfer to another school. Moreover, to cite one additional possible outcome, New York now requires *all* colleges and universities within the state (public and private institutions alike) to document any judicial finding of responsibility for "significant misconduct" on a graduate's permanent academic transcript.

Let's focus on the word "permanent" in the preceding sentence. Your academic transcript is the official record of your college career. You'll have to submit it whenever you apply to graduate school or professional school, and sometimes you'll need it for post-college employment. In time, other states may follow New York's lead and implement such regulations, if they haven't done so already. You absolutely do *not* want a finding of significant misconduct on your record—much less permanently attached to your transcript!

For all these reasons—the external ones and the even more important internal ones—it's smart to be thoughtful in regulating your actions according to your values. Don't place yourself in a situation where you might be more likely to do something hurtful or just plain stupid—perhaps because your judgment was impaired by drugs or alcohol. You might end up doing something you'll regret for the rest of your life. And *don't ever take advantage of someone else* whose judgment has been compromised by *their* use of alcohol or drugs and who, therefore, cannot give full, informed consent. There can be *no* excuse for doing that! Ever. Respect and value your fellow students. Watch out for your friends and even for people who are not your friends. You never know when someone will require your help or when you might need theirs.

PREJUDICE AND BIGOTRY

Being respectful of others also means being unwilling to tolerate physical or verbal assaults—undeserved mockery, derision, or threats—that are rooted in racial prejudice or any other kind of bigotry, whether they're aimed at you, someone else, or a group on campus. The Black Lives Matter (BLM) movement has brought new awareness and attention (especially within the white population) to issues of persistent racial injustice across our society. But of course, members of other groups, too, can be subjected to verbal or even physical assaults just because of their personal identity. Our country is becoming more attentive, for example, to harassment and other forms of violence directed against citizens of Asian and Pacific Island heritage. But people of many other backgrounds and identities—especially the LGBTQ+ community—all too often find themselves targeted in such attacks. Unfortunately, in recent years, we've witnessed a troubling increase in such incidents across our nation, including a significant rise in antisemitic and Islamophobic assaults. These actions result from prejudicial attitudes I referenced a few pages back, and which have long histories.

Students can also find themselves mocked, attacked, or marginalized because of their *religious beliefs*. Freedom of religion—enshrined as the separation of Church and State in the Constitution's First Amendment—is a right not only for citizens of the United States, it is also a right for all people, as acknowledged by the United Nations in its Universal Declaration of Human Rights.[93] You should expect these rights and protections to be affirmed and safeguarded at your college or university. Whether you are religious or not, it is important that you respect your peer's beliefs.

In short, bias-related physical or verbal assaults have no place in our democratic republic, in which the Constitution affirms the equal rights of *all* persons to be protected in their life, liberty, and property. And they certainly have *no place* on a college or university campus, where *every* community member deserves an equal chance to enjoy the full rights and benefits of membership.[94]

So, *look for ways in which you can be part of the solution at your school.* A commitment to protecting our shared human rights,

---

[93] The Universal Declaration of Human Rights was approved by the United Nations General Assembly in Paris on December 10, 1948. It has been translated into over five hundred languages. Article 18 affirms that all persons have "the right to freedom of thought, conscience and religion; this right includes freedom to change [one's] religion or belief, and freedom, either alone or in community with others and in public or private, to manifest [one's] religion or belief in teaching, practice, worship and observance." See the full document at https://www.un.org/en/about-us/universal-declaration-of-human-rights.

[94] For more information on this topic, see Dr. Beverly Daniel Tatum's book, *Why Are All the Black Kids Sitting Together in the Cafeteria?*, which is referenced in Additional Resources. This is a comprehensive and highly informative treatment of diversity and inclusion in colleges and universities, both historically and today.

practicing civic virtues, and living out your own moral code sometimes requires standing up *against* injustice and *for* equal opportunity for everyone. We all have an obligation to interact with one another respectfully, and acting out of prejudice represents a notorious expression of disrespect. No matter your personal background, you will have opportunities—both in your classes and in your cocurricular life—to become better educated about historical issues involving injustice, and where those challenges still remain within our society. (As author William Faulkner wrote, "The past is never dead. It's not even past.") Appreciate those learning opportunities and avail yourself of them whenever you can.

But we all need to do more than just *learn* about these issues. As President Biden said, when he signed the bipartisan COVID-19 Hate Crimes Act[95] in May 2021, "Silence is complicity. And we cannot be complicit. We have to speak out. We have to act."[96] So, learn how *you* can speak up to challenge someone who makes an offensive or insensitive remark or who acts in a hurtful way toward someone else. (Many schools offer programs that teach students how to do this.) *Stand with* and *speak up for* someone who is the target of such remarks or actions. If you don't, other people will legitimately construe your silence as consent.

---

[95] This bill was specifically created to curtail acts of violence against the Asian American and Pacific Islander (AAPI) Community.

[96] Joe Biden, "Remarks by President Biden at the Signing of the COVID-19 Hate Crimes Act," The White House, May 20, 2021, https://www.whitehouse.gov/briefing-room/speeches-remarks/2021/05/20/remarks-by-president-biden-at-signing-of-the-covid-19-hate-crimes-act/.

FREE SPEECH ON YOUR CAMPUS

Let's be very clear that verbal assaults directed against either individuals or groups *differ from protected free speech*. Especially on a college or university campus, it's crucial to understand the difference and appreciate the importance of defending uncomfortable, challenging, or even unpopular speech about important issues. College-level inquiry requires the intellectual space to interrogate "dangerous" ideas and raise provocative questions across the broadest range of topics.

No one deserves to be personally attacked. Ever. But in a college or university community, all of us should be prepared to have our *ideas* challenged or interrogated—even if this process sometimes makes us feel uncomfortable. It's not always easy to draw a bright line between the two—between protected speech and challenging inquiry on the one hand, and verbal assaults or hate speech on the other. But, again, the distinction is real. Part of being an educated citizen is understanding the difference and making the effort to tease it out in individual situations.

There will be many occasions for you to reflect on the difference between engaging in a complex, challenging, or uncomfortable conversation and attacking someone verbally. So, pay attention to the language people around you are using. *Don't be afraid to talk to them about it*—to invite them to consider their exact words, and to interrogate their implicit background assumptions. This goes for you as well: It's always important to reflect on what *you* are saying and assuming, and about the words *you* are using. *And always be prepared to listen to what others are saying in turn*. As I've said, we all can benefit from cultivating our intellectual humility. Being purposeful in doing so can help dial back the intense feelings that can so easily escalate and short-circuit mutual understanding.

Your instincts should be able to guide you in most situations. But there may be times in your college career when it's not all that simple to distinguish a distressing-but-legitimate conversation from one in which intellectual freedom has given way to hateful expression. At that moment, you will need to reflect about what is going on and engage in candid conversation about it. Your school's faculty members and administrators will be thinking about these issues, too, and should be able to offer guidance. By participating thoughtfully in such conversations, you will be helping your college or university foster the campus climate necessary to discuss and debate difficult political or ethical issues.

This subject took on a high level of urgency in the context of the war between the state of Israel and the Palestinian military organization Hamas that occurred in fall and winter 2023, which I've already referenced above. Supporters of the opposing sides protested on many college and university campuses, and the strong emotions associated with this conflict, gave rise to all manner of statements. In some cases, what was said was considered by some to rise to the level of hate-speech—specifically, either antisemitism or Islamophobia—and some protests even led to physical confrontations. In too many cases, students on various sides of this issue came to feel unsafe on their campuses.

As difficult as it is to do in practice, we need to commit to lowering the level of tension around such divisive issues. Especially on college or university campuses, we need to be able to discuss them vigorously but without resorting to hate-speech Admittedly, this can be exceedingly difficult to do; it can require courage. Given the levels of anger we now routinely see on social media and elsewhere (including so often in political speech), it is tempting to use harsh or threatening language immediately when engaging with an issue that evokes our passions. At such moments, it is helpful to remind ourselves of our responsibility to afford others the same level of respect we would expect for ourselves. Showing basic respect for others requires that we not demonize them just because we disagree, even in cases where so much can seem to be at stake. One of the most important goals of a college education should be to learn how to do this, even when it is difficult. In fact, these complicated situations often present opportunities for learning on all sides, if we can just find the courage to take advantage of them in this way.

Many schools have issued statements about campus speech.[97] It's a good idea to find out if your college or university has one and, if it does, to familiarize yourself with it. It's no secret that colleges and universities can struggle with these questions, in both classrooms and more public spaces. But *freedom of speech and inquiry* are so fundamental to the life of a college or university— and are so basic to our democracy—that we all should pay close attention when these values are challenged.

For example, shouting down a speaker who has been invited to your campus runs contrary to the basic principles of any respectable college or university. If you strongly disagree with a speaker, you have many appropriate options: You don't have to go to the event at all. You might protest *respectfully* outside it. If you choose to attend, you can listen what the speaker has to say and then challenge them with your own questions. Doing so raises the prospect of learning for everyone—even you.

---

[97] One of the best is Denison University's document, "Freedom of Expression and Academic Freedom," which derives, in part, from a similar statement issued by the University of Chicago, https://catalog.denison.edu/catalog/history-mission-values/expression-academic-freedom/.

Besides, if you think it's okay to shout down *this* speaker, what happens at a later moment, if others decide to silence someone who's been invited to campus by you or a group with whom you identify? What happens then to protections for *your* freedom of speech and access to ideas? As an informed, responsible citizen, it's important for you to think about these matters, both while you are in college and throughout your post-college life.[98]

One way to act on any concerns you might have about speech on your campus is to join or even start a student organization dedicated to promoting dialogue across difference. Here's an example of a student who did just that:

Fostering campus dialogue: Zachary R. Wood

> Before Zachary Wood became a student at Williams College in Williamstown, Massachusetts, he'd already lived a challenging life. His parents divorced when he was still in grade school; his mother was alternately loving and abusive; having enough money was frequently an issue for them. Growing up as a young Black man, he personally experienced racism in its various forms.
>
> But he also was fortunate to have supportive, loving relationships with his father and other relatives who did their best to help him develop into a person with substantial dreams, along with the ability—and the determination—to pursue them. He movingly relates his story of

---

[98]   As you can imagine, a great deal has been said and written about this complex topic. I list two thoughtful and informative books in Additional Resources.

growing up and living through his college years (which he highly valued and enjoyed) in his memoir, *Uncensored: My Life and Uncomfortable Conversations at the Intersection of Black and White America.*[99]

As a college student, Zachary was committed to learning as much as he could about the widest range of subjects and from as many people as he could get to know—especially people whose beliefs and perspectives differed from his. In his book, he describes how he pursued his goals purposefully and with passion. Early on in his time at Williams, he joined a campus organization dedicated to bringing controversial speakers to campus to catalyze dialogue, even if those conversations sometimes turned out to be difficult. The organization was called Uncomfortable Learning, and in time, Zachary became its president.

Uncomfortable Learning lived up to its name by inviting to campus controversial speakers who might not always be well received by some individuals or student groups. Those talks, however, embodied the aspirations of liberal learning by enabling audience members to consider, interrogate, and challenge diverse points of view— views that they might not agree with or even find distressing. The events added to the richness of

---

[99] Please see Additional Resources.

campus conversations and encouraged all college community members to consider a broader range of ideas.

Since graduating, Zachary has pursued a successful writing and speaking career. His articles have appeared in several publications, including the *Wall Street Journal*, the *Washington Post*, the *Huffington Post*, the *Nation*, the *Weekly Standard*, and *Inside Higher Ed*. Zachary continues to have high aspirations. His remarkable college career and his continuing work afterward clearly show how one committed person can make a difference.

***

CYBERBULLYING

In recent decades, the problem of bullying at all educational levels, including at colleges and universities, has attracted increased attention. It's hardly a new issue. As long as there have been human beings, some individuals have sought to elevate their own social status by threatening, harassing, intimidating, or otherwise diminishing others. Today, we see so many examples of obnoxious, hurtful, and hateful actions in films, on television, and across social media that it's hardly surprising that some young people copy such behaviors.

It's another unhappy-but-undeniable fact of contemporary life that social media platforms now afford seemingly limitless opportunities for people to attack others verbally—whether they know them personally or not. At the extreme, this behavior becomes *cyberbullying*. Worst of all, some social media platforms enable people to do this anonymously, in a thoroughly *cowardly* way. So far, this problem has proven largely intractable in society at large; unfortunately, it also is a growing issue on college and university campuses, where it's no easier to solve.

As we consider this problem and what can be done about it, it's helpful to start with a definition from the US government website, stopbullying.gov:

> Cyberbullying is bullying that takes place over digital devices like cell phones, computers, and tablets. Cyberbullying can occur through SMS, text, and apps, or online in social media, forums, or gaming where people can view, participate in, or share content. Cyberbullying includes sending, posting, or sharing negative, harmful, false, or mean content about someone else. It can include sharing personal or private information about someone else causing embarrassment or humiliation. Some cyberbullying crosses the line into unlawful or criminal behavior.[100]

Another organization, the Cyberbullying Research Center, emphasizes that cyberbullying, by definition, involves multiple, repetitive instances of such behavior, and that it "is actually harassment taken to the next level."[101] The latest available research indicates that nearly 60 percent of high school students have

---

[100] "What is Cyberbullying?" Stopbullying.gov, November 5, 2021, https://www.stopbullying.gov/cyberbullying/what-is-it.

[101] Cyberbullying Research Center, "What is Cyberbullying?" Cyberbullying Research Center, accessed November 25, 2023, https://cyberbullying.org/what-is-cyberbullying.

experienced cyberbullying or on-line harassment,[102] and, as I said, it's becoming more of a problem in colleges and universities. In some cases, cyberbullying can be accompanied by physical bullying when a perpetrator is not satisfied with simply doing damage in cyberspace.

At the time of this writing, all fifty states have passed anti-bullying laws, and every state except Alaska has enacted anti-cyberbullying statutes as well. Such laws typically require schools to take steps to deal with cyberbullying, and they sometimes provide legal tools to do so. (This is especially true if it involves physical threats.) But since this is a relatively new area of legislation, these laws continue to evolve. And unfortunately, school administrators at all levels often feel that they are being asked to solve a society-wide problem but are given insufficient resources to do so.

Colleges and universities typically forbid such behavior, and they can impose penalties on someone who's responsible for launching or participating in a cyberbullying attack. In extreme cases (again, especially those that include physical threats), a college or university can go to court to force an internet platform to reveal the name(s) of a cyberbully (or bullies) hiding behind the cloak of anonymity. Such behavior definitely deserves to come with consequences. No one should be able to get away with attacking another person online, just as no one should be able to avoid punishment for physically attacking someone else.

But why does cyberbullying happen in the first place?

Some people do it just to intimidate or hurt someone else, and there can *never* be an excuse for such meanness. But some college students resort to cyberbullying in a misguided attempt

---

[102] Monica Anderson, "A Majority of Teens Have Experienced Some Form of Cyberbullying," Pew Research Center, September 27, 2023, https://www.pewresearch.org/internet/2018/09/27/a-majority-of-teens-have-experienced-some-form-of-cyberbullying/

to remedy a wrong or a perceived wrong. Perhaps they or a friend have been the victim of sexual harassment or assault, and they're not satisfied with their school's response. They don't feel justice has been done. So, they believe they are justified in using social media to attack the person they hold responsible. This impulse to engage in what is essentially cyber-vigilantism may be understandable, but let me point to four reasons why it's wrong—and why *you* should *never* do it.

First, once you launch a cyberattack against someone, you immediately lose control of what you've done. You can't prevent others from piling on or from forwarding your post, even beyond your college or university community. At that point, there's no way to prevent people in the wider world from jumping in as well—which so many people are inclined to do today, even when they don't know anything at all about the person they're attacking or what they've supposedly done. At that point, your cyberbullying attack has become fully public and possibly viral. So, even if you change your mind at a later point—if, for whatever reason, you come to regret what you've done—there's little or nothing you can do to reverse the damage you've already caused to the targeted individual or their reputation. You also will have opened yourself to possible disciplinary action by your college and to potential legal liability—for example, a civil lawsuit by the target of your attack—or, in some extreme cases, to criminal charges.

Second, in the context of *doing the right thing*, it's important to acknowledge that cyberbullying is profoundly *unfair*. It's extremely difficult and often impossible to defend yourself once you've been attacked in cyberspace. This means that the targeted person is automatically deprived of an essential right that we all enjoy as both members of a college community and citizens of our nation: *the right to defend yourself against accusations*. This is why there are formal processes—in both colleges and universities and in law courts—to adjudicate claims of wrongdoing. Moreover, even when you disagree with the outcome of a particular judicial proceeding, it's important to remember that the same procedural rules that protected the accused person in this case are also there to protect *your* rights in the future, should *you* ever be accused of wrongdoing. And you never know when you might need that protection.

Third, even if a person did something very wrong, it's almost never an ethically justifiable or effective way to remedy the situation by adding another wrong action on top of the original one.

And lastly, by engaging in cyberbullying, you're reinforcing the idea that it is a culturally acceptable practice—that it's okay to behave this way, either at your school or in our broader society. By contributing to that culture, you're helping to make the world a *worse* place for everyone. This means that you're increasing the chances that *you* might become the target of such an attack in the future. Our actions have consequences, frequently unexpected ones.

So, what can you, personally, do about the problem of cyberbullying?

First, doing the right thing means *deciding not to become part of the problem.* As I've emphasized throughout this book, you *always* have a choice. Above and beyond the considerations I've just discussed, it's important to understand that cyberbullying typically carries enormous social and psychological consequences for the person who is targeted. In some extreme cases, people have felt so harassed that they've transferred to another school, and some have even committed suicide. For this and for all the reasons I've just given, you can—and *should*—choose *not* to engage in such behavior. *Never* start. And even if you might have done it before, now is the time to determine *never to do it again*.

A second way to help is *to become an ally to a friend or class-mate who's being attacked in this way*. You can stand with them by offering support and encouragement. Even more importantly, if you know who is doing the cyberbullying, you can stand up to that person (or persons) and push back. You can tell them to stop. Admittedly, this can be difficult—it can require a measure of courage, because pushing back might even lead the cyberbully to target *you*. For this reason, it can be a good idea to engage other friends to join you in standing up for your friend and to the people responsible. Either way, you can support the victim of the attack. Even if the cyberbullies don't listen, you'll have done the right thing.

Third, you can encourage your friend to check out the resources that are available to them. Below are four helpful ones, two of which I've already mentioned.

Your college or university likely offers campus-based resources to assist in dealing with cyberbullying, and you can encourage and assist your friend in accessing them.

The counseling center and the office of student life would be good places to start. Some schools have established an administrative office or a committee to address cyberbullying and support individuals who are targeted. Princeton University, for example, has created such a

The US Government site: https://www.stopbullying.gov

The Cyberbullying Research Center: https://cyberbullying.org

The Pen America Online Harassment Field Manual: https://onlineharassmentfieldmanual.pen.org

UNICEF, "Cyberbullying: What is it and how to stop it": https://www.unicef.org/end-violence/how-to-stop-cyberbullying

special response group, and it's reasonable to expect more colleges and universities to follow suit in the future. If your school doesn't already have this dedicated resource, you might approach someone in your student affairs office about working with them to establish one. That could be a great project to take on—a terrific way to leave your school better than you found it. (We'll have more to say about this in Chapter 8.)

But what if you find yourself on the receiving end of a cyberbullying attack?

The unfortunate truth, as I've indicated, is that there are no easy answers. If you can, it's often best to begin by just ignoring what someone is saying about you online. Perhaps you can block them from contacting you. In this way, you won't reinforce their behavior by responding, and you also can use it as an opportunity to build your own resilience. But I'm not at all trying to minimize the problem or deny the terrible costs this activity can impose on someone who is victimized. When such harassment becomes severe and repeated, ignoring it may well cease to be a realistic option.

In that case, both the resources at your school and the websites I've referenced above represent good places to look for information and assistance. I also hope you're fortunate enough to have friends who will stand up with you and for you. So, don't be afraid to talk with them about what you're facing and see what they are willing (and able) to do on your behalf. It's also prudent to collect evidence, for example, by saving texts or screenshots of the obnoxious social media posts. This material will help you in reporting the problem and, I hope, addressing it.

Above all, you absolutely should inform the appropriate office or person on campus of your concerns. Again, this will usually be the office of student life or student affairs, but it might also be your school's Title IX Coordinator. You can speak with your academic advisor or another sympathetic professor, coach, or staff member you've met. See what your college or university can do to help. Try to work with a responsible person to devise an action plan—something you and they (and possibly your friends) can do together. It's reasonable to expect these college or university officials to keep your conversation confidential, at least at first. But if you want them to take some kind of action, be aware that they likely will need to share your story with others. In an extreme case, you and your family can consider taking legal action against the person or persons who are responsible. This is not a step to be taken lightly, but it remains an option of last resort.

As I said at the start of this section, cyberbullying remains a significant societal problem—and, in many ways, it can feel like an unsolvable one. As with our society as a whole, colleges and universities are limited in what they can do in response to an instance of cyberbullying. Many times, unhappily, they may not be able to do much at all. Which means that people all too often get away with this hurtful behavior. (As I look back at my own presidency, I regret that I wasn't able to do more to address this issue on my campus.) But none of this means we have to accept an unjust situation without actively confronting it. And if people don't try to solve it, then this problem is guaranteed only to get worse.

Cyberbullying is a *social* problem. It's caused by peoples' actions people—individually and collectively—and it's supported by social structures and commercial entities we've permitted to exist, primarily unregulated social media. As such, it's one more example of a wicked problem facing us all, which means we all have a role in remedying it. I certainly can't point to a magic bullet that will make it stop. But I can assure you that resolving it begins with raising awareness, on all our parts, and then looking for both personal and, yes, political ways to reduce and ideally eliminate it altogether.

ACADEMIC HONESTY

One of the most important sections of your school's student conduct code relates to academic honesty. It goes without saying that this should be a fundamental concern for *all* members of any educational institution.

As a student, you need to count on the integrity of your teachers. You depend on the fact that they know what they're talking about. You also deserve to be confident that they will honestly acknowledge those times when they might be unsure about something—for example, when they might not immediately know the answer to a question that has come up in class. (No one can know *everything* about any field.) Finally, you should be able to assume that your professors are careful to describe the full range of perspectives within their discipline—including credible views about a topic or question that differ from those *they* happen to favor.

Likewise, when you submit a writing assignment, an exam, or a project to be evaluated—*when you sign your name to it*—your professor needs to be able to trust that you produced the work the way it was supposed to have been done. The basic expectation here is that *you take credit only for work you've completed appropriately*. This is a major way to do the right thing in college: *to resist the impulse to take the easy way out by cheating on an assignment or test*.

Unfortunately, many campuses are seeing a troubling increase in instances of academic dishonesty. Please avoid becoming part of this problem too. Some students give in to the temptation to cheat because they assume—quite wrongly!—that their primary academic goal in college is only to get good grades, by any means whatever. Sure, grades are important. But their true value comes in reflecting what you've learned. It's never worth it to act dishonestly just to get a better evaluation—a point we'll come back to in a moment.

Your school most likely has prepared a helpful publication that explains how to avoid plagiarism and other forms of academic dishonesty. Make sure you obtain a copy—or review it online—and familiarize yourself with the principles it explains. It will include guidelines for properly citing someone else's words, ideas, or images so you can appropriately include those things in a paper you're writing or project you're completing.

If you run into a gray area where you're not sure how the academic honesty rules apply, be sure to check *before* you complete and submit the assignment. Ask for clarification from your professor, your TA, someone in the writing center, your academic advisor, or some other knowledgeable person. But always remember that, in the end, *you* are responsible for following the rules relating to academic honesty, for the work you sign your name to. Don't risk making a misstep simply because you were confused or just too lazy to check.

Recently, as we discussed in Chapter 1, a new crop of computer programs has appeared: generative artificial intelligence programs. These AI tools are easy to access, can respond to questions, and are capable of producing text good enough to pass for something a human being has written. The most well-known program is ChatGPT, but others are available, and still others are being developed.

The public launch of ChatGPT prompted two immediate responses: First, some students were tempted to use it to cheat on written assignments and tests, leading teachers to look for ways to detect work that had been produced by the program, something people are continuing to do. Second, some concerned educators moved to ban such programs—to restrict access to them on their school computer systems and, more generally, to forbid students from using them. But right away, it became pretty clear that neither of these workarounds was likely to be successful.

What you're now far more likely to encounter in your college career are a variety of emerging approaches to this developing technology. For example, you'll probably find more in-class writing assignments, quizzes, and tests, and perhaps fewer traditional paper and take-home test assignments than in the past.

But more interestingly, you're likely to see your professors experimenting with ways to incorporate this new technology in your classes—so that, in the end, it becomes one more tool available for you to use, just like calculators and spell-check programs. In addition, colleges and universities are now beginning to revise their academic honesty policies to provide guidance for how to employ this new technology with integrity.

Most of all, I hope—and, in fact, I *expect*—that your professors will employ this technology to help you gain a more sophisticated understanding of AI itself—both its promises and its limitations. As I commented in Chapter 1, we all need to come to terms with the increasing integration of AI in virtually all aspects of our lives. It's likely that you'll be using AI-related tools in your post-college work. So, you'll need to determine how much you can trust a given program and how to check what it's "telling" you. For example, students who naively trust a program like ChatGPT—say, to write a paper for them—will discover that it frequently makes factual errors and has other shortcomings as well.

It also will be important to resist the very human temptation to ascribe more understanding to AI programs than they warrant. As more professors incorporate generative AI in your classes, you will have opportunities to develop a more sophisticated understanding of this technology, which will serve you well in the future.

So, to repeat what I wrote earlier, the basic expectation remains the same: that you take credit only for work you have done within the guidelines of the assignment. If you're unclear about the rules or find yourself struggling with what to do, talk with your professor or TA to clarify the expectations or, possibly, to get help (or extra time, if needed) to complete it. This counts as a useful general guideline: Even if you have to turn in a paper late or postpone taking an exam, it's better to accept a lower grade but understand the material or complete the assignment with integrity.

Please understand that your college or university takes its academic honesty regulations seriously. This means that *taking credit for someone else's ideas without giving proper acknowledgement* or otherwise *cheating on an assignment, test, or exam* is not only ethically unacceptable but can also subject you to a range of penalties—whether it's a lowered grade or failure on that assignment or exam, failure of the entire course, suspension, or expulsion. And any of these outcomes can potentially result in a permanent blot on your transcript, which we've talked about already.

But it's also instructive to consider the issue of academic honesty from another perspective—not just in the context of your college years but in terms of your future life and that of your fellow citizens. Imagine that you or someone you love experiences a heart attack. In that instance, how would you feel if you learned that the attending physician or surgeon had cheated their way through medical school? Or imagine that you need the services of an attorney to assist you in a complex legal matter involving financial or even criminal risk. How would you feel if you were to discover that your lawyer had cheated their way through law school? Or what if the architect who designed your dream home turned out to have fraudulent credentials? You see the point.

The answers to these questions are entirely obvious, and their implications apply to *you*, right now. *Preserve your self-respect and integrity by practicing academic honesty all the time.* Make sure you don't risk becoming someone whose degree is tainted by cheating. Honestly earning your diploma is one more important step toward becoming someone others can trust and respect. *Do the right thing!*

MORAL HUMILITY

Cultivating an attitude of *moral humility* about our personal ethical decision-making helps us do the right thing consistently. It's similar to the attitude of *intellectual humility* regarding our beliefs, which we talked about in Chapter 6. An attitude of moral humility comes from recognizing those times when we've failed to fulfill an ethical obligation—whether it's to care for someone else, to be respectful to them (or to ourselves), or something else. In short, when we've *failed* to do the right thing.

There are very few moral saints among us, and I'm *not* at all calling upon you to become one. (Believe me, I've certainly had to own up to ethical lapses in my own life.) At those times when we betray our own best values, we need to be honest in owning our mistakes and asking forgiveness from those whom we've harmed. And just as in the case of other kinds of failure, we need to *learn* from those moments of moral failure too. We can always reflect on where and why we went wrong, and then resolve not to make a similar mistake in the future.

Realizing that we fail to do the right thing more often than we might want to admit helps us avoid falling into the attitude of arrogant self-righteousness—the feeling that we are morally superior to everyone else. (Guess what? *None* of us is!) It also sets the stage to forgive others when *they* miss the ethical mark.

Writing in the context of Christianity, Dr. Martin Luther King, Jr. commented, "Forgiveness is not an occasional act; it is a constant attitude." Likewise, journalist Nathan Hersh observed that the Jewish tradition also emphasizes the importance of accepting an apology and offering forgiveness:

> One of Judaism's most famous sages, the 12th-century philosopher Maimonides, made clear the role the forgiver should play ... [in helping] the wrongdoer overcome [their] ignorance and then [forgiving them]. Maimonides said: "One must not show himself cruel by not accepting an apology; he should be easily pacified, and provoked with difficulty. When an offender asks his forgiveness, he should give it wholeheartedly and with a willing spirit."[103]

When we are honest enough to acknowledge our own ethical shortcomings, we open a space in our hearts to cultivate both the "constant attitude" of forgiveness recommended by Dr. King and the generosity described by Maimonides and referenced by Mr.

---

[103] Nathan Hersh, "Whoopi Goldberg Apologized. Punishing Her Further Is Un-Jewish," *New York Times*, February 9, 2022, https://www.nytimes.com/2022/02/09/opinion/whoopi-goldberg-the-viewapology.html?referringSource=articleShare.

Hirsh. Doing so enhances our capacity to forgive others—and ourselves too! To repair as best we can whatever damage we may have caused. To learn from these experiences and resolve to do better next time. And above all, to approach someone who might have wronged us with the kind of generous spirit we hope others would display when we are at fault.

WHY LIVE A PRINCIPLED LIFE?

There are many ways to justify the idea that we all should live principled lives—that we all should do the right thing. Religious teachings frequently emphasize acting morally. But let me appeal to a very simple idea that can be instructive whether one is religious or not: *care*. You may have noticed that I've used this notion multiple times already throughout this book. It's an important concept, though it can easily be confused with a different one: *empathy*. The two are related, but they're not the same.

Empathy is a basic human psychological capacity—literally the ability to *feel with* someone else: to share their emotions, their joy, or their pain. (In extreme cases, the inability of a person to experience empathy can be a pathological condition.) And this kind of fellow feeling often becomes the basis for caring; we frequently care for those we can empathize with, and conversely, we usually can empathize with those we care about.

Caring, however, is a more active and a more broadly applicable attitude. First, it denotes not only feeling but also *doing*. To care for someone else, in the fullest sense, is not just to *feel* a certain way toward them but to *act* on their behalf—to do the right thing *for them*. Moreover, it's quite possible to *care* for someone we don't personally know or even someone we dislike. You can donate funds to assist people suffering from the war in Ukraine or victims of a natural disaster in some far corner of the globe. Or you can help out a classmate who's struggling with, say, a math problem—even though they've not been kind to you in the past and you don't particularly *like* them. In other words, we can't always choose to empathize with someone, but we can choose to *care* about them.[104]

Mature and thoughtful adults understand that the universe does not revolve around them—that other people have value too. As I've emphasized, other persons deserve our respect and consideration—just as we deserve theirs. If you think about people you look up to, I suspect you'll find that the best of them care about others first and themselves second. They care that their actions do not cause needless pain, suffering, or grief to others. They care enough about fairness not to press their own advantage to someone else's disadvantage. They care that the world should be a place that is good and equitable for everyone, not only for themselves. And they do their part to help make it so. They express their caring through acts of thoughtfulness and kindness. They look for ways to foster caring communities based on mutual respect. They understand that by acting in these ways, they're helping to build a better human community in which *everyone* can flourish. Why wouldn't *you* choose to be that sort of person?

Living the kind of life I'm describing also requires us to care about *truth*—about being honest with ourselves and with others, and about holding beliefs that are well-founded and justified, not only ones that are convenient or popular. Mature and respectful adults understand that muddled or false beliefs provide a shaky foundation, at best, for deciding how to act and that dishonesty

---

[104] Saul J. Weiner, MD, makes the case for distinguishing empathy from care in Chapter 6 of *On Becoming a Healer: The Journey from Patient Care to Caring about Your Patients* (Baltimore: Johns Hopkins University Press, 2020).

represents a terrible basis for interacting with other people. Cultivating the various dimensions of caring builds your capacity to do the right thing and helps you move the world, bit by bit, toward being a better place for everyone.

FINDING THE COURAGE TO CARE AND DO THE RIGHT THING

At the beginning of this chapter, I said that our problem is seldom being confused about what is the right thing to do. The real problem is usually finding the courage to do it. Previously, in Chapter 6, I linked courage to love. That connection comes into play here as well.

You may be aware that the ancient Greeks distinguished two sorts of love: The first, *eros*, represents the more common meaning of love in contemporary usage; it denotes a romantic or sexual interest in or attachment to another person and, obviously, is the root of the word "erotic." The second sense, *agape*, is a notion that was taken up by the early Christians; it denotes a general (non-erotic) love of others, a concern for their welfare. This is the love parents have for a child, for example, but it applies much more broadly.

My use of the term "love"—here and throughout this book—clearly calls upon the second of these two meanings. As in the case of care, love—in the sense of *agape* and as opposed to *eros*—needn't be attached to a personal relationship, much less a romantic one. Fundamentally, it's a *willingness or a commitment to do good for someone else*.

As an example, consider the following story of love and courage from the 1960s Civil Rights movement:

Confronting hate with love: David Hartsough

Quaker peace activist David Hartsough describes how he discovered the power of love in the act of nonviolence at a 1960 lunch counter sit-in protesting segregation in Arlington, Virginia:

"Love your enemies...do good to those who hate you."

I was meditating on those words when I heard a voice behind me say, "Get out of this store in two seconds, or I'm going to stab this through your heart." I glanced behind me at a man with the most terrible look of hatred I had ever seen. His eyes blazed, his jaw quivered, and his shaking hand held a switchblade—about half an inch from my heart....

I turned around and tried my best to smile. Looking him in the eye, I said to him, "Friend, do what you believe is right, and I will still try to love you." Both his jaw and his hand dropped. Miraculously, he turned away and walked out of the store.

That was the most powerful experience of my twenty years of life. It confirmed my belief in the power of love, the power of goodness, the power of God working through us to overcome hatred and violence. I had a profound sense that nonviolence really works. At that moment, nonviolence became much more than a philosophical idea or a tactic that had once made a difference in Gandhi's India. It became the way I wanted to relate to other human beings, a way of life, a way of working for change.

My response had touched something in my accuser. He had seen me as an enemy. But through my response, I believe I became a human being to him. The humanity in each of us touched.[105]

***

Many religions call upon their followers to love and care for people they do not know or who have done them harm. But there are countless instances of such caring that are not necessarily linked to religion. For example, soldiers can love their country and thus their fellow citizens—most of whom they couldn't possibly know—so much that they willingly give up their lives to defend them. Firefighters frequently risk their lives to protect people they've never met. Recall the courageous NYFD members who rushed into the burning Twin Towers on 9/11, realizing full well that they might not return. Tragically, 343 did not.

More recently, in the early days of the COVID-19 pandemic, before there were vaccines or even effective treatment protocols, we witnessed selfless and, indeed, heroic acts by thousands of doctors, nurses, EMTs, first responders, and other frontline

---

[105] David Hartsough with Joyce Hollyday, *Waging Peace: Global Adventures of a Lifelong Activist* (Oakland: PM Press, 2014), 19–20; Richard Rohr, "Nonviolence: A Nonviolent Love," Center for Action and Contemplation, October 23, 2022, https://cac.org/daily-meditations/a-nonviolent-love-2022-10-23/.

health care workers. They stepped up to treat patients when they were exhausted by the sheer volume of cases, and at considerable risk to their own safety. It's easy to multiply such examples. But all these people could not have acted so unselfishly if they did not care—in the deep sense we are invoking here—about the people they had sworn to serve and protect. Viktor Frankl defines love as "active caring for others," and the people I've just referenced truly have embraced a form of life that expresses such unselfish service to others.

In the context of your own life, here and now, you can choose to care about your fellow students—in fact to love them, in the sense we've been discussing—so that you commit to doing right by them. This level of caring can inspire the courage necessary to stand up to peer pressure when it might be pushing you in the other direction. It also can help to ground new grown-up friendships that are able to weather "the slings and arrows of outrageous fortune"—which life hurls at all of us and which can tear apart more superficial relationships based only upon self-interest or other kinds of surface-level attraction.

It's entirely up to you. Choosing to nurture a deep commitment to caring for others can guide you in developing the qualities of character that will serve you well, both in the years immediately ahead and then long past your graduation. This effort can become a powerful part of your college experience and, after that, of your life's journey. It will help you develop into a person who not only merits respect but who is, in fact, very much respected by others. *Do the right thing!*

SUMMING UP—CHAPTER 7

- In most cases, reminding yourself to do the right thing is enough to clarify an ethical choice you're facing. Doing the right thing starts with respecting both others and yourself.

- But sometimes we do encounter a complex ethical situation that does not admit of a neat resolution. In those cases, we need to bring to bear the higher cognitive skills we've been developing in college and sometimes hold competing ideas in balance, as we search for a solution.

- Become familiar with your college or university's student code of conduct; it will let you know what your school expects of you as a member of your campus community. Pay special attention to the sections that deal with academic honesty.

- College students often encounter challenges to their values in regard to incidents of bigotry or prejudice on campus, in cases of sexual- or gender-related misconduct, around issues of free speech, cyberbullying, and temptations to cheat in their academic work. Avoiding these pitfalls will help you become a person you can be proud of, and it will earn you the respect of others. Doing the right thing will also keep you from having to explain a serious judicial ruling attached to your permanent transcript.

- Cultivating an attitude of moral humility—akin to intellectual humility—starts with honestly acknowledging our ethical failures. We can learn from those lapses, and we can also become more generous in forgiving the moral shortcomings of others.

- Understanding that *no* person is the center of the universe—that others have intrinsic value too—can help to foster attitudes of care and love (*agape*): an active concern for the wellbeing of others. Your time as a college student will provide abundant opportunities to build a character that will sustain you long after you graduate from college.

This time in your life calls for a determined focus on *you*: on what you're learning and on your personal growth. But any human life is deeply imbedded in human communities; and those communities, too, deserve our interest and care—even during your college years. So, I ask that you pay attention to that aspect of your new campus life as well. In the next chapter, we'll see what this might mean for you.

CHAPTER 8

PRACTICE GIVING BACK AND
PAYING IT FORWARD

Be ashamed to die until you have won some victory for humanity.
—*Horace Mann*

I've already asked you to imagine how you'll feel at your college or university commencement. Now let's think ahead even further. When you've earned your bachelor's degree, you'll join the less than 40 percent of US citizens who have attained this level of formal education. Forty percent! That's a surprisingly small proportion for such a wealthy and accomplished nation. Globally, the figure is even lower. It varies widely by country, but overall, fewer than 10 percent of all people living today have earned a college degree.

This means that, in the broader context of the planet we inhabit together, it remains an enormous privilege just to be able to *attend* college. And notice that we're *not* talking about entitlement. None of us has a *right* to membership in our college or university community. Each of us has to earn our place every single day. And by the way, this comment applies to everyone: not only to you and your fellow students but also to each member of the faculty, staff, and administration at your school. It was equally true for me as a college president. We all are privileged but *not* entitled to be members of a college or university community.

PRIVILEGE AND RESPONSIBILITY

You've probably heard it said that with privilege comes responsibility. In that spirit, I want to suggest that the unparalleled opportunities you now have before you give rise to a proportional obligation *to give back and to pay it forward*. This is especially true if your economic situation or family background has made it relatively easy for you to afford a college education. But it's still true, even if attending your school presents you and your family with substantial financial or other hardships. No matter how hard you have to work—and how many sacrifices you and your family have to make—the opportunities you enjoy for attending and succeeding at college still place you in a position of privilege relative to so many other people in both our nation and the world. This is not at all about guilt, by the way. Rather, it's about acknowledging that *the chance to earn a college education represents a unique opportunity to benefit from what the larger human community has made available to you*—an opportunity not available to so many others.

So, as you embark on your college journey, consider asking some additional "big questions":

- How will I choose to give back in response to everything that's been given to me?
- How can I pay it forward to help others realize the advantages from which I have benefited?

- What am I prepared to do to meet this challenge—not just for my undergraduate years but for the rest of my life?

In his sentence quoted at the start of this chapter, the nineteenth-century American educator Horace Mann reduces these questions to a single one: What victory will *you* win for humanity?[106]

YOU CAN MAKE AN IMMEDIATE DIFFERENCE ON YOUR CAMPUS

Your college or university is a great place to start. *What are you prepared to do to win your first victory there—to leave your new school better than you found it?*

A college campus is an incredibly complex network of interconnected people, offices, and operations. It's obviously an educational enterprise in its classrooms, labs, and studios, and its cocurricular opportunities. But most colleges and universities also resemble small cities: they include restaurants/food courts (dining spaces), hotels (residence halls), arts districts (art galleries and theaters), intercollegiate teams, a sports complex (with gyms and fitness facilities, a swimming pool, and a full athletic staff), a medical clinic/hospital (health services), a psychological counseling center, a job counseling service (career development office), possibly a daycare center, certainly a library, and for many community members, they are places of employment. But despite offering all these advantages, every school has areas where things could be improved. This means that your campus will present

---

[106] Mann's exhortation—"Be ashamed to die until you have won some victory for humanity"—has long been the motto of Antioch College in Yellow Springs, Ohio.

many possibilities for you to begin giving back and paying it forward. You can choose to make a modest contribution or a more substantial one. Either way, *every* student can make a difference.

You can begin with small steps. Pick up a piece of paper someone carelessly dropped on campus and deposit it in the proper receptacle. (What if everyone did this?) When you enter or exit a building, hold the door for the next person, and thank someone who holds the door for you. Look for other ways to perform small, random acts of kindness. You never know how far the ripples from a small gift to another person can travel.

Then broaden your vision. In your very first year, you can *begin to look for your personal cause on campus*. Among the different offices and functions that make up your college or university, find a place where your interests and abilities intersect with the needs of your community—perhaps in a student organization or club that aims to make a positive difference in some way. At their best, these organizations exemplify active care and concern for others. They also give you the chance to employ your positive freedom that we've emphasized so much—to do something you've decided is worth doing in collaboration with others. *So, consider joining a campus service club. Pitch in. Exercise your leadership (and followership) skills. Engage your creative powers. Make a difference!*

We know that everyone wants to *belong* somewhere. One question new students often face is whether they are going to feel like they belong at their school. No matter how large or small it may be, your campus community may seem a bit intimidating at first. It may not be immediately evident where you, personally, are going to find your niche. But it helps to realize that every college or university is actually a *community of communities*. The key to finding your own place is identifying those smaller, micro-communities that offer you a chance to connect with others.

If you're a varsity athlete, you already have your team. If you're a musician or dancer, you'll surely meet other students who share your interest and with whom you'll perform. If you have a campus work-study job, you'll likely meet student coworkers. For anyone, as you progress through your classes, you can count on connecting with other students in your chosen field of study.

But you don't need to wait until you've declared a major. As I've suggested here and in the preceding chapter, you can start right away, by exploring the various clubs and organizations on your campus. You could look for one that reflects an interest you already have or check out one that represents a possible new interest—especially dedicated to making your school a better institution. As you join in that activity, you'll find an immediate secondary benefit: a ready-made micro-community of fellow students who will be glad to welcome you as a new member. And if possible, don't settle for finding just one micro-community; look for others where you can belong as well. Here are two stories of students who discovered their own ways to make a difference as undergraduates:

Motivating change on campus: Jonathan's story

Jonathan was a student who struggled with eating issues and weight gain for much of his young life. He also was an athlete (ice hockey), but in his pre-college years, he still never seemed to identify the right foods to be as healthy and fit as he wanted to be.

When he first came to Skidmore, he didn't find the dining hall food to be as nutritious as it could—and should—have been. So, rather than just complain to his friends, Jon started a student organization aimed at improving the situation: the Skidmore Nutrition Action Council (SNAC). He and a small group of like-minded peers researched how the college could provide healthier options. They worked with the folks in Dining Services to develop those alternatives, and they engaged other students to identify the kinds of food they were interested in eating.

SNAC made a difference right away! Starting then and over succeeding years, Dining Services developed a broader range of nutritious, organic, and locally-sourced food options. This may not seem like a large victory, but it was an important one, both for Jon and for the students who came after him.

In his academic work, Jon pursued a double major in chemistry and health and human physiological sciences, and he did research with one of his professors into the molecular mechanisms that cause obesity and diabetes. After graduating, he went on to the University of Pennsylvania to earn a master's in public health in epidemiology and a combined MD/PhD in in cell and molecular biology. He then completed a post-doc at the Washington University Medical School in St. Louis, Missouri.

Jon still maintains a strong interest in nutrition. He's continuing his research on obesity and diabetes in his own lab at Washington University. He says, "I feel fortunate to have found a career that still gives me butterflies and that is driven by passion." At the time of writing, Jon also has served as a member of Skidmore's Board of Trustees for ten years.

Leading to make a difference: Nigel's story

Nigel was the first student from his Atlanta high school to attend Skidmore, and he had never even traveled to New York state before arriving for his first year. He had an unfortunate experience early on in Saratoga Springs when someone said to him, as a Black male, that Skidmore "probably wasn't the place for him." He was "devastated" by this thoughtless (and completely inaccurate!) comment, but his mother said to him that he'd "come too far to go back now." So, Nigel leaned into the project of being a college student and, in his first semester, ran for class president. In a crowded field of candidates, he won and set out to understand how student government worked and how he could best make a difference.

Then, on Halloween night of his first semester, tragedy struck. A group of first-year students were on a road walking back to campus after an off-campus party when they were hit by a car driven by a drunk driver (someone who was not a student). Several were severely injured, and one was killed.

The campus was thrown into shock and mourning. A memorial event was immediately planned, and it was attended by over one thousand students, faculty members, staff members, and others. The parents of the deceased student and those who had been injured were there as well.

Barely two months into his term as first-year class president, Nigel was called upon to speak at the memorial service (along with several others, including me as the college President). Understandably, he found this a daunting assignment—one that could intimidate anyone. How do you choose the right words at such a moment? How do you speak on behalf of your classmates and all the other students who were feeling such a terrible sense of loss? What do you say to the grieving families and to the hundreds in attendance?

Once again, Nigel stepped up to do what was difficult: to meet this challenge. He talked honestly about his own experience of community on campus, which he already had come to value. He expressed the deep feelings of grief he himself was experiencing and that he knew others were feeling as well. In the face of such an overwhelming loss, his eloquent remarks helped to bring a sense of healing to his fellow students. It was a marvelous act of service.

Then, in the very next semester, the campus again experienced another unexpected and shattering tragedy. A second student from the same first-year class lost his life in an off-campus accident (at another university in another state, where he had been visiting). We gathered once more to mourn his death, and again Nigel came forward with words of consolation for his fellow students and the family of the student who had died.

For the next three years, Nigel worked with his peers to preserve and cherish the memory of their departed classmates. Three years later, as the time for their commencement approached, he consulted both his classmates and college administrators to assure that the two students who couldn't be there to share that moment with everyone else would be remembered and appropriately honored. Among other things, we awarded each of them a Skidmore degree, which their families gratefully accepted.

In all that he did, Nigel made a real difference—for his classmates, for the families of the students, and for the college as a whole. In his time at Skidmore, he worked in many other ways to make it a more inclusive school and to help other students, who initially may have wondered whether *they* would belong and find their place. His peers were deeply grateful for his contributions.

Nigel has gone on to begin a career in banking. He earned an MBA at Emory University, and he is now a member of Skidmore's Board of Trustees too. And I'm pleased to say that Nigel's high school in Atlanta has continued to send students north to attend his alma mater.

***

As these two stories suggest, you can set out to make a difference, or you can find yourself thrust into a situation that calls upon you to step forward. Either way there will be multiple opportunities for every student to leave their college or university better than they found it—whether in large ways or small ones. It's just a matter of becoming aware of the possibilities and then deciding to act.

LOOK BEYOND YOUR CAMPUS

The world is a fine place and worth fighting for.
—Ernest Hemingway

Next, why not raise your sights to the world beyond the borders of your school? To your local community, your state, your country, and our planet as a whole. I hope you agree with Hemingway that our world is indeed "a fine place" and is certainly "worth fighting for"! It goes without saying that it's the only one we have. So, consider how you want *your* world to be tomorrow, for the rest of your life, and in the yet-more-distant future. What would a more just, sustainable, and satisfactory planet look like? What are you prepared to do to help bring that brave new world into being? What are *you* willing to fight for? You can immediately begin to practice being a caring, informed, and responsible citizen of our larger human community.

In fact, young people everywhere are doing this—leading the fight against climate change, promoting more sensible and effective firearm safety laws, or finding other ways to make a difference. If you too have been involved in such a project in high school (or even earlier), good for you! You can continue your efforts in your new local community. Or you can find new ways to be of service. But even if you've never volunteered before, you can discover some way to make a difference in the lives of people who live just beyond the boundaries of your college or university.

Making a difference in the world: Greta Thunberg's story

I've already mentioned Greta Thunberg (in Chapter 3), and you've probably heard about her on your own. As a fifteen-year-old high school student in Stockholm, Sweden, she launched a global wave of student activism in response to the global climate crisis, a cause she continues to champion to this day. She's received a great deal of recognition for her work (including an invitation to address the United Nations). Most important of all, she's inspired thousands of young people across the world to take up the cause of fighting climate change in active and innovative ways. Both individuals and governments have listened to their call for change. Greta's example shows how one creative, committed person can make a real difference on a planetary scale.

***

But you don't have to become an internationally famous activist to effect genuine change in people's lives. Consider the story of Johane who came to study in the US from Swaziland, Africa.

Making a difference in the world: Johane's story

At Skidmore, Johane created a self-determined major in public health. In his junior year, he received funding from the college to undertake a summer project in his home country—conducting public health research on social and cultural factors relating to the spread of HIV/AIDS. This is an important topic anywhere but especially in Africa, where rates of transmission remain quite high. Johane's findings were taken up immediately by the Swaziland government and used to make changes in national public health policy.

Johane has gone on to complete a master's degree in public health at Columbia University. He's currently working as a research program manager with the Department of Veterans Affairs in the Bronx, New York. His position initially focused just on infectious diseases (COVID-19, obviously, became a key topic of concern), but through his leadership, his program has expanded to include many more divisions (for example, cardiology, spinal cord injury, and primary care, along with eight others). Johane now directs a seventeen-person team, and his people work with twenty-five physicians across all the covered specialties. His undergraduate experience in his interdisciplinary self-determined major gave him essential knowledge and skills that he's used to establish and lead a diverse multidisciplinary research division.

For now, Johane remains focused on enhancing the quality of care for the veterans who are his clients. But he still plans, at some later stage in his career, to be active in improving healthcare systems in developing countries—especially his native Swaziland. He's currently involved in an HIV study through Harvard University, funded by the National Institutes of Health (NIH), that addresses issues in both the US and several African nations.

***

There are countless other stories of students at colleges and universities across our nation and around the world who are actively working to contribute to the greater good. But I hope these examples might inspire you to make some "no small plans" of your own to fight for a better world. Opportunities to make a difference are limited only by your interest, imagination, and willingness to make the required effort.

As you reflect upon the broader world beyond your college or university, consider, too, how important it is for all of us to participate in the political processes of our democracy, which we first talked about in Chapter 1. Assuming you're eligible, it's important to make sure you're registered to vote—either at home or in your new college town—and then vote whenever the opportunity presents itself. Try to resist going into political hibernation, as some people do, between national presidential elections. Though midterm elections often motivate much lower voter turnouts than general elections, they can have enormous consequences. So, it was a very healthy sign that the 2022 US midterm elections inspired so many young people—and so many on college and university campuses—to make their voices heard through their votes.

As an informed, responsible, and caring citizen, you'll want to keep up with both the national political questions of the day and the local issues in your city or town that directly affect your life and the lives of others in your college or university community. Talk with your friends about these things. If you have a special interest in politics, you could join a campus political club, volunteer in a political campaign, or help with a campus voter registration drive. There are many ways to be involved and make a difference. A campus can sometimes seem isolated from its surrounding community; being a college or university student can feel like you're living in a bubble. But you aren't! Thinking this way is *not* helpful, and it's good to resist the impulse to do so. Whether we're aware of it or not, our lives are interconnected; we share a common fate.

NOT WAITING TO DO WHAT YOU CAN

It is not your duty to finish the work, but
neither are you at liberty to neglect it.
—Rabbi Tarfon

How wonderful it is that nobody need wait a single
moment before starting to improve the world.
—Anne Frank

None of us can solve all the world's problems. In Chapter 7, I said that I'm *not* at all calling upon you to become a moral saint. In this chapter, I'm *not* challenging you to go out and personally save the world. Very few of us can become a Greta Thunberg. Moreover, it can take time to discover a cause that inspires your passion— the "victory for humanity" you choose to win. And there will be many competing demands upon your time in college and later. But each of us can acknowledge that we are inescapably members of the interconnected and interdependent human community with a responsibility to contribute to it. We can decide where to direct our efforts to make a difference of some kind.

Anne Frank has come to be identified with the sentence from her diary quoted above. Most likely, you've read it before. You'll recall that she wrote that comment, along with many others, expressing an inspiring faith in humankind during one of history's darkest hours—in World War II when she, her family, and several others hid for two years in Amsterdam from the Germans who had invaded the country. Because they were all Jews, they had good reason to fear for their lives. As you also surely know, the Nazis eventually discovered their refuge and subsequently sent Anne and everyone who had lived with her to the death camps. Her father was the only family member to survive the war.

Even though Anne's faith in humanity could not save her and most of the people she loved, her determined expression of hope in the midst of such horrific circumstances stands as an uplifting example for us all. She intended her diary to be a private record of her experiences, the personal reflections of an adolescent girl coming of age. But her words have given encouragement to so many who have learned of her story. No matter what our personal situation, none of us has to wait a single minute to begin making a difference in some way.

GRATITUDE

Let us be grateful to people who make us happy; they are the charming gardeners who make our souls blossom.
—*Marcel Proust*

Think back to when you were applying to college. That process is certainly demanding, and many students understandably find it stressful. Perhaps it was for you. You might even know how many other applicants were rejected by the school you ultimately chose to attend. You are where you are today because your college or university determined that *you* could take best advantage of what it has to offer—that *you* were prepared to succeed there. You deserve to be proud of getting to where you are today, and I sincerely hope you feel this way.

We all have the right to be proud of our accomplishments. But no matter how hard you had to work to get where you are, *you did not get there alone.* And no matter how difficult the road ahead may be—and how hard you are prepared to work to realize your "no small plans"—you won't achieve your new goals without assistance from many others along the way. *None of us ever succeeds at anything totally on our own.*

So, I also sincerely hope that reflecting on this reality—and, as I said before, recognizing the enormous privilege represented by the opportunity to pursue a college education—gives rise to feelings of gratitude. Mature and thoughtful people understand

and celebrate what they owe to those who have preceded and supported them along their way. They give thanks.

Expressing gratitude: J. Herman Blake's story

A distinguished professor of sociology, researcher, and academic administrator, J. Herman Blake, PhD, has frequently been honored by his colleagues in the academic world and is often called upon to speak across the country. Regardless of the occasion, he begins every public address by talking about someone from his past who positively influenced his life: a teacher, a colleague, a friend. Dr. Blake always describes what they did for him and thanks them by name. In doing so, he sends the message to his audience that none of us is too important to say "thank you" to those who lifted us up along the way and helped us get to where we are today. That's why he makes sure that expressing gratitude always comes before anything else he might have to say.

Expressing gratitude: Oliver Sacks's story

Just weeks before his death from metastatic cancer, the renowned medical researcher, author, and storyteller Dr. Oliver Sacks wrote the following lines:

"I cannot pretend that I am without fear. But my predominant feeling is one of gratitude. I have loved and been loved; I have been given much and I have given something in return; I have read and traveled and thought and written.... Above all, I have been a sentient being, a thinking animal, on this beautiful planet, and that in itself has been an enormous privilege and adventure."[107]

***

It surely would be a blessing for any of us to be able to face the end of our days expressing such thoughts about our own life. But we don't have to wait until then. We all can learn from these and many other examples of people whose lives remind us of the beauty of a generous spirit. And we can apply their lessons in our own lives. Each of us can commit to cultivating our personal sense of gratitude and looking for opportunities to communicate it.

In that spirit, I invite you to take just a moment to reflect on how much *you* owe to

- a teacher who inspired, pushed, or supported you at a crucial juncture in your earlier education—especially during COVID;
- a coach or mentor who gave you guidance, helped you through a rough patch, or kicked your butt in motivating you to perform beyond your own expectations;
- a minister, priest, rabbi, imam, or other spiritual advisor who became a resource for you at a time when you were searching for answers;
- a friend who was there for you in good and tough times alike and who will continue to be there for you in the future when you need an encouraging word, a shoulder to cry on, or just a laugh;

---

[107] Oliver Sacks, *Gratitude* (New York: Knopf, 2015), see Additional Resources.

- and above all, to your parents and other family members who have been there for you in so many ways and who will continue to have your back during your undergraduate years and beyond.

Why not make it a point to say "thank you" to at least some of these folks before you set out upon your college adventure? Or the next time you speak with them? In fact, it would be terrific to do something really old-fashioned: *write* them a note. You could do this electronically, but a hand-written note from you would be particularly meaningful, especially since we receive so few of them these days. Since we don't always pause to feel and express our gratitude, I guarantee you that anyone would deeply appreciate hearing from you in this way.

And then consider giving the additional gift of staying connected. From time to time, tell someone who helped you along your way how things are going for you in college. They will continue to care about you and will want to know what you're up to. And don't forget to ask about *them*—they need to know *you* still care about *them* too! Above all, it would be terrific to commit to living your college life in ways that give you many new occasions both to experience and express pride and gratitude.

GIVING BACK TO YOUR SCHOOL AND PAYING IT FORWARD

Lastly, your college or university needs you to understand that even schools with the highest levels of tuition and fees receive only a portion of their operating revenues from that source. The rest comes from endowment, external grants, and the financial generosity of alumni, parents, and friends. Think of the buildings and other facilities that were waiting for you when you arrived.

Most of them probably bear the names of donors whose philanthropy brought those buildings into existence. In addition, many faculty members and other key people on your campus (including athletic coaches and administrators) hold positions funded by endowments, which were provided by donors who chose to make a difference. If you are receiving financial aid, you are benefitting directly from such generosity as well. The list goes on.

Following your graduation, as a proud member of your college or university's alumni population, you too will be called upon to help support your alma mater and future generations of students. Please understand that even small gifts can add up to significant resources for your school; *no gift is ever too small to matter*. Your university or college also may invite you to be an alumni volunteer or to serve in some other capacity. Whatever your future circumstances, you'll find many ways both to give back in appreciation of the benefits *you* received and to "pay it forward" to help lift up those countless students yet to come. And these ideas apply to your high school as well. Don't forget to include that important institution in your gratitude and philanthropy!

SUMMING UP—CHAPTER 8

- Having access to a college education places you in a position of significant privilege relative to the majority of people in the US and to an even larger majority of the world's population. With such privilege comes responsibility, both to give back and pay it forward.
- Your campus is a great place to start. It will afford you many opportunities to make a difference for your school. Your contribution can be small or large, but look for a way to do something positive.

- Ask another "big question": What are *you* willing to fight for in the larger world? What "victory for humanity" are you willing to work for? There are so many opportunities here too! You don't need to save the entire world. Just find a place to start.
- No matter how hard we work to accomplish our goals, we never get there alone. Realizing the assistance we've received from others—yet another form of privilege—naturally gives rise to experiencing gratitude. Take a moment to thank those who've been so influential in your life, including your college or university.
- Remember to include your college or university (and your high school) in your philanthropy, and stay involved through volunteering, if you can.

So far, you've been reading a lot of things that might fall into the "yeah-sure-I'll-get-to-that-someday" category. Okay. That's an understandable reaction. But thinking this way can lead to mistakes you might regret later. We'll see what this means in the next chapter, the final one in the student section of this book.

CHAPTER 9

BEGIN NOW!

What you can do, or dream you can, begin it,
Boldness has genius, power, and magic in it...
Begin it, and the work will be completed!
—Johann Wolfgang von Goethe, *Faustus*[108]

M y final challenge to you, as a brand-new college or university student, is the simplest. But it may be the most important of all. So, even if you forget everything else you've read up to now—though I earnestly hope you won't!—please remember this: *Your college career begins the very first day you walk on to your new campus (or take your first remote course), not* next week, *not* next semester, *not* next year. It begins *on that first day!* So, resolve that, when that day comes, *you will commit to begin to take full advantage of these next few precious years of your life. Begin now!*

---

[108] Johann Wolfgang von Goethe, *Faustus: A Dramatic Mystery*, trans. John Anster (London: A. Spottiswoode, New-Street-Square, 1835).

QUESTIONS ABOUT YOU

For one last time, I'll ask you to think ahead to your college graduation. At that moment, the people you care about the most—your parents, friends, respected professors, and coaches; deans of admission in law schools, medical schools, business schools, or graduate schools; potential employers; and many others—will ask how you've spent your undergraduate years. They will want to know what you've made of your opportunities.

Here's just one example of what I'm talking about. When I was an academic dean, part of my job was to fill out recommendation forms for seniors who were applying to graduate or professional schools. Here are some typical questions from the "Dean's Form" portion of a national law school's application:

- Did this student choose demanding courses or less challenging options?
- Was this person ever subject to disciplinary action by the college or university?
- In what ways did this person distinguish themself in their college career?

These questions illustrate the kind of things people will ask about your precious college years. *What will you have to say to them?*

Today, we might find an additional question:

- Are there any embarrassing photos or hurtful (or just plain stupid or nasty) posts by this student on Facebook, Instagram, Snapchat, Twitter, TikTok, or some other social media platform?

The point is that posts you might already have outgrown and even come to regret by the time you graduate will nevertheless be available on the Internet *forever*, to *anyone* who chooses to search your name. *Forever!* So, be smart and protect your online reputation as carefully as you would guard your reputation among people who know you personally. Your decisions can have lifelong implications; make sure they are good ones.

Back to our main question: Four years from now, *what will people read in the personal college narrative you'll be composing through everything you do?* How will the dean of your college or university be able to fill out that "dean's form" for *you*? What will a potential employer who's ready to offer you your dream job uncover among your old social media pages? How will it influence their final decision?

In that spirit, here's one more question to consider. Imagine you are talking with a potential employer—someone who is hiring for a position you'd really like to have. Then imagine that, at the end of the interview, your would-be boss asks,

- "Why should I hire *you*?"

What will you have to say? What will you include in your "elevator speech" to demonstrate how you stand out from all the other applicants being considered?

You could start by highlighting your muscular work ethic, which you've developed through four years of intense academic heavy lifting (in those demanding courses you chose). After that, you should be able to talk in some detail about what you've learned and how those skills and abilities can benefit your future employer. You can describe the cognitive skills you've enhanced in your major. For example, one anthropology grad I've met says, "My major taught me how to understand people."

It's especially compelling if you can point to one or more substantial projects you've completed—especially if you can show

how those projects relate to what you would be doing in your new job. Next, it would be terrific if you can make the case that you've strengthened the key general intellectual skills and abilities that you've added to your intellectual toolkit—which we first talked about all the way back in Chapter 1. The topics we've discussed in this book give you plenty of material to compose a compelling response to your potential employer's question. The same goes for an interview with the dean of admissions at a graduate school, law school, medical school, and so on. But it all depends on how effectively you've used your time.

NO REGRETS

Throughout my entire academic career, I *never once* spoke with a graduating senior who regretted creating a record of significant achievements. *No one* ever expressed remorse over earning Latin honors (graduating *cum laude*, *magna cum laude*, or *summa cum laude*), being named to Phi Beta Kappa (the oldest academic honor society in the US), or receiving some other academic award or honor. I *never* heard a graduating senior say they were sorry about having achieved success in athletics, excelling in performing arts, or facing a difficult choice among multiple offers from graduate schools, law schools, medical schools, business schools, or would-be employers. And to return to the topic of this chapter, in all my years of congratulating seniors as they walked across the commencement stage, no one ever said to me, "I really wish I'd played around more in my freshman year." *No one!*

On the other hand, did I ever talk with seniors who deeply regretted having blown off their first semester (or their first year) of college, who'd wasted that precious time with too much partying, too much alcohol or drugs, and not enough attention to their academic work? Have I known students who became academically disqualified and didn't even make it back for their second semester or their sophomore year? Or could I tell you about students who regretted being suspended or expelled because they committed academic dishonesty or violated some other significant rule in the student code of conduct? Did I ever meet seniors who *just* missed earning a major academic honor, who failed to gain admission to the graduate or professional program they really wanted, or who weren't offered the corporate position they'd tried so hard to get? Students who faced limited post-grad opportunities all because they dug themselves into an academic hole their first year and never managed to climb out of it again? Graduates who would have loved nothing more than to be able to go back and do that first year over again? (Spoiler Alert #2: *You can't!*) You bet I did!

In Chapter 4, I mentioned the "danger zone"—your first six weeks on campus—when new students are most at risk for overuse of alcohol, sexual misconduct, and other such missteps. Sometimes these problems arise in the context of pledging a fraternity or sorority, which I also talked about earlier (in Chapter 4). I'm not denying that fraternities and sororities can offer many benefits. At their best, they foster deep and lasting friendships, provide service to their campus or larger community, and function as important micro-communities, especially within larger universities.

But they can also have serious downsides: Pledging can require so much time (and result in so much lost sleep and other disruptions to your schedule) that your academic performance can be significantly degraded. At the worse extreme, as we saw, illegal hazing has put pledges in situations where they have suffered serious injuries and even death. In response, some schools have banned (some or all) Greek organizations. Many others have moved pledging to the second semester of the first year or, even better, to sophomore year. Deferring this process until those later times helps to remove unneeded distractions from your crucial first term. Fully committing to getting off to a great start in college may require *you* to make the decision to delay pledging on your own. It's certainly something to consider.

If you're thinking about joining a sorority or fraternity—either at the start of your first year or later on—please do so with your eyes wide open to potential problems. And always remember that it's *never* appropriate to abandon your own moral judgment about someone else's actions or your own. So, please do not let your desire to become part of a group—whether it's a Greek organization or any other group, formal or informal—prevent you from doing the right thing. If you find yourself in a situation where you or your peers (for example, your fellow pledges) are being told to engage in humiliating or even potentially life-threatening behavior, most commonly, by consuming dangerous amounts of alcohol in a short time, do the right thing. *Find the courage to say "no."* Too many parents (and even *one* instance is too many!) have had to deal with the death of a child due to illegal hazing. Do not allow yourself or one of your friends to become yet another tragic statistic. And less dramatically, do not allow your first academic year to become a casualty of pledging a Greek organization.

YOUR MANTRA FOR SUCCESS

> *Do the difficult things while they are easy and do the great things while they are small. A journey of a thousand miles must begin with a single step.*
> —*Lao Tzu*

Is it possible to recover from a disastrous first semester in college or other serious trouble you've gotten into? Yes. It's difficult, but it can be done. However, since you're now thinking so purposefully about how to launch your highly successful undergraduate career, *why would you willingly choose to take on such a burden?* It's like starting a Marathon five miles behind everyone else and having to carry a fifty-pound backpack the rest of the way.

Think back to Chapter 2, when we talked at some length about your newfound autonomy. We emphasized how important it is to embrace your new *positive* freedom, take charge of what you do, and especially manage the time you suddenly hold in your own hands. Then think back to Chapter 3, when we talked about how to set inspiring goals—those "no small plans"—for your college years and for the rest of your life. These ideas come together with what I'm now recommending you take as your new mantra: *Begin now! Begin now to embrace your new freedom—to take full charge of your life! Begin now to get your new college journey off to a terrific start. Begin now to lay the foundation for making and then carrying out your "no small plans." Begin now!*

SO WHAT?

The charge to begin now has immediate practical implications for your first few weeks of college. You see, many college classes follow a roughly similar pattern: the first half of a course may be relatively light on work that you have to turn in, while the final weeks of the semester or quarter become more intense. In some classes, your first graded assignment may not come until the midterm; in others, most or all of your grade will depend on a final exam, project, or paper.

Why is this important?

Because it can be all too easy to fall into a sense of comfort and complacency in your early college days. You might feel you have more free time on your hands than you anticipated, and you might begin to think that college really isn't all that tough after all. (Spoiler Alert #3: It will become more demanding each year.) This risk is especially seductive for first-year students who are still learning about the rhythms of a college semester (or quarter).

To begin now means to look past these first impressions—to *not* allow yourself to coast at the start of your first semester or quarter, regardless of the academic demands (or lack of demands) you're feeling at that point. It's far more advisable to get to work right away: Keep up with your course readings and other assignments; if possible, get ahead of them. Read through each course syllabus at the beginning of the class to see what you will be facing later in the term (papers, lab reports, presentations, exams, etc.). Plan (in writing) how (and when!) you'll meet those responsibilities—for example, decide when you'll start working on that first paper. And when you do this, make sure you look at *all* your courses *together*, to see when an assignment for one might overlap with work you have to do in another. As we said in Chapter 3, be intentional about structuring your daily and weekly schedule and managing your time in a purposeful way.

Most of all, I highly recommend getting into the mindset, immediately, that you are here to *explore new things* and discover new ways to learn. What a privilege to have four years as a member of a community of scholars—for "learning among friends," as Kenyon College says! You'll likely never have a comparable opportunity again. So, be *intentionally curious*. Look for something interesting in every class you take, in every lecture, play, or concert you attend, in every conversation you have. If you make that commitment to yourself early on, then how about including it as a part of your personal mission statement?

In short, do not become the person at commencement who wishes they could go back in time and redo their first college semester or quarter or year! Don't burden yourself with a load of regret you'll have to lug across that graduation stage ... and forever after. *Don't squander this precious, once-in-a-lifetime opportunity!* To say all this more positively, *not only embrace your new freedom but also honor all the people in your life who did so much—and who may have sacrificed so much—to give you the privilege of gaining a college education. Honor yourself and your enormous potential!* Immediately start to take the steps we've discussed that will ensure you'll make the most of your own "journey of a thousand miles." *Begin now!*

BEGIN NOW...AGAIN

> *It does not matter how many times you get knocked down, but how many times you get up.*
> —Vince Lombardi

I've been urging you to adopt "begin now!" as your new mantra from the start of your very first college semester or quarter, and I absolutely don't want you to lose sight of that advice. But we've also talked about (in Chapter 6) how your college life will invariably throw you some curves. Some of your plans will not work out as expected. The gnarly wave you try to catch may toss you underwater and leave you gasping for air. Your resolution to get up every morning and take a run collides with last night's late study session, and you're just too darn tired to answer your alarm. You give it your best shot, but you still crash and burn in that challenging class. As I've said, *every* person will inevitably experience failures, small and larger ones, many times throughout their lives.

When you experience a setback, you always have at least two choices: feel sorry for yourself and quit, or pick yourself up and start over. Legendary NFL coach Vince Lombardi certainly knew a lot about getting knocked down. It was an essential aspect of the game he loved and to which he dedicated his life. And it's absolutely part of the game for *you*, as it is for us all. When life knocks you down, you need to get back up.

You can invoke your new mantra on these occasions, too. At that tough moment, you can challenge yourself, once again, to *begin now! To start over, to set a new goal, to chart a new direction, to resolve to be more disciplined in the future, to do whatever it takes to overcome your setback.* It's never too late to learn from your experiences and do what you need to do better the next time around. *In short, it's never too late to begin now!*

LEAVING, LEARNING, AND LIVING

> *I've learned that I still have a lot to learn.*
> —*Maya Angelou*

Even when you've earned your undergraduate degree, you will not have completed your education. Not by a long shot. That's why a college or university graduation is formally called a commencement. Yes, it's certainly an ending to what I hope will be a wonderful time in your life. But even more, it's a new beginning. As I said in the first chapter of this book, you'll always have the opportunity to learn new things throughout your professional life. Moreover, when you graduate you won't have resolved all those "big questions" you've been asking. In fact, if your school has done its job, you'll come away with many more questions than answers. At the same time, you'll have the profound satisfaction of thinking—and, in many ways, of *knowing*—about both yourself and the world in so many fresh, exciting, deeper, and more mature ways.

In short, when you graduate, you absolutely will *not* have all the answers. As Maya Angelou reminds us, *none* of us ever has all the answers, no matter how long we live or how many academic letters we get to list behind our names. In fact, the only people who no longer have questions—who may *believe* they have all the answers—are those who've stopped thinking and learning. One of the saddest sights is someone who has walked away from their natural curiosity. And in today's world, both your career and your personal growth will absolutely stall out if you fail to keep learning. You'll also fall short of meeting your continuing responsibilities as an informed, caring, and responsible citizen.

My challenge to you, therefore, is to carry with you, through commencement and beyond, the basic liberal learning intellectual toolkit we've been talking about since the first chapter—a set of skills, knowledge, and habits of mind that will enable you to continue to learn as long as you live. You'll call upon those capacities in a professional environment that, more than anything else, will be marked by an ever-accelerating rate of change. *Your future success in that professional world will depend enormously on becoming a self-directed, lifelong learner.* But the same is equally true for both your personal life and your civic life. *Stay curious! Embrace the challenge of continuing to learn, now and for the rest of your life.*

ONE LAST GIFT FROM YOUR ALMA MATER

Having completed your time as an undergraduate, you'll be carrying away one additional legacy from your alma mater. Your college or university will have become an important part of your personal identity. I hope, as you go forward, you'll be proud to tell others that you're a graduate of your school. That's certainly been true for me, and the realization of just how much my college experience helped form who I am has only grown over the years. In fact, very few days go by when I don't put on my Notre Dame class ring. It's a constant reminder of the values of the university that launched my own journey into adult life.

The same is true for my most recent school, Skidmore. After we'd been there for a time, the college's alumni association made my wife Marie and me honorary alumni. We now wear our Skidmore class rings frequently—and proudly. Many schools foster a strong sense of identity and belonging, so I hope you'll find it easy to relate to these sentiments regarding your own college or university.

But we're talking about much more than just nostalgia for those good old college days, or any sense of prestige that might be associated with your school's name. Back in Chapter 3, I mentioned said that every college or university has a mission statement, and I encouraged you not only to become familiar with the one at your school but also to craft a personal mission statement of your own. Whenever you think about it, your personal statement should remind you of your highest values and aspirations.

Likewise, your college or university most likely has a short phrase or motto that encapsulates an important core of its mission. I've already cited Notre Dame's question, "What would *you* fight for?" But you also may have seen another phrase that is associated with that university: "Play like a champion today." It's on a sign that hangs outside the home locker room in the football stadium. On their way to taking the playing field before every home game, each member of the football team taps that sign. Many other colleges and universities have similar athletic traditions. The point, of course, is to remind each team member of the standard of excellence they're expected to meet in the coming game.

There are plenty of these statements, and their meaning extends far beyond athletics. We've seen that the motto at Antioch College is "Be ashamed to die until you have won some victory for humanity"; Skidmore says, "Creative Thought Matters." Here's a sample of some others (many of which were originally written in Latin):

- **Amherst College**: Let them give light to the world.
- **Boston College**: Ever to excel.
- **Bryn Mawr College**: I delight in the truth.
- **Champlain College**: Let us dare.
- **Dillard University**: From confidence, courage.
- **Harvard**: Truth.
- **Rensselaer Polytechnic Institute**: Why not change the world?
- **University of Michigan**: Arts, Knowledge, Truth.
- **University of Oregon**: Mind moves mountains.
- **The United States Military Academy at West Point**: Duty, honor, country.
- **Yale University**: Light and truth.

Admittedly, these statements can sound corny to contemporary ears. But you can get past that—especially when the phrase is associated with the college or university you've grown to love.

And in fact, these phrases encapsulate worthy aspirations for us all. So, if you haven't seen them already, I suggest again that you look up your school's mission statement and motto—to see how they express what your college or university is all about, what *it* stands for. And what *you* should stand for too!

This may also sound corny, but each day before I sit down at my desk to write, I find it useful to take just a moment to remind myself that *creative thought matters*; to commit to *playing like a champion*; to try to bring a little more *light and truth* to the world; and to ask *what would I fight for*? These four phrases remind me of ideals I've tried to use in defining who I am—elements taken from schools that have meant so much to me. I also glance at my personal mission statement. Thinking of these things gets me in the right mindset to make my best effort in whatever I'm trying to accomplish in the next few hours.

What would it be like if *you* were to do something similar? To take to heart that sentence or phrase from your own alma mater that expresses its purpose and is intended to inspire its students, faculty, staff, and alumni. We all need occasional reminders of what we're most committed to doing—of what we've determined our life is *for*. Dialing up your school's motto—along with your personal mission statement—can inspire *you* to do your best every day.

SUMMING UP—CHAPTER 9

- The personal narrative you'll write during your time in college starts on day one—not next semester or next year. Your new mantra for success: *Begin now!*
- Thinking about the questions people will ask you when you graduate can help to focus your attention on what's

most important as you launch your new college adventure—and how to avoid regrets later on.

- You can also invoke your new mantra when you experience (inevitable) failures and setbacks. It's never too late to *begin now (again)!*
- When you graduate, you still won't have all the answers—though you should have some more sophisticated questions. Determine to retain your curiosity and set out to be a lifelong learner.
- Cherish the fundamental ideals of your school. Make those values part of your personal mission statement and let them inspire you every day for the rest of your life.

SUMMING UP—PART TWO

That's it! Just eight pretty straightforward steps to become a highly successful college student. Eight ways to get a running start and then stay focused on the finish line throughout your entire undergraduate career:

1. Take charge of your new college life—understand and embrace your new level of positive freedom.
2. Make "no small plans" for your college years and for your post-college life, and commit to doing what it takes to make them real.
3. Take charge of caring for yourself—assume responsibility for your physical well-being.
4. Assume responsibility for your emotional, mental, and spiritual well-being. But don't hesitate to ask for help when you need it.

5. Take good risks—the ones that pay dividends by stretching you intellectually and personally.
6. Do the right thing—live a principled life, respect and care for others, and offer forgiveness when it's called for.
7. Decide what your own "victory for humanity" will be; and don't wait to start on it—practice giving back, paying it forward, and expressing gratitude.
8. Above all, *begin now!* to make the most of your college career, and then continue to be inspired by what you've learned at your alma mater and by its fundamental values.

As you kick off your college journey, taking time to think about these challenges will help keep you on track to becoming a truly free, self-regulating, and highly successful adult human being—as well as a caring, informed, and responsible citizen.

When you take on these challenges, you will recognize—*and respect!*—yourself as someone who truly has embraced your new freedom by taking full advantage of the amazing opportunities your college or university offers. Someone who is preparing to navigate the ever-changing waters of today's professional world. Someone who is committed to leaving the human community a better place than they found it. Above all, someone who will be fully prepared to take the next step in your life—whatever *you* decide it will be.

The final part of this book continues our conversation but now with a focus on your parents. The remaining two chapters talk about their continuing role in your college life—presenting some ideas about how together you can use your college years to lay a foundation for an even more satisfying grownup relationship with then in the decades to come.

So, I'll ask that you share the next part of this book with your parents. But it's okay for you to read it too; in fact, I encourage you to do so.

PART THREE

FOR PARENTS, AN IMPORTANT
SUPPORTING ROLE

CHAPTER 10
PARTNERING AND EMPOWERING

Whatever they grow up to be, they are still our children,
and the one most important of all things we can give to
them is unconditional love. Not a love that depends on
anything at all except that they are our children.
—Rosaleen Dickson

So far, we've been focused on the college student's experience, and so, in the preceding chapters, "you" and "your" have primarily referred to them. Now, in these final two chapters, these words will (mostly) shift to denote *you*, their parents, as we talk about the college years from *your* perspective. I would ask you to approach this part of the book as a parent-to-parent conversation. As I said in the Introduction and as you'll see again a few pages from now, I've been through this experience too—not just as a college professor and administrator but also as the father of two college graduates.

I'll start by assuming you've already read what I've said in the pages addressed to your student. If not, I would again encourage you to do so. When I gave the talks that prompted this book, parents often commented that they heard echoes of things they had been saying to their kids all along. They also said it was useful for their child to hear these ideas from someone who's *not* their parent. So, the high bid is that the earlier chapters have included some familiar themes that led you to feel that we are on the same page. I hope you were heartened to have those aspects of your parenting reinforced in another voice. Those chapters also contain information that's potentially helpful to you, as your child begins their college journey.

Whether you're a veteran college parent or all of this seems quite unfamiliar, you still have many more years of life experience than your child—and, consequently, a greater store of wisdom to draw upon. Accordingly, there are only two chapters for you. They aim to help *you* survive the next few years on good terms with your student, with their university or college, and with yourself. They suggest ways you can contribute to making your student's undergraduate career productive and fulfilling and making commencement a moment of genuine celebration for them, for you, and for everyone else who cares for them so much.

YOU STILL MATTER...A LOT!

Your child's developmental arc through their high school years has been preparing everyone for them to leave home. If your experience has been at all typical, this time has been marked by many mixed emotions—on your part and your student's. There's probably been some friction, at least from time to time. On many days, no doubt, you were very ready for them to fly the nest ("You have two choices: either go off to college or I'll have to strangle you!"), while on other days you (and they) couldn't quite bear the thought of them leaving. All of this is pretty normal, of course, just part of the deal in parenting a teenager.

As you and your student have discussed their choice of a college or university, you may have realized some unexpected dividends. To the extent that you've been involved in that process, it's likely helped both you and your student begin exploring their life goals and considering how various schools might best help to achieve them. Road trips to visit prospective colleges or universities can also provide some powerful moments of parent-child bonding. Together, these shared experiences should have helped everyone begin to feel that the impending departure really is going to happen—that your student is ready to let go of the trapeze. More than anything, I hope that throughout this process, your child has continued to feel your love and support. In the best of all possible worlds, they've even paused to express some appreciation for everything *you've* done for them so far. Hope springs eternal!

Whatever the nature of your relationship with your prospective college student, let me assure you that, even though things will change as they head off to campus, your connection will remain an extremely important one for both you and them—now and in all the years to come. But at this point, as they make this next big step from late adolescence to early adulthood, your relationship needs to take on a different shape. This may seem an obvious point. But it's useful to be intentional in coming to terms with it. So, I hope the following pages will help you get your mind around the changes that inevitably will be taking place.

Nevertheless, your new college student's enhanced level of autonomy, which I've been emphasizing throughout the preceding chapters, does not at all mean their life will suddenly become totally separate from yours—regardless of how far away their college or university may be from your home or how removed their new situation may feel. Everyone needs support, advice, and encouragement, no matter where we are on our life's odyssey. And contrary to all available evidence, your student still places an enormous value on *your* opinion and, yes, on your *approval*—even if they seldom get around to admitting it. Holding on to this belief, especially in moments when it might not seem so evident, can encourage you in your still-important role as a partner in your kid's college experience.

STAYING IN TOUCH

One positive aspect of contemporary life is that there are so many ways for parents and their new college student to stay connected. Cell phones, texts, email (which, admittedly, a lot of young people feel is *way* too out-of-date), and various social media platforms combined with real-time visual options such as FaceTime and Zoom make it pretty easy to remain in touch and aware of what's going on, on both sides of the relationship. Call me crazy, but the possibility of actually exchanging written cards or letters is still in the mix as well.

The electronic platforms present creative opportunities that we simply didn't have even a few years back. For example, during the COVID-19 lockdown, one mother I know formed the habit of sitting down to an occasional afternoon tea with her daughter—sharing conversation and their choice of teas and enjoying their favorite matching mugs. When the daughter went away to college, they continued this new tradition with scheduled weekly afternoon Zoom-teas. They caught up in a resonant and familiar way; they still enjoyed their choice of teas in the same matching mugs; and the visual connection also allowed the daughter to check in on the family dogs. This small ritual was fun and worked for them. But there are myriad variations on this theme that you could imagine and explore with your student.

It's certainly possible to overdo all this connectivity, of course. Too much of a good thing really can be too much, and we'll return to this theme in the next chapter. But for now, let's just celebrate the fact that options for communication are significantly less limited today than even a few years ago.

LISTENING AND SUPPORTING

Both at the start of their college years and later on, *please talk with your student about how their "no small plans"* (which we discussed in Chapter 3) *are coming together.* You need to give your student the emotional space to begin formulating those ideas, and it's very helpful to remember that this process can take a long time—sometimes years—and that it's not always linear. But it can be enormously important for parents to offer their encouragement and continuing support. This becomes especially true if your student is beginning to envision a future for themselves that looks quite different from anything they—or you!—might have imagined before.

So, if your student chooses to bounce some ideas off you, terrific! Try to approach those discussions as brainstorming sessions: it's fine to raise a few questions (for example, "Have you thought about…?"), but it's definitely *not* the time to be judgmental or to rule anything out (no matter how farfetched an idea might seem). Keep reminding yourself that your student is just exploring *possibilities*. There's a long way to go before they'll be ready to *act* on them—a lot of time left for them to change their mind. Ideally, you can be a great source of questions for them to consider and even, possibly, some advice (e.g., if you're considering *x*, then it probably would be a good idea to think about doing *y* and *z*). But in the end, your student needs to own their plans and decide how to make them real. So, give them room to construct their own big dreams.

Here's a powerful question for all of us parents: *What could this amazing young person do, if they were absolutely convinced they have our total, unconditional love, support, and commitment?* We should never pass on an opportunity to assure our kids that we have their back and that we're confident in their ability to envision and then realize their big dreams, however crazy they might sound to us.

TWO KEY MESSAGES

Next, it's helpful for parents *to reinforce the dual message that (1) college is a once-in-a-lifetime opportunity and (2) it really is a full-time job for a student, with academic work at its center.* It's good for parents to keep these priorities in mind as well. Many students will have other obligations, including the need to earn a portion of the money to finance their education. Those responsibilities certainly are important and can often mean the difference between a student's being able to go to college or not. I get it. And I absolutely honor both the student who has to work extra hours to earn those necessary funds and the family that has to sacrifice financially (and otherwise) to make the college opportunity possible. Making it all work out can be a huge undertaking. But anything parents can do to keep this burden from becoming excessive—from hindering the student's ability to succeed at their *primary* academic job—will be beneficial. So, please encourage your student to maintain their focus on what's most important.

This could turn out to be more of an issue if your child will continue to live at home. In that situation, everyone should try to be mindful of the new college student's need for some physical and psychological space to concentrate on their academic work. With a stay-at-home student, college might feel, to a parent, like it's just an extension of high school. But the reality is very different. A new college student will be facing unfamiliar academic demands, an increased workload, and a higher level of personal responsibility for meeting those new requirements. So, whenever possible, please do have a frank conversation about their needs and be as generous as you can in minimizing requests for your student to perform other tasks (for example, helping to care for siblings).

As I've already observed, a successful college career requires commitment and, often, some level of sacrifice from *both* students and parents. It is absolutely a team effort—a genuine partnership. But at this point, you'll most likely need to negotiate a new "contract" about who's going to be doing what. It may sound clichéd, but it's nonetheless true: *each side in this negotiation will likely have to compromise.* Sorting out differing family expectations—and sometimes dicey conversations about those expectations—are often part of this new beginning. We'll return to the idea of the parent-student "contract" in Chapter 11.

Of course, college should also be fun for your student—not just work all the time. Ideally, there should be room for a social life, clubs, varsity or intramural sports or other fitness activities, and so many other things that can enrich an undergraduate experience and contribute to the personal development that also is such an important priority in the college years. But, as I've already said to your student, they need to keep all these aspects of their college life in balance. Parents, if you want your child to get everything they can out of this time—and, dare I say, everything *you* are paying for, or at least helping to pay for—there needs to be a high level of focus, on their part, on their primary academic work, along with a comparable level of understanding from you about what counts the most. You can help them maintain that focus.

Toward that end, here's another question you can ask your child anytime you speak with them: *What have you done today that makes you proud?* It's all about encouraging them to keep their eyes on the prize.

CONNECTING WITH OTHER PARENTS

Another great way for parents to make the college experience more enjoyable, for you *and* your child, is to *connect with other parents*. There are many ways to do this. If your student plays a varsity sport, you already have a ready-made community with other team parents, as you know from your earlier experience. But even if your student is not involved in athletics, there are many other ways to make those contacts. Just as in high school, there often are informal parent groups associated the team-like activities your student may be involved in. And you will certainly meet parents of their closest friends, roommates, or housemates. Eventually, you may encounter parents of their fellow majors, but that's probably a few years away. In any event, you can ask your student to introduce you to their friends' parents when you visit. There may be opportunities to share a meal or attend a campus activity, and that, too, will give you some sense of how your student is spending their time.

Many colleges and universities today sponsor parent organizations that hold events to put parents in touch with school administrators, professors, and staff members. If that's an option at your student's school, you might consider participating. It's a great way to find out what's going on without having to bug your student too much about it. And it's one more way to meet other parents.

Be aware, however, that these organizations are frequently connected to fundraising. So, there might be a request for a donation—an *optional* one—somewhere down the line. As I said to your student in Chapter 8, it's useful to understand that even the full comprehensive fee charged by a college or university, however much it may be, covers only a fraction of the cost of a year of education. (These ratios differ at different institutions.) Schools depend on proceeds from their endowment, other sources of revenue, and fundraising to close that gap.

When I was a president, I especially valued donations from parents who were grateful for their students' experience because their generosity strongly indicated that the college was doing something right with regard to their children. If you regularly engage in philanthropy, it would be wonderful to include your student's school in your giving. But even so, *no parent should feel pressure to contribute anything beyond what you already are providing in tuition and fees.* As I said, any donations should be *optional.*

A WINDOW INTO YOUR STUDENT'S NEW ACADEMIC WORLD

Here's another idea that may seem obvious, but even so, it's one that can be enriching and fun for both students and parents: *talk with them about their classes.* But don't just settle for "Yeah, they're fine." Or "They're going OK." (I realize that, if your student is a male, those sentences may well count as fully expressed thoughts.)

Ask them which course is their favorite, then see if they're willing to share a copy of that syllabus. Talk through it with them. And don't be afraid to ask if there's a course they're struggling with or don't particularly like. It can be informative to hear about those experiences as well—especially if you can get them to say more about *why* they're feeling especially challenged. Ask if there's some topic or reading that they find particularly interesting—something you all can talk about. Perhaps your student can send that reading to you electronically. Or maybe you already have that book or can get your hands on it from a local library. Sharing a reading experience can create a ready-made topic of conversation for the next time you get together.

You can do the same with a paper or class assignment your student has completed—ideally one they're especially proud of. Ask them to share a copy with you and talk about it with them. They might need to explain it to you—after all, *they* are taking the course, not *you*, and the subject may be unfamiliar. But it can be fun to have them to teach *you* something for a change! However it works out, it's an opportunity for everyone to expand their horizons. So, take advantage of the fact that it's easy (and basically cost-free) to exchange many of these materials electronically.

These suggestions all represent potential conversation-starters for when a student returns home for breaks in the academic year. They're also a great way for parents to get a "twofer" out of the enterprise: to actively share, to learn from, and to enjoy some part of your student's new college academic life.

BE PREPARED FOR INTELLECTUAL CHANGE

Education draws out the uniqueness of people to be
all that they can be in the light of their irreducible
singularity. It is the maturation and cultivation of
spiritually intact and morally equipped human beings.
—Cornel West and Jeremy Tate[109]

For a first-time student, heading off to college is like crossing the frontier into a strange new land—to an unaccustomed social community and a realm of unfamiliar ideas with novel intellectual challenges. It can be disorienting if not overwhelming at first, and most students need some time to adjust. For parents, your job is to give them the time, emotional space, and encouragement *to accomplish that work on their own.*

Earlier in Chapter 6, I invited your student to entertain some of the perennial "big questions" that people have wrestled with for centuries. *Please encourage them to do this as well. But then be prepared for the intellectual changes—the dislocation, discomfort, sometimes even the alienation—that might follow.* You may well see signs of this in their very first term (maybe during a first visit home): your student exploring some unfamiliar ideas and trying potential new beliefs on for size, maybe even some ideas you find a bit disturbing. The transformation from high school student to college student can be striking. Young people can alter what they believe, how they view the world, and how they regard themselves.

If you see these kinds of changes taking place, it doesn't mean that your child has found yet another way to rebel against your influence. (It's really *not* about you!) It probably means that both

---

109   Cornel West and Jeremy Tate, "Howard University's Removal of Classics is a Spiritual Catastrophe," *Washington Post*, April 19, 2021, https://www. washingtonpost.com/opinions/2021/04/19/cornel-west-howard-classics/.

your student and their college or university are doing their jobs. College students should be exposed to ideas they've never considered before, and it can take them a while to navigate those previously unexplored conceptual landscapes.

This doesn't mean they'll totally change their minds about what they've believed in the past—much less abandon the basic values you've worked so hard to instill in them over the years. In fact, they may actually end up appreciating and reaffirming those longstanding beliefs and values, though ideally in a more sophisticated and nuanced way. Also, just because they're attracted to some new idea today, it's by no means inevitable that they'll still embrace it tomorrow. But they do need the latitude to find their way through those regions of thought that will broaden their intellect. So, please be patient with them as they take their initial steps on this journey.

A course of undergraduate studies truly is an odyssey, and students do change along the way, often profoundly. There is a reason that the conventional age of a first-year student, in most of the world and across most of history, is eighteen or nineteen. This moment represents the start of adulthood, and the "coming-of-age" narrative about college students is real. In the years between now and commencement, they will likely develop more profoundly—both cognitively and psychologically—than at any other time in their lives. A second-year student is significantly unlike a first-year, and both are very different from a senior. It's remarkable how much intellectual and personal maturity students gain across their undergraduate years, provided they take the job of being a student seriously.

Watching this all happen, as a parent, can be enormously rewarding. It can also be a bit unsettling, to see these changes in someone you have nurtured for so long, know so well, and still love so dearly. This can be especially true if you personally are unfamiliar with what your student is experiencing in their new college life. But this transition can be disruptive for *any* family, regardless of the parents' educational background or previous experience. Just like *any* stage of parenting, parent-child relations in the college years can lead to frustration, on *both* sides of the table. The best strategy is to anticipate that these episodes might happen and then work through them with love and good will. Forewarned is forearmed. Try to keep in mind what I said above in Chapter 1: at its best, a college education is intended to teach students *to think for themselves*. And they sometimes will start to do this in ways that can seem unfamiliar, perplexing, and even challenging to their parents. But in the end, creating this capacity for critical and independent thought is a major goal of a course of undergraduate studies. *Your* job is to keep the lines of communication open.

EXPECT THEM TO CHANGE DIRECTION

To continue with this theme: *be prepared for a new student to change their mind about what they want to do, both in college and afterward.* For most students, this is a natural part of the developmental process. For parents, it helps to remind ourselves that it's not possible to know, in advance, just where this journey will lead, and that *the best plans*—the ones that stand the best chance of coming to fruition—ultimately, are *the ones students create for themselves.*

Jason's Story

> When my wife Marie and I sent our son Jason off to college, he was purposeful about three goals: he wanted to attend a school with strong

academic programs, he wanted to play football, and he wanted to go into any field other than medicine. (He was very clear—and vocal— about all these ideas, but especially about that last point; initially, he thought he wanted to become an architect.) As things worked out, Jason attended an Ivy League university, he played football for four years, and he ultimately decided to major in history. But by the end of his sophomore year, his "no small plans" for his life had shifted dramatically.

He decided he wanted to become a physician after all, despite his earlier aversion to that career path. After graduating with his history major (having written his senior thesis on the development of American medicine during the Civil War), he did a post-graduate year of studies back home with us at the University of Redlands to complete the pre-med science requirements he was unable to finish in college (because of his relatively late decision to go that route).

Next, he spent a year in an internship at a New York City teaching hospital. He then attended medical school, did a residency in surgery, completed three years of research in a stem-cell lab, and finally completed his studies with a three-and-one-half-year cardiothoracic surgery fellowship back in New York City.

Yes, Jason's medical training took forever! But he persisted, and it was totally worth it for him. Today he is an attending physician—a practicing cardiothoracic surgeon—and an associate professor in a major university medical school with its own teaching hospital. You just never know.

Elizabeth's Story

In high school, our daughter Elizabeth was decidedly an academic "late-bloomer." But she eventually found inspiration on her school's speech and debate team, in its outstanding theater program, in an AP American History class, and on the water polo team. In college, at a strong liberal arts university on the West Coast, she continued to play water polo and was named a team captain as a senior. Initially, she thought she would study either theater or government. But pretty early on, she too changed her mind and set her sights on becoming a filmmaker. She built a solid liberal arts foundation and graduated as a communications and film studies major.

Liz then set off for Los Angeles. Breaking into the film industry is hard for anyone. Her first job was in the mailroom of a major talent agency (still a typical way for aspiring filmmakers to begin), and she felt very fortunate to have landed it! Then, through a number of promotions and job changes across the kind of unpredictable (and impoverished!) apprenticeship that is so common in Hollywood, she developed her own vision of the work that suited her best (producing) and the type of films she specifically wanted to make (edgy treatments of timely themes).

After several years and a couple of lucky breaks, she ended up in the movie production company of her dreams, Fox Searchlight. There she worked on a number of exciting films—including *Slumdog Millionaire*, which won the Academy Award for Best Picture. Her journey continued after that, and she landed her next job as an associate producer on a film she really believed in, working with some emerging young filmmakers (including an aspiring actress named Greta Gerwig). At no point was any of this easy for her. And it was never totally clear how it would all work out. But, in the end, it made her incredibly happy to experience several successes in pursuing her dreams.

Tragically, Liz passed away at far too early an age. She was taken from us only ten years after her college graduation by a medical condition—type 1 diabetes—that she contracted in her senior year of college. But she had followed her passion and packed an enormous amount of life into each of the too few years allotted to her. There was so much more she had wanted to do. But she took tremendous delight and satisfaction in everything she had been able to accomplish.

Liz followed a path we might not have encouraged at first, though we take comfort now in the firm conviction that it turned out to be absolutely the right one for her. Her narrative came to a distressing and premature end, though no more so than the stories so many other parents, sadly, could tell.

We continue to honor and cherish Elizabeth's memory every single day—sometimes with tears, more often with pride and joy. Realizing she was able to pursue the "no small plans" she created for herself, and that meant so much to her, continues to provide us solace even in the face of such a profound loss.

**

These two tales of revised plans, altered directions, and turns of fortune are hardly unique—especially today, when there is such fluidity in the professional world—and so many graduates will find themselves doing things they'd never even considered just a few years earlier. Indeed, many college students will change their minds and shift directions—oftentimes, more than once. Others will remain laser-focused on a goal they set early on. But either way, their undergraduate careers need to prepare them not just for the launch into the next stage of their lives after college but also for the many chapters to follow, especially those they can't even begin to imagine when they graduate. Each of our own children certainly came to appreciate the various ways their liberal educations positioned them to be successful across all the dimensions of their post-college lives.

For parents, as your student goes through this process, *your job is to continue loving them—and to listen, listen, listen, encourage them, offer advice (when asked!), support them in all the ways you can, then listen, listen, and listen some more.* Try not to judge. Let them experiment with new ideas, new ways of being themselves, and most importantly with their own "no small plans" for their college career and their life beyond. *Trust them. Trust their school. And above all, trust the foundation you've given them for everything they are doing now.* You will all get through it.

LET THEM CHOOSE THEIR MAJOR, BUT ENCOURAGE THEM TO STUDY BROADLY

For these and many other reasons, as I first discussed in Chapter 1, it's enormously important for students to select a course of study—a major, a combination of majors, a major and a minor, whatever—based on *their* interests. Or, even better, on a *passion* for some field of learning they've discovered. *Not* on someone else's ideas about what they should become. Not even yours! *You'll be doing your student a major service if you give them the freedom, encouragement, and support to make these decisions driven by their own best judgment.*

As I also explained in Chapter 1, in our complicated and ever-changing world, a solid grounding in liberal learning, combined with virtually *any* major, represents the best possible foundation for a lifetime of professional success, personal flourishing, and responsible citizenship. *Which particular major they choose really matters less than you might think.* Most students, in fact, go on to do something more or less removed—often, something entirely different—from what they studied in college. (A 2013 study found that less than 30 percent of college grads were doing something related to their major. A more recent study by the Federal Reserve Bank of New York suggests that this figure has remained largely unchanged.[110]) Moreover, and this is the most important point, the *narrower* a field of study, the *shorter* its useful life in today's professional environment.

Having said all this however, I want to make a special pitch for encouraging your student to include at least one or two courses in the physical, biological, or mathematical sciences (including computer science) somewhere in their academic program—even if it is not required at their school. There are all kinds of strong reasons to major in a science these days. If a student is so inclined, that's great! But some experience with college-level science should be a component in *any* program of studies, regardless of a student's major.

An art history major's story

Not long ago, I heard about a graduate from a highly regarded national liberal arts college who majored in art history and is presently working as a curator in an art museum. His alma mater did not have a general education science requirement, and so he avoided taking any science classes as an undergraduate. But he recently commented to his parents that he wished he had elected some science courses, because he would have been better positioned to understand the

---

110 Brad Plumer, "Only 27 percent of college grads have a job related to their major," *Washington Post*, May 20, 2013, https://www.washingtonpost.com/news/wonk/wp/2013/05/20/only-27-percent-of-college-grads-have-a-job-related-to-their-major/. The more recent study is "The Labor Market for Recent College Graduates," The Federal Reserve Bank of New York, November 8, 2023, https://www.newyorkfed.org/research/college labor market#--:explore:unemployment.

fine points of maintaining and preserving art-
works—a process he's responsible for managing
in his current position.

***

As this story illustrates, taking one or more science classes along
the way, whether required or not, can turn out to be enormously
helpful down the line, even if it may not seem that way at the time
to a student. Exposure to science helps broaden their conceptual
horizons, and there are many ways for it to be useful in both their
professional life and certainly—in an era when so many public
policy issues have important scientific dimensions—in their role
as an informed, responsible citizen.

Next, let me put in a word for the humanities, the social sciences, and the arts. Today, fewer students are majoring in these
areas than in the past. Parents sometimes fear that such academic
programs do not prepare their students for success in the job market. In some cases, elected political leaders try to score cheap rhe-
torical points by disparaging such majors as "useless"—i.e., unval-
ued in the job market—and even threatening to defund them in
state colleges and universities.

True, those fields may not always relate directly or obviously
to a *first* post-college job. But this impression can also be misleading. (For example, federal and state governments employ surprisingly large numbers of archeology and anthropology majors.)
Moreover, studies have shown that, later in their careers, graduates who have majored in these disciplines tend to catch up with
and ultimately *surpass* people who elected more narrowly focused
undergraduate programs—whether we're talking about positions
attained or salaries. Indeed, humanities, social sciences, and arts

majors are actually *overrepresented* in the ranks of highly success-ful business CEOs.

To cite another interesting data point, medical schools now tend to favor humanities graduates (who also have completed the science prerequisites, of course) over science majors because they tend to relate better to their patients, making them more effective physicians. There are research studies that support this idea. And this preference certainly helped our son gain admission to medi-cal school in a highly competitive field. As just one more exam-ple of what I'm talking about, consider Ted Turner, the founder of CNN, who pretty much invented the cable news industry and clearly enjoyed a successful business career. As an undergrad, Turner started as a classics major before switching to econom-ics. The point is that there are *many* pathways to professional accomplishment.

Beyond such job-related considerations, the arts, humanities, and social sciences are important because they speak to essential dimensions of the human spirit. Their contributions to a life of human flourishing retain their value—and in fact, often become increasingly appreciated—long after graduation. They also play important roles in cultivating the capacities for empathy and understanding others (even when they present as "different") that are essential to good citizenship.

THINKING ABOUT YOUR STUDENT'S CUIRRICULAR CHOICES

My larger plea is to resist the understandable impulse to see a col-lege education in purely transactional terms, as merely a means to an end—specifically as just a way to land a well-paying job. It should have this benefit, of course; that outcome is undeniably important. But an undergraduate degree is so much more than a ticket to a particular employment track. Indeed, for it to be worth the time, effort, and expense, it needs to position a graduate to meet the broadest possible range of future challenges.

But even in purely professional terms, to repeat what I've said several times already: in ten to twenty years, today's graduates may be working in fields that had not even been invented when they were in college. On average, they will experience *nine* different careers in their professional lifetimes—not nine *jobs*, nine different *careers*! This is a fact of the modern professional world. It means that *flexibility of mind*, a *creative imagination*, the ability to *draw upon knowledge and information from a variety of disciplines*, and most of all *the capacity to continue to learn* are some of the most valuable attributes one can take away from an undergraduate education.

Equipped with the range of skills outlined earlier in Chapter 1 and a willingness to acquire the more specialized knowledge required in the professional field(s) of their choosing, a college graduate should be prepared to succeed in virtually any line of work. Sure, they may need to pursue additional training or post-graduate studies at some point in their professional life. But a broad and rich undergraduate experience will best equip them to succeed in doing so.

For several decades, the American Association of Colleges and Universities (AAC&U), has sponsored extensive research surveying the heads of large and small companies (regional, national, and global ones) about what skills they value most and therefore seek in new employees. Those of us in the academy were not surprised that the views of these employers align remarkably well with the liberal arts learning outcomes outlined in Chapter 1 and that I've been promoting throughout this book. The business leaders surveyed reported that they highly regard skills such as *clear writing* and *effective expression*; the *ability to work in teams*; *critical thinking*; the *capacity to analyze, interpret, and synthesize data*; *creative thinking*; and *the ability to communicate and work with people from different cultural backgrounds*, among others. And they look for those skills in the people they want to hire.[111]

Finally, if you're still not convinced that a student's best course of study is the one that most inspires their interest and catalyzes their energy, please consider this: research has shown that *students do measurably better, not only in college but in their lives after college, when they pursue a major they really want to study*. This research surveyed students at a variety of institutions, including the US military academies.

More generally, psychological studies have demonstrated time and again that intrinsic—internal—motivation is much more powerful than extrinsic—external—motivation. So, *please resist the urge to impose any preconceived ideas upon your student about their choice of major, even if what they select might not make much sense to you at the time. And please don't pressure them to choose a degree path simply because it appears to offer immediate job prospects after they graduate.*

Certainly, if a professional or pre-professional field sparks their interest—or better, their *passion*—they should go for it! But no student should be *defensive* in choosing a major. That is, they should *not* select one just because they—or you, as a parent—might be fearful about their immediate job prospects after college. There simply is no straight-line path from most undergrad majors to success in today's professional world. The broader and

---

111   The AAC&U recently repeated that survey, and the new results were consistent with the earlier ones. See Colleen Flaherty, "What Employers Want," *Inside Higher Education*, April 6, 2021, https://www.insidehighered.com/news/2021/04/06/aacu-survey-finds-employers-want-candidates-liberal-arts-skills-cite-preparedness.

deeper the intellectual skillset students gain in college, the greater their chances for professional success in the future. *In short, your best course is to empower and support your student to trust their instincts and interests in guiding them to the best path through their undergraduate years and into their life beyond.*

SUMMING UP—CHAPTER 10

- Whether or not they show it, your new college or university student still cares about your opinion very much. You still matter a lot! The most important thing you can do for them is to give them your unconditional love and support.
- This moment also represents an inflection point in your relationship with your child—an opportunity for you to develop, with them, a new partnership in which they play more of a leading role. It can be helpful to connect with other college parents who are going through the same process.
- I encourage you to talk with your student about what they're studying, learning, and thinking. But your emphasis should be on *listening*. It's a terrific idea to read something they are studying that interests them and ask then to share some work that they are especially proud of.
- Be prepared for some disruption—new ways of thinking, new ideas they are exploring, and so on. And don't be surprised when they change their mind (sometimes again and again).
- Encourage them to study broadly—to develop the intellectual toolkit we talked about in Chapter 1, but let *them* choose a major that excites their interest.

We've been talking about your student's choices regarding their course of studies and other life decisions. But what about *you*? What about issues *you* may encounter as a college parent—especially when things might seem to be going wrong with your student or, more generally, about letting go? We'll consider these topics in the next and final chapter.

CHAPTER 11
LETTING GO

I believe the light that shines on you will shine on you forever.
And though I can't guarantee there's nothing
scary hiding under your bed,
I'm gonna stand guard like a postcard of a golden retriever
And never leave 'til I leave you with a sweet dream in your head.
—*Paul Simon*[112]

Starting with the very first paragraph of the Introduction, nearly everything I've said in this book has been about letting go of the old and embracing the new. In a sentence, the whole purpose of letting go of the familiar is to connect with something even better. For the new college student, it's time to let go of beliefs about the world and attitudes about who they are that were appropriate for someone at earlier stages of life. But no longer. In going to college, they should expect to be challenged to embrace a higher and richer understanding of all those

---

[112] Paul Simon, "Father and Daughter," track 11 on *Surprise*, Warner Bros, 2006.

things—starting with unaccustomed levels of autonomy and personal responsibility.

There's another element of letting go that also has been implicit all along, but now needs to be brought forward to center stage. It's the final and most poignant challenge for both students and parents. For everyone involved, the challenge is to let go of your familiar and more or less comfortable relationship and reshape it into something new and untried, yet rich in promise.

PARENTING'S CENTRAL DILEMMA

> *You'll fly away. But take my hand until that day.*
> —*Dar Williams*[113]

For parents, this can be the tough one. So, let's talk about it directly and frankly, parent-to-parent. Since your child first entered your life, you've been living with an acute dilemma at the heart of parenting: At the beginning of that journey, when you initially came face-to-face with that precious and vulnerable tiny person, you were genetically predisposed to respond with a kind of overwhelming love most of us could never have imagined before that instant. The profound emotions that nearly every parent experiences with a new child usually include a powerful recognition of just how defenseless this small human being is, and how totally dependent they are upon *you* to care, nurture, and protect them from harm.

Realizing the fragility of this tiny person—who eventually will have to go out into that sometimes harsh and heartless world, whose potential threats and tribulations parents understand all

---

[113] Dar Williams, "The One Who Knows," track 6 on *The Beauty of the Rain*, Razor & Tie, 2003.

too well—is, I believe, a critical foundation of *moral reasoning.* In a deep and visceral way, parenthood enables us to see with brand new eyes and care with a brand new sensibility about not only our own children but also our fellow human beings and the world we inhabit together. This experience can lead to sometimes new and unfamiliar value judgments about the world our children eventually will inherit—about how we want it to operate and how we want other people to behave.

On the one hand, most parents would aspire for that world to be fair, equitable, and sustainable—a place in which this young person you love unconditionally and without reservation will be able not just to survive but to thrive. A world that enables them to fulfill their potential and pursue a life of full human flourishing. Not a world that threatens their safety or places obstacles in their path. This is the first horn of the parenting dilemma: *the natural desire and responsibility of parents to protect their children at all costs*—not only by providing what they need immediately but also by imagining a world for them to live in that may be substantially different from the one we all actually inhabit.

On the other hand, and this is the second horn of the dilemma, in becoming a parent you also have taken on the project of *preparing that fragile young creature to develop their own capacity to leave your protection at some point in the distant future,* to make their own way in our imperfect world. Accordingly, effective parents realize early on that they *cannot* give in to the urge to encase their child in Bubble Wrap. Getting dirty, falling off a bike, skinning knees, learning up close and personal how to deal with bullies and other nasty people, climbing trees, falling out of trees, and perhaps even breaking a bone or two along the way are all things that happen in a normal, healthy childhood—one that teaches young people to pick themselves up when life knocks them down.

Ditto for the intellectual "skinned knees" they are likely to receive in school. Grit, resilience, and emotional agility are three of the most important lessons we need to teach our children. But admittedly, they also can be incredibly difficult to impart.

This double-sided mission of parenting—needing (and wanting!) to protect your child while, at the same time, preparing them to function as an autonomous person in a sometimes-hostile world—can occasionally leave any parent conflicted, dazed, and confused. This may well be even more the case today than in the past. Now it seems that everyone expects us to be *perfect parents raising perfect children*.

Popular culture tells us at every turn that, as parents, we dare not allow the slightest harm to befall our precious offspring. We face tremendous pressure to schedule their every minute, to fill their calendars with experiences that will prepare them for the future (not to mention enhancing their college-admission résumés). Above all, it can seem like we're expected to insulate them from failure. Nevertheless, at the same time, we also need to be getting that child ready to walk out our front door forever, to make their own decisions and solve their own problems. All the while loving them more every day (well, at least *most* days) and sometimes wanting nothing more than to hold them close.

Our charge as parents, therefore, is to turn this parenting dilemma into a dialectic: to chart a direction that honors each set of legitimate-but-competing demands, by coming up with a *synthesis* that (somehow) balances both sides of this equation. I don't have to tell you it's not easy. The difficult truth, which you no doubt know very well, is that there is no hard-and-fast formula for doing this—there's no parenting algorithm. You might even say that parenting is just another of those wicked problems we discussed in Chapter 1. Nobody can give us the rules that guarantee how to find that virtuous mean between the two unhappy extremes. Nevertheless, there are many voices out there telling us that this or that is the *one, true method for effective parenting.*

But children, parents, and families are unique in so many ways. One size (of parenting) absolutely does *not* fit all! Reassuringly, the *New York Times* columnist Jessica Grose writes that

> Having read parenting literature for years, having seen trends come and go and having witnessed the individuality of my own kids and their peers and the differences in their family situations, I'm confident that there are numerous ways to raise thriving kids without cleaving precisely to one parenting dogma.[114]

Indeed, the best most of us can do, most of the time, is to steer a zig-zag course between those two extremes I've identified. It's like tacking a sailboat into the wind. The important thing is to keep making headway toward that far harbor on the distant shore. In the process, we have to depend upon our own experience and judgment, maybe the occasional article or book that speaks to us, and the wisdom of our family and friends who have sailed these waters before us. We also need to expect that not everything will always go as planned.

---

[114] Jessica Grose, "I'll Say It Again: There's More Than One Way To Raise Kids Who Thrive," *New York Times,* March 9, 2022, https://www.nytimes.com/2022/03/09/opinion/tiktok-parenting-philosophy.html.

PARENTING'S GREAT TEMPTATION

Sometimes love means letting go when you want to hold on tighter.
—*Melissa Marr*

As we've worked our way through this complex assignment, most of us have probably happened upon a parent-child moment that seemed just perfect, one we were tempted to fasten on forever. MIT physicist Dr. Alan Lightman has written a wonderfully creative small book, *Einstein's Dreams*. In each chapter, he imagines a possible world in which time works differently from the way we actually experience it. In one world, time is circular—endlessly repeating; in another, time moves backward; in yet another, time has ceased to "flow" at all. In this unchanging world,

> Raindrops hang motionless in the air. Pendulums of clocks float mid-swing. Dogs raise their muzzles in silent howls. Pedestrians are frozen on the dusty streets, their legs cocked as if held by strings...

> And so, at the place where time stands still, one sees parents clutching their children, in a frozen embrace that will never let go. The beautiful young daughter with blue eyes and blond hair will never stop smiling the smile she smiles now, will never lose this soft pink glow on her cheeks, will never grow wrinkled or tired, will never get injured, will never unlearn what her parents have taught her, will never think thoughts that her parents don't know, will never know evil, will never tell her parents that she does not love them, will never leave her room with the view of

the ocean, will never stop touching her parents
as she does now.[115]

This image surely tugs at the heartstrings of any parent.

But in the end, none of us would choose this arrested world.
We want our children to become their own strong, self-directed,
independent persons—even knowing full well that growing up
carries inevitable risk and potential heartbreak, both for them and
for us. For students, you may have struggled to help your parents
realize that they cannot hold you in that "frozen embrace." For
parents, let's be brutally honest: Your child is mostly gone already.
When was the last time you truly were in charge of their life? But
now they'll be traveling much further—growing into their new
autonomous self and increasing the emotional distance between
them and you.

We parents can be of two minds about all this: we want them
to be independent, and yet we want them still to need us. We're
proud of that self-assured young person (or even that nervous
and uncertain young person) heading off to new adventures.
And yet we also want them to be that child who still clings tightly
to us while we wipe away their tears. In other words, there is a
part of us that wouldn't mind that timeless world. But it's not our
world. And, students, it is decidedly not *your* world. Once again,
no responsible parent would ever choose it—even with full fore-
knowledge of a tragedy that was going to play out for that child
later on in real life. So, here's the bottom line: That once-distant
moment has arrived. *Both parents and students need to let go of so
much of what you had before.*

---

[115]   Alan Lightman, *Einstein's Dreams* (New York: Vintage Books, 2004).

Are you homesick? A student's story

A few years ago, I came across a story of a young woman whose parents had dropped her off at college. After the usual round of goodbyes, they headed back home. Several days passed, and the parents hadn't yet heard from their new college student. After waiting a while longer, they finally broke down and gave her a call. The conversation went something like this:

PARENT #1: Hi, honey. How are you doing?

DAUGHTER: Fine. I'm doing just fine.

PARENT #2: We're glad to hear you're okay. Are you feeling homesick at all?

DAUGHTER: Nope. I like my roommates. I'm beginning to find my way around campus. And I think I'm going to enjoy my classes.

PARENT #1: Well...are any of your *friends* homesick?

DAUGHTER: [after a pregnant pause] Only the ones with dogs.

***

I'm sharing this vignette with you because it's important to understand just where we parents fit into *the college student's great chain of being*:

My dog or cat (or other pets)
My (old and new) friends
My professors, coaches, et al.
My parents

Fortunately, this classification isn't eternally fixed, and it will definitely change over time. Even before their college graduation, your student will almost certainly begin revising their worldview, and you'll likely move back up in the rankings. You'll also become considerably *smarter* than you were when they were in high school! As Mark Twain observed,

> When I was a boy of 14, my father was so ignorant I could hardly stand to have the old man around. But when I got to be 21, I was astonished at how much the old man had learned in seven years.

So, parents, there's a lot to look forward to. But for now, it's good to approach this new stage of your parent-child relationship with an appropriate level of self-awareness and humility.

RESPONDING TO YOUR COLLEGE STUDENT'S EMOTIONAL UPS AND DOWNS

New college students sometimes do get homesick, of course. As I confessed in Chapter 5, I too experienced some homesickness at the start of my own first year in university. For a couple of days, I even considered transferring to another school, but I'm very glad I didn't.

This story is hardly uncommon. Many new college students initially and understandably find themselves a bit unmoored. As I've said, it's not unusual for anyone to doubt their ability to make it in such an unfamiliar environment. But then, soon enough or at least over time, most students do manage—on their own—to work through and overcome those feelings of separation, loss, and self-doubt. They begin to let go of the past and focus on their future.

But to be sure, some parents will experience a very different phone call from the one on which we eavesdropped above: a phone call from their new college student who definitely sounds distressed. Perhaps it's a daughter who is in tears and just doesn't know what to do about some problem she's run into. She sounds totally lost. A parent's natural first response can be to jump in the car and rush to help—to throw her a lifeline.

If you do get this phone call, *please resist that impulse!* In the vast majority of cases, dropping everything to help is exactly the wrong thing to do. Usually what happens is that the conversation ends, and then the parents don't hear from their child again for a couple of days. So, they stew about it until their concern overcomes their reticence, and they call back. But this time, their student sounds fine (see the preceding vignette). And if the parents happen to mention that unsettling earlier phone call, the student may barely seem to remember it.

Please don't misunderstand what I'm saying. *At that moment*—during that disquieting earlier call—*what your child was going through was fully real to them.* Their feelings were entirely genuine. They very much needed to hear your voice and to share with you whatever they were experiencing. They needed to unload. Most of all, they needed someone who loves them to just *listen*.

But there's so much going on in their new life, with new experiences coming at them so fast and furiously, that they usually move on from such an episode pretty quickly. *Your job is to give them the chance to do that.* If some helpful bit of advice occurs to you, don't hesitate to offer it. But most likely, that's not what your student most needs at that instant. As I said, what they really need is for you to simply *listen.* What they *don't* need is for you to show up at their door and try to solve the problem for them. In the vast majority of cases, they'll be able to do just fine on their own.

GROUND YOUR HELICOPTER, PARK YOUR SNOWPLOW

In earlier times—certainly during *my* undergrad years—the primary model for parenting a college student was pretty much *fire and forget.* That may be a bit of an exaggeration. But students *were* expected to manage largely on their own. And if something went wrong, it was assumed to be the student's fault—and *their* responsibility to fix it—not the school's.

No so much today. I observed in the preceding chapter that cell phones, texting, social media, and the like make it far easier than ever for parents to stay connected with their college student. Overall, this is a positive development. But in some cases, it's *far too easy* for parents to become immersed in their college student's life. You've probably heard the expression "helicopter parents." It's been around for longer than you might realize; higher education professionals started using it in the late 1960s and early '70s. It refers to parents who insist on hovering over their children and involving themselves in their lives to a disruptive extent. The most aggressive ones came to be known as "Black Hawk parents."

More recently, as you also may be aware, a couple of new phrases have entered the lexicon: "snowplow parents" and "curling parents." These well-meaning folks don't just hover; they do everything in their power to plow or sweep away all possible obstacles from their child's path. They try to remake their student's world into a frictionless ice rink, where no adversity or harm can possibly befall them. Snowplow parents, especially those with economic resources, can go a long way toward preventing their children from having to solve *any* problems on their own. Some have gone so far as trying to personally run interference for their student, not just in college but in graduate or professional school, and even later in employment situations. (Spoiler Alert #4: *These efforts definitely do not end well... for the child or the parents. No employer wants to hire someone if it means onboarding their snowplow parents too!*)

In the final analysis, therefore, neither students nor parents are well served by this kind of overprotectiveness. Even though maintaining such an overreaching and ongoing presence in a student's life might appear (to some people) to be a viable short-term parenting strategy, in the long run, it turns out to be disastrous, especially for the child. It can totally derail a young person's project of becoming an autonomous adult. It can arrest their emotional development and prevent them from learning how to cope with the adult world on its own terms. In the most extreme cases, what's required is a total parent-ectomy: removing the parent(s) from the student's life entirely. But *no one*—neither the parents nor the school nor the student—wants things to get to that point! So, parents, please take these remarks as a cautionary tale—no doubt an unnecessary one for most of you who are reading this book, but one worth reflecting upon nonetheless.

If you've been even somewhat over-protective in your child's earlier life, the transition to college affords you a prime opportunity to recalibrate your relationship. You can start by cutting the cellphone/texting umbilical cord, or at least dialing back the frequency and intensity of your conversations. Here's a good rule of thumb: *let your student take the lead in determining the type and frequency of their interactions with you.* Maybe even work out an explicit compact with them: that you will talk, text, etc., once or twice a week, on given days—whatever arrangement makes everyone most comfortable. As I've said, FaceTime, Zoom, and the like offer great ways to stay connected today. But let your child take the upper hand in determining how, and how often, you touch base.

More broadly, students, it's time to give yourself the opportunity to assume responsibility for your life and, especially, to work through your own problems. This is one essential aspect of moving into adulthood. *So, students, you need to let go of constant parental input into everything you do—regardless of how comfortable that might seem. Parents, you've got to let them go so they can truly develop into their own autonomous self.* Does this amount to a no-contact order? Not at all! The point is that parents and their new college student need to *collaborate* to determine the happy mean between too little interaction and too much.

INTERACTING WITH YOUR STUDENT'S SCHOOL

Parents, if you're able to participate in the portion of the school's new-student orientation designed for you—and I very much hope you can—you'll most likely be introduced to a number of administrators and other staff members who serve in student affairs, academic affairs, and other areas on campus who will become important allies and resources for your new college student. And if you can't attend orientation, you can find that information on the school's website. Either way, you'll see that today's colleges and universities deploy an impressive array of offices and professionals whose job is to assist and support students, much more so than in former years (when most of us were in school). These positions include trained resident assistants (RAs) in dorms, academic advisors, writing centers, tutors, professional clinicians in the counseling center, and many others.

You can and *should encourage your student to learn about those resources and take advantage of them as needed.* Other than in exceptional circumstances, however, *it's best not to make those contacts yourself.* For example, if your student has documented special academic needs or a learning disability, encourage *them,* first, to seek out the appropriate support office on campus and, second, to speak with each of their professors at the *beginning* of the academic term, to arrange for the necessary accommodations in their classes. You can assure them that this is a normal practice in universities and colleges today and that there should be no stigma attached to it.

It's also helpful to remind your student—and perhaps yourself—that they have the space and the support to make discoveries on their own. For example, a roommate who at first seems unpromising can turn out, in the fullness of time, to become a lifelong friend. A class that initially seemed off-putting and uninteresting can, by the end of the term, become a springboard to choosing that subject as a major. You get the point.

But, as time goes on, *if you feel that something is going seriously wrong with your student—if the wheels really seem to be coming off in some way—it's important to follow your well-honed parental instincts.* In that case, please reach out to one of those administrators or offices I referenced in the opening paragraphs of this section, whom you encountered during new-parent orientation. If you don't know exactly whom to contact, reach out to the office of student affairs or the office of student life (whatever that division is called in your child's school), and talk with the person you reach about your concerns. They should be able to put you in contact with someone who can help.

The point is *to direct your call at an appropriate institutional level*: That is, if your student seems to be having serious personal or social problems (for example, significant roommate issues, depression, anxiety, etc.), call the office of student affairs. *But please* don't *call your student's RA*. If your student has run into an academic problem they can't seem to resolve, call the academic dean's office (or, if there is one, the dean of first-year studies). *Please* do not *call your student's professor or academic advisor directly.* The guiding principle here is that *parents should avoid coming between their student and the college or university professionals the student needs to be working with on a regular basis.* It's imperative *not* to take those relationships out of your student's hands.

Again, whomever you speak with should be able to direct you to the appropriate office or person. Talk with them, explain your concerns, and hear what they have to say. Then, let that person do some discrete checking to see if any kind of intervention might, in fact, be indicated. Someone should get back to you—either to reassure you that things really are okay or to let you know what they discovered and what they plan to do.

At the same time, please be aware that sometimes the college or university staff will be constrained by legal privacy restrictions—some of which are mandated in federal laws (especially FERPA and HIPAA[116])—that prevent their disclosing to you as much information about your student as you might think you're

---

[116] FERPA is the Family Educational Rights and Privacy Act (1974), which protects the privacy of educational records; HIPAA is the Health Insurance Portability and Accountability Act (1996), which pertains to the privacy of medical records.

entitled to have. For example, most colleges and universities will not automatically send you copies of your student's grades. They usually offer your student the option to grant permission for them to do so, but this requires their signing the appropriate authorizing form, usually through the Registrar's Office. These restrictions reflect one more significant difference between high school and a college or university.

To summarize, for parents: in that *rare* instance in which your intuition tells you something is going quite wrong with your child, trust your instincts. But then *let the school's administrators do their work to make sure there's not a serious problem after all; if there is, let them do what they can to make things better.* The school should be prepared to partner with you in these cases. But as I've emphasized, in the vast majority of instances, it's best to give your student the space and time to solve their own problems. Even if they seem to be struggling a bit, take the long view. Don't deprive them of the opportunity to learn from the experience of dealing with a difficult situation as an autonomous adult. *It's time to let them go.*

TRANSITIONING TO JUNIOR PARTNER

> *Give the ones you love wings to fly, roots to*
> *come back and reasons to stay.*
> —*Dalai Lama XIV*

In the previous chapter, I suggested that parents still can and should be important partners in their student's college career. So, what I've been saying just now may sound at odds with those earlier comments. It's really not, and it might be helpful to think of it this way: The notion of being a *partner* with your student is a useful metaphor. But your student now needs to receive a promotion—to become a more *senior partner* in the firm and assume more responsibility for their relationship with you. While a parent's job is still enormously important, your role now needs to become more secondary: less about managing and directing; more about coaching and cheerleading from the sidelines. A *junior partner*, if you will.

Something else I said before also remains true: your student still cares about you, respects your opinion, and wants your approval—probably more than anyone else in the world and much more so than they may want to let on. But it's time for students, too, to begin relating to your parents in new and different (adult) ways than you did before. Again, for both sides, *it's time to let go.*

This young person has been under your care for plus-or-minus eighteen years. You've nurtured their development. You've been a steward of their education. You've given them a foundation of values they will depend upon for the rest of their lives. Now it's time to trust that you've done the best possible parenting job you could. None of us ever gets everything totally right. *There's simply no such thing as "perfect parenting,"* whatever *that* might even mean! But if you've given them the gifts of unconditional love and your most thoughtful guidance, then you've done your part. You've been good enough.

Now it's time to take your own leap of faith. Trust that *you've* prepared them for this new stage in their lives and trust them to do *their* part to go on from here. Stay involved as a supporter, as a mentor, and an enthusiastic and vocal cheerleader—as the one who still loves and cares for this young person more than anyone else on the planet. But at the same time, be intentional in saying to yourselves (and *mean* it!): *We've got to let them go.*

SUMMING UP—CHAPTER 11

- This book has been all about letting go of the old and taking hold of the new. For parents, the responsibility to protect a child who's growing up while preparing them eventually to set out on their own presents the central dilemma of parenting. You've worked to balance these two obligations across your years with your child. During their teenage years, you've given them an increasing measure of (negative) freedom.

- But now it's time to let go in a new way. It's important to resist the temptation to hold on too tightly or to rush in to solve a problem your student has encountered. Let them learn by solving their problems themselves.

- If you sense that something is going seriously wrong with your student, don't hesitate to contact their school *at the appropriate level*. But it's never a good idea to inject yourself into the working relationship you child needs to have with a faculty or staff member. Let the appropriate people at the college or university check to see if there's really a problem and, if so, to see what they can do to intervene.

- In Chapter 10, we talked about your *partnership* with your student; now it's time for you to transition to the role of *junior partner*. As parents, our ultimate act of love is to let them go.

SUMMING UP—PART THREE

So, there it is: Two pretty straightforward sets of ideas about how parents can best support a new college student as they to take those important first steps in their college career and continue on to success both there and in life beyond. Two ways for parents to encourage their student to get a running start and stay focused on the finish line throughout their undergraduate years.

1. *For parents, stay engaged. But be the right kind of partner on this journey. Your primary job is to listen to and support them. But have some fun along the way too. At the same time, be prepared for discomfort, dislocation, changes in direction, and other signs of growth—see them as markers that both your student and their college are doing their jobs.*

2. *For both students and parents, it's time to be intentional about letting go of the past and focusing on the future.*

When we send our kids off to college, it may feel like the most difficult portion of our parenting job is done. More often than not, that turns out to be true; sometimes, unfortunately, it doesn't. The truth is that we *never* stop being their parents. But even so, it's undoubtedly the case that you've passed an enormously important marker in your life, in your child's life, and in the life of your family.

So, parents, after you've said your (more or less tearful) goodbyes and your young person has taken up their new station as a college or university student, allow yourself a moment or two for a quiet celebration of your own. Raise a glass to both your student and to *you*. You've earned it!

My fondest wish for you is that there will be many more celebrations yet to come. But for now, give yourself permission to mark and enjoy this significant milestone. You absolutely deserve it!

PARTING THOUGHTS

Oh, wonder!
How many goodly creatures are there here!
How beauteous mankind is!
O brave new world, that has such people in it!
—William Shakespeare, The Tempest

Everyone involved in the transition to college—the new student, parents, family members, and those who teach and work at their college or university—is about to begin the remarkable undertaking that is an undergraduate odyssey. For parents and the school's faculty, staff, and administrators—regardless of how many times some of you have been through it—every student's arrival is truly a new beginning. And especially so for the student! The most breathtaking quality of this moment, is that it's impossible to tell just where it will lead. But I guarantee that, if everyone does their part, amazing things will happen.

To the student: As Shakespeare has it, the new world you are about to enter is "brave" indeed! As you take the first steps into your new life as a truly autonomous, responsible adult, your college years are just the starting point. You can't predict just what will happen or who you'll meet along the way. But I can guarantee that you will encounter a great many "goodly" people, from whom you can learn more than you ever imagined—if you open yourself to them.

I've already said quite a bit about the importance of friendship. But it's a solid bet that by the end of *your very first week* on campus you'll have connected with people who quite literally will become some of your most important friends *for the rest of your life*! This pattern has been repeated countless times, across generations of students and alumni. Indeed, I still highly value my close relationships with friends I met during my own first days as an undergrad.

For all its troubles, our world remains full of *wonder*—if we just allow ourselves to see it. It's the only one we have, and to repeat Hemingway's comment one final time, it definitely *is* "worth fighting for." So, let it speak to you. My final hope, therefore, is that you *always embrace and cherish your newfound autonomy, your friends, your curiosity, and your sense of wonder about the world—and that you nurture a lifelong commitment to making a difference in it.*

To parents: Have faith in both your student and in the professional educators who will be there to guide them for the next few years. You can take a measure of encouragement from the fact that so many students (and their parents!) have traveled this road before. No human institution is ever perfect. But there is wisdom deeply embedded in both the structures and the people who make up our colleges and universities—both across their long histories and in their present incarnations. Supported by your ongoing unconditional love and (an *appropriate* level of) continuing engagement, your student will emerge as truly a "beauteous and goodly creature."

At that point, this young person who now is preparing to walk out your door will come back into your life in a welcome new way. They will be older, smarter, more mature, and even more interesting than they are at present. They will have become someone you really will want to hang out with: To sit down with over a cup of coffee, or tea, or a beer, or whatever. To talk, to share stories. Just to enjoy being together again. You have that to look forward to.

To everyone: Determine not to waste a single precious moment of the college experience. Begin now! to do all in your power to make the best possible use of the remarkable gifts of time and opportunity that these years represent. Make sure that on commencement day the graduate can look back with pride and honestly say that they left everything on the field—that they took full advantage of every minute they were privileged to spend as a student at their chosen college or university. *Commit to playing like a champion every single day!*

ADDITIONAL RESOURCES

There is a substantial literature devoted to colleges, universities, students, and parents. What follows is a highly curated list of titles, any of which you might check out, should you be inclined to look further into one or more of the topics I've touched upon above.

Diversity and inclusion on the college campus

❖ Tatum, Beverly Daniel. *Why Are All the Black Kids Sitting Together in the Cafeteria? And Other Conversations About Race*, revised ed. New York: Basic Books, 2017.

Free speech/campus speech

❖ Ben-Porath, Sigal R. *Free Speech On Campus*. Philadelphia: University of Pennsylvania Press, 2017.

❖ Strossen, Nadine. *Hate: Why We Should Resist It with Free Speech, Not Censorship*. New York: Oxford University Press, 2018.

❖ Wood, Zachary R. *Uncensored: My Life and Uncomfortable Conversations at the Intersection of Black and White America*. New York: Dutton, 2018.

Liberal education/liberal learning/college life

❖ Bruni, Frank. *Where You Go Is Not Who You'll Be: An Antidote to the College Admissions Mania*. New York: Grand Central Publishing, 2016.

❖ Delbanco, Andrew. *College: What It Was, Is, and Should Be*. Princeton: Princeton University Press, 2012.

❖ Detweiler, Richard A. *The Evidence Liberal Arts Needs: Lives of Consequence, Inquiry, and Accomplishment*. Cambridge: The MIT Press, 2021.

❖ Epstein, David. *Range: Why Generalists Triumph in a Specialized World*. New York: Riverhead Books, 2019.

❖ Kluge, P. F. *Alma Mater: A College Homecoming*. Reading: Addison-Wesley, 1993.

❖ Light, Richard J. *Making the Most of College: Students Speak Their Minds*. Cambridge: Harvard University Press, 2001.

❖ Nussbaum, Martha. *Cultivating Humanity: A Classical Defense of Reform in Liberal Education*. Cambridge: Harvard University Press, 1997.

❖ Zakaria, Fareed. *In Defense of a Liberal Education*. New York: W. W. Norton & Company, 2015.

Parenting college-aged students

❖ Levin Coburn, Karen and Lawrence Treeger, Madge. *Letting Go: A Parents' Guide to Understanding the College Years*, 3rd ed. New York: HarperCollins, 1997.

❖ Denworth, Lydia. "Age of Opportunity: A refined understanding of the adolescent brain could lead to improvements in education and mental health," *Scientific American* 324, no. 5 (May 2021): 57–61.

❖ Duckworth, Angela. *Grit: The Power of Passion and Perseverance.* New York: Scribner, 2016.

Taking charge of your most precious resource: Time

❖ Carroll, Ryder. *The Bullet Journal Method: Track the Past, Order the Present, Design the Future.* New York: Portfolio, 2018.
❖ Clear, James. *Atomic Habits: An Easy & Proven Way to Build Good Habits & Break Bad Ones.* New York: Avery, 2018.
❖ Newport, Cal. *Deep Work: Rules for Focused Success in a Distracted World.* New York: Grand Central Publishing, 2016.

A well-lived life

❖ Blanke, Gail. *Between Trapezes: Flying into a New Life with the Greatest of Ease.* New York: Rodale, 2004.
❖ Emmons, Robert A. *Thanks!: How Practicing Gratitude Can Make You Happier.* New York: HarperOne, 2008.
❖ Lightman, Alan. *In Praise of Wasting Time.* New York: Simon & Schuster/TED, 2018.
❖ McRaven, William H. *Make Your Bed: Little Things That Can Change Your Life... And Maybe the World.* New York: Grand Central Publishing, 2017.
❖ Sacks, Oliver. *Gratitude.* New York: Knopf, 2015.
❖ Wallace, David Foster. *This is Water: Some Thoughts, Delivered on a Significant Occasion, about Living a Compassionate Life.* New York: Little, Brown and Company, 2009.

ACKNOWLEDGMENTS

As noted in the Introduction, the ideas in this book came together over quite a few years. Their present formulation and expression owe more than I possibly can express to good advice and incredibly helpful comments on earlier drafts from many friends and colleagues: John Barkett, Beau Breslin, Judy Campbell, Kim Crabbe, Carolyn Higbie, John Hurley, Alan Lightman, John R. (Rick) MacArthur, Virginia Murphy-Berman, Thomas Henry Pope, John A. Roush, Sara Schupf, Daniel G. Stroup, Adam S. Weinberg, and Robert Weisbuch. They provided encouragement, as well as thoughtful critiques and so many useful ideas—often quite developed and detailed ones—that are reflected throughout the final product. W. Rochelle Calhoun and, again, Carolyn Higbie offered especially helpful guidance regarding the timely topic of cyberbullying. These friends and colleagues will recognize their ideas scattered throughout this book.

Appreciation is due to Rowe Davenport, who read and commented on the manuscript from a high school student's perspective. Likewise, great thanks are due to all the former Skidmore students who gave permission to use their stories, ensured that the details in those narratives were accurate, and often made other helpful suggestions as well. Nigel, especially, provided extremely useful comments that improved the text well beyond the part that talked specifically about him.

Special thanks go to Howard Gardner and Wendy Fischman, who were kind enough to share prepublication results from their important new study, *The Real World of College: What Higher Education Is and What It Can Be* (MIT Press, 2022). They also provided encouraging and enormously useful comments and suggestions after carefully reviewing several earlier versions.

University of Redlands President Emeritus James R. Appleton offered thoughtful, supportive, and valuable comments on an early draft that prompted a number of substantive revisions to subsequent iterations. When he was my boss at Redlands, Jim modeled for me how to speak to new parents, showing what was most helpful for them to hear. He will recognize at least one sentence that I appropriated directly from talks he gave each year to that group at "the dear olde U of R." I am grateful to him for this and many other things.

I also owe a significant debt of gratitude to another former Redlands colleague, Nancy Carrick, who reported to me, first, as Associate Dean and then as Dean of the College of Arts and Sciences. Nancy did not review this manuscript. But through our work together, she gave me fresh regard for thorough and rigorous editing, along with an understanding of the effort that needs to go into that phase of composition. All of which added considerable value to my efforts as an author on so many occasions and eventually to this project.

Appreciation is due as well to my longtime friend Larry Connor, Managing Partner of The Connor Group. The first principle in his organization's corporate culture is "Do The Right Thing," which I appropriated with his blessing, as the organizing exhortation in Chapter 7. It's certainly not a novel idea. But Larry's use of it in his company's documents inspired me to see it in a new light.

I owe another substantial debt of gratitude to Edgar Wachenheim III—a highly successful investment professional, an author in his own right, a Skidmore parent and former trustee, and a friend. Ed offered much encouragement and contributed invaluable prepublication assistance in connecting me with both Howard Gardner and my agents, Peter and Amy Bernstein.

Peter and Amy provided incredibly helpful instruction about the unfamiliar (to me) world of commercial publishing, as they pushed me to turn both the book proposal and the manuscript into something an editor might seriously consider. They also introduced me to my prepublication editor Will Weisser, who continued my education and provided invaluable assistance in producing the final text of both the book proposal and parts of the manuscript. Without their help, this book never would have come to market, and the final version would lack any number of improvements. Thanks are due as well to Ella Haney Foulds for her vital assistance in securing the requisite permissions for the many quotations that appear in the text.

Heartfelt thanks to Debra Englander, Consulting Editor at Post Hill Press, for deciding to take on this book, and to Caitlin Burdette, Managing Editor, for skillfully guiding it through production. Ashlyn Inman's careful copy editing not only cleaned up and normed the text but also resulted in a great many substantive improvements.

Jason Glotzbach gave several earlier versions of the manuscript a thoughtful read and offered insightful comments and suggestions; he also granted me permission to include both his and his sister's stories. Additionally, more thanks than I possibly could ever express go to my perennial first and last reader, Marie Glotzbach: my full partner throughout the Skidmore presidency (and, indeed, across my entire academic career), toughest critic, the source of so many creative ideas for the text (starting with the talks on which it is based), my greatest source of inspiration, and my most enthusiastic cheerleader.

The reactions, additions, critical comments, and other suggestions contributed by the above-cited individuals—most of which I happily incorporated—significantly improved the final version of this book. I am more grateful to them than they can realize. But of course, any remaining deficiencies and infelicities remain my responsibility.

Finally, I owe an enormous debt to the many generations of new students and their parents who listened to (or suffered through) my remarks in the Opening Convocations that kicked off their undergraduate careers at Skidmore College. As I mention in the Introduction, their positive responses first prompted me to consider turning those talks into this book. *Heartfelt thanks and three hearty cheers* to them for their attention and encouragement on those occasions and so many others! And most especially, sincere appreciation to thousands of Skidmore parents for entrusting their children to the college during my presidential years—one of the most profound leaps of faith imaginable.

ABOUT THE AUTHOR

Photo courtesy of Skidmore College

D r. Philip A. Glotzbach served as president of Skidmore College for seventeen years. During that time, he led initiatives to enhance its academic offerings, student body diversity, finances and financial aid, infrastructure and physical landscape, and national reputation. Prior to arriving at Skidmore, Glotzbach served as dean of the College of Arts and Sciences and then vice president for Academic Affairs at the University of Redlands. He began his career in the Department of Philosophy at Denison University, where he taught for fifteen years. Across his academic career, he has written, spoken, and consulted on a broad range of topics. He is well-known as a commentator and outspoken champion of American higher education.

Glotzbach earned his BA in philosophy at the University of Notre Dame (*summa cum laude and Phi Beta Kappa*), and his MA, M.Phil., and Ph.D. in philosophy at Yale University. He has received honorary degrees from Centre College, Denison University, and Skidmore College.